RESERVE STOCK

KU-275-321

B.C.H.E. - LIBRARY

00075478

John Lawrence

Ulysses
in the Raj

RESERVE STOCK

Captain Paul Nicachi (Norris), the author, as an officer in the 7th Rajput Regiment during World War II

Ulysses
in the Raj

by
Paul Byron Norris

BACSA
PUTNEY, LONDON
1992

Published by the British Association
for Cemeteries in South Asia (BACSA)

Secretary: Theon Wilkinson MBE
76½ Chartfield Avenue
London SW15 6HQ

© *Copyright 1992 Paul Byron Norris*

*All rights reserved. No part of this publication may be reproduced, stored
in a retrieval system or transmitted, in any form or by any means, electronic,
mechanical, photocopying, recording or otherwise, without the prior
permission of the copyright owner.*

ISBN 0 907799 46 9

RESERVE STOCK
LAWRENCE COLLECTION

BATH COLLEGE OF
HIGHER EDUCATION
NEWTON PARK LIBRARY

DISCARD
954.03 NOR

SUPPLIER
DonL

Cover, maps and plan adapted by: Rosemarie Wilkinson

Typeset by: Professional Presentation, 3 Prairie Road, Addlestone, Surrey

Printed by: The Chameleon Press Ltd., 5-25 Burr Road, Wandsworth SW18 4SG

Contents

Illustrations & Maps

Cover sketch of Greek Memorial, Dacca (see pages 89-91)

BACSA acknowledges and thanks all those who provided photographs

Foreword

'Ulysses in the Raj' is the twentieth in a series of books about Europeans in South Asia, written by a BACSA member, published by BACSA for BACSA members with a wider public in mind and particularly those who have a special interest in the Greek families that migrated from their homeland to India in the 18th and 19th centuries.

The author, himself of Greek descent, writes with rare insight on the historical background of this dispersion of Greeks into the far corners of Europe and Asia and then follows the fortunes of some of the most notable families that went to India with details of his own as a sample of the lives they led and the careers they followed. There is the striving for acceptance within the British social circle while retaining their distinctive cultural identity and at the same time adapting to Indian conditions; a three-way cultural tug-of-war which they managed so successfully.

This is a unique account and the Appendices at the back give most valuable information on all the recorded Greek Merchants in Bengal and northern India between 1750 and 1853, a rich source for future researchers.

Introduction & Acknowledgements

The real genesis of this book goes back to my boyhood in India when my grandfather, Menelaus Panioti Nicachi, used to tell me stories about his Greek forbears, his boyhood in Calcutta and his service with Ralli Brothers. Nearly a whole lifetime has passed since then and it was only in 1982 that I began to explore my paternal ancestry, a project I had long considered but deferred because of the pressures of life and my own indolence. Once I had begun I was soon caught by the fascination of the search and its wider implications of Greek trade in India and the Hellenic presence in Bengal. At an early stage of my work I was fortunate to learn of the existence of BACSA which I immediately joined.

Reading the numbers of 'Chowkidar' I began to see that there was a greater potential readership for books about India than I had previously realised, so I was encouraged to extend my genealogical researches to a study of the Greek presence in Bengal and northern India. This little book is the result.

It makes no pretensions to be a work of scholarship for it would have required almost a lifetime of research, far greater knowledge of Greek and more historical expertise than I possess to have written such a book. I will be happy if it manages to catch the attention of the general reader interested in the history of British India and serves as an elementary introduction to the student. As far as I am aware, it is the first of its kind on this subject in English. The only book I know which deals with the Greek presence in Bengal is Spiros Loukatos' 'Greeks and Philhellenes in India during the Greek War of Independence' which I have made considerable use of, but it has not been translated into English and only deals with a small portion of the period I have attempted to cover.

Despite the title of my book, its range is largely limited to Bengal and northern India. Chapter eight gives a brief, rather inadequate account of 'Ralli Brothers' but a thorough examination of the work of this great trading corporation would involve massive research and still remains to be written. The last two chapters concentrate mainly but not exclusively on the history of two Greek families, the Paniotys and the Nicachis, which may serve as a sort of sample of a much wider and more extensive Greek presence in India.

This book would not have been completed had it not been for the generous encouragement and help of Theon Wilkinson. I owe a debt of gratitude to Mr W. Saumarez Smith for having procured for me copies of the inscriptions on the Dacca Greek Memorial through the British High Commission; to Guy Evans, Zoë Yalland and Bishop Timotheos Catsiyannis for the loan of interesting material; to Father Vincent Pizzala, O.P., and Jeremy Thomas for translations from the Greek and to the staff of the India Office Library, Miss Marie Aspioti, Mrs Marie Therianou and Mr Nondas Stamatopoulos of Corfu for their courteous assistance. My wife Maureen has bravely and unselfishly accomplished the task of typing my untidy and difficult manuscript and for this, as for her constant help and encouragement, I am deeply grateful.

P.B.N.
Kenilworth. 1991

*To the memory
of my grandparents,
Ione Panioty
and
Menelaus Panioti Nicachi
and
for
Maureen, Josephine,
Richard, Damien
and Alexandra.*

The young man, showing no signs of fear, replied: "My name is Acoetis. I come from Maeonia. My parents were humble people. My father could not leave me any fields to plough with strong oxen, or any woolly sheep or cattle. He had no property apart from his skill, and when he died he could leave me nothing but the open sea. So I took to the sea".

'Stories of the Greeks' Rex Warner

But if we forgot our own dead, who upon earth would remember them? Is it folly to rescue from oblivion those ghosts once vital as ourselves? For my part, I believe that the love of the past, which is felt by so many, has elemental roots to be cherished by us all.

Lady Wilson

1

The Source: Greek Traders in the Ottoman Empire

The isles of Greece, the isles of Greece!
Where burning Sappho loved and sung,
Where grew the arts of war and peace,
Where Delos rose and Phoebus sprung!
Eternal summer gild them yet,
But all, except their sun, is set.   (Byron)

On Tuesday May 29, 1453, the Ottoman Army of Sultan Mehmet captured Constantinople, the Imperial capital of the Byzantine Empire whose last Emperor, Constantine Palaeologus, died fighting to preserve the honour of the Christian God and His Holy City. For a thousand years it had been the centre of a polity which was both the prolongation of the Roman, and a Greek Orthodox Empire, whose armies had been the eastern bastion of Christendom against the onslaught of Islam. Now it had fallen, never to rise again as a Christian citadel. By the time that Sultan Mehmet died in 1481, Turkish armies had overrun the Balkans and were threatening southern Italy. The long, dark night of the Greek race had descended with the setting of the Byzantine sun.

From the end of the 16th to the beginning of the 19th century three things kept the Greek sense of race alive: the Orthodox Church with its hieratic rituals and gilded piety, the wiles of the Phanariot families of Constantinople and the Greek ability to master the sea and use its highways to live by trade. It was not the Classical but the Christian heritage of Orthodoxy, so rich in its texture of worship and so contrasted with the stark puritanism of Islam, that gave the Greeks continuity with their Byzantine past. Turkish ineptness at, and scorn for, diplomacy led to a truly unique situation - the diplomacy of this Muslim Empire was almost wholly in the hands of a few Phanariot families of Constantinople[1]. In the bare, iron mountains of the Maini, in Laecadaemonia (home of the ancient Spartans), the Turks never conquered. An English traveller of the 18th century observed that the Greeks "have in this corner resisted all the efforts of the Turks, to whom they pay neither tribute nor obedience, and who dare not approach the country. They are all robbers, or rather, pirates, and infest these seas with small armed boats which pillage all the small craft from port to port."[2] On the westward side of the Morean peninsula the Venetian Lion protected the inhabitants of Corfu and the Ionian Islands who, under their protectors, fought off the Turkish challenge and never succumbed to Ottoman rule.

But it was the Mediterranean and its extensions that provided the Greeks with their greatest opportunity for racial assertion and covert independence. "The Turks traditionally scorned commerce as unbefitting an imperial race and the Greeks were eager to assume the mercantile mantle in the Ottoman Empire, taking over from the Armenians and Jews who had dominated Ottoman commerce during the early centuries after the fall of Constantinople. The bulk of the export, import and carrying trade of the Ottoman Empire was in the hands of the Greeks, and towns and cities such as Joannina, Smyrna, Thessalonica, Patras and Alexandria became thriving centres of Greek commerce."[3]

The ports of Italy were 'invaded' by a tide of Greek merchants and sailors. By the 16th century Ancona had granted privileges to Greeks from Vallona, the Gulf of Arta and Joannina and many large Greek colonies had established themselves in Venice, Trieste, Livorno, Naples and even Marseilles, and these had attracted many of the most enterprising and prosperous of Greek merchants.[4] Trieste, particularly, was a great channel for Greek trade and many Greek houses were established here with connections with others in Vienna, Leipzig and other towns in Germany.[5] In Ancona, too, small trading was particularly in the hands of the Greeks who arrived ships loaded with merchandise - cheese, spices and wines - and exchanged them for goods desired in the Levant - gold and silver specie, Holland draperies but particularly firearms.[6] Greek sailors "from islands with no arable land and who were therefore destined to roam the world" rounded the capes of Italy to Naples, Livorno and Marseilles. In October 1787 the Russian Consul at Messina observed that in every year sixty or more Greek ships passed through the Straits of Messina to these ports.[7]

It was not long before Greek traders began to penetrate central Europe. They took advantage of the steady advance of Austrian power in the 18th century against the Turks. In 1739 the Austrian border was pushed eastwards to the junction of the Sava and the Danube, and the Habsburg government began to colonize these new territories with Greeks.[8] By the end of this century there were 80,000 Greek families living in the Hapsburg territories. The English traveller Moritt, passing through Hungary in the last years of the century, said that eastwards from Hermanstaat "we were travelling in a Greek country"[9]. From Austria Greeks, propelled by their own adventurous momentum, passed into Germany and the rest of Europe, using credit facilities provided by bankers in Amsterdam. Goethe recalled in his autobiography being charmed as a young man by the traditional dress worn by Greeks at the Leipzig fair.

Even more extraordinary was the Greek penetration of the lands belonging to the Czar of Russia. The silver mines of Nerchinsk in Siberia were first worked by Greek entrepreneurs as early as 1691,[10] and Greek fur buyers were observed operating in the Altay region.[11] On January 20, 1794, when the Irbit fair opened, an intrepid French traveller, Jean Gmelin observed that "the roads were thronged with horses, men and sledges.....I saw there Greeks, Bukhars and

Tartars of all kinds.....the Greeks brought with them foreign goods purchased at Archangel such as French wines and spirits."[12] Catherine the Great was not slow to appreciate the thrust and initiative of these Hellenic merchants and, after the Russian conquest of the northern borders of the Black Sea from the Turks, she attracted Greek settlers to Odessa, Mariupol and Tagranog and enabled Greek merchants to sail the Black Sea flying the Russian flag.

In the Levant and the eastern Mediterranean, Greek enterprise swept everything before it and soon became the dominating commercial power in the region. The Greek mercantile marine "expanded dramatically in the last decades of the 18th and the first two decades of the 19th centuries, under the impetus of the French Revolutionary and Napoleonic Wars, which afforded enterprising Greek captains plentiful and profitable opportunities for blockade running. Much of the Greek merchant fleet was based on what was known as the three 'Nautical Islands': Psara, Spetses and, the most important, Hydra. During this period the Greeks had eclipsed the French in the trade of the eastern Mediterranean."[13] A French visitor in 1820 noticed that in Hydra "a host of ships fill the harbour, go on frequent visits to neighbouring coasts or carry far abroad the produce of Europe, Asia or Africa, and even the rich superabundance of India". Moritt in 1796 says "we hear of nothing but successes of the French, Amsterdam taken, etc. As the Turks always judge of nations by their success, they are all sansculottes. The Greeks, for this reason, are all on the other side."

Even the trade between the Levant and England was invaded by these jaunty entrepreneurs. From Smyrna in 1804 the English merchants of the Levant Company were protesting to the British Consul about the increasing incursion of Greeks into their monopoly of trade between the Levant and the British Isles. "It would be trespassing unnecessarily on your time" they write with commendable urbanity "to dwell on the character and nature of the mercantile spirit of the Greeks; for this must be familiar to you as it is to us....it appears to us that to transfer the trade carried on by British subjects into the hands of Greeks cannot possibly be of benefit to the nation". The reason for Greek success emerges indirectly in this petition: "our principals would not find the Greeks better able to serve them than we can, although they might offer their services on more moderate terms." The petition ends with a fine flourish of Anglo-Saxon superiority "The Honour, Probity, Prudence, conduct and zeal of a British Merchant are well enough established in every quarter of the globe, and will not assuredly suffer by comparison with the Greeks, whose speculative spirit and slavish subjection to an arbitrary government must ever render them a dangerous factor".[14]

'Slavish subjection' was certainly the lot of the majority of Greeks and, more especially, of the other Balkan and Asiatic subjects of the Turks but, for the Greeks, there were rays of sunlight which broke through the dark clouds of Ottoman tyranny. Many of the Greek islands never bore the harsh yoke placed on the diaspora Greeks in the Balkans and Asia Minor. "The Cyclades and all the islands in that part are entirely in the hands of Greeks and the Turks make them pay an annual tribute and give them very little other trouble," observes Moritt. "Zea, Tenos and Mycone (Mykonos) are barren and rocky, but from the peace and freedom they live in, are much cultivated."[15] The island of Chios was also exceptional in the degree of prosperity and autonomy that it enjoyed, and nearby Psara (Syra) was one of the most important ports and trading centres of Greece, "floating at the maritime crossroads of Asia, Thrace, Crete, the Greek mainland and the archipelago".[16]

Perhaps the greatest degree of prosperity enjoyed under alien rule was in the maritime island of Hydra. Nature had dealt it a poor hand - a barren rocky island "the pastorage of which" says Moritt, the blunt Yorkshire squire, "would hardly feed a horse." Perhaps for this very reason the Hydriotes, unable to support themselves by agriculture, took to the sea and became the greatest carrying traders in the Eastern Mediterranean. Their principal cargo was grain exported largely to France and Genoa. "The Hydriote ships, many of them three, four or five hundred tons, purchased their cargoes of corn in Greece, Egypt or Asia Minor; much of it from the Morea, Thessaly or Macedonia; and carrying it down the Mediterranean, obtained a ready sale, occasionally at a profit of 40 or 50 percent upon the cargo".[17] The manner of conducting this trade was highly original and may be described as an experiment in democratic capitalism. The capitalists of Hydra, frequently former merchant captains, lent money to commercial adventurers at interest but on no more than a verbal contract. The captains of the ships engaging in the trade (usually the owners of the vessels) acted as agents in these transactions. "Every person on board their ships, even to the cabin boy, has a share in the speculation, either in lieu of wages....or by the investment of savings which anyone may have made. Every Hydriote sailor is therefore, more or less a merchant, and is furnished with the strongest motive to habitual industry, in the opportunity of thereby advancing his fortune in life".[18] Their sailors were reckoned as amongst the most skilful in the Mediterranean and their town a hive of maritime activity.

Less ethical but no less daring in their activities were the rough Maniot pirates whose "vessels would lie in wait for Turkish and Venetian convoys between Crete and Cape Matapan, and, being too small to attack them in bulk, pounce on laggards and strays, board them, or force them on to the rocks. They were frequently in league with captains from the islands, particularly from Cephalonia".[19] They were not the only pirates in the Mediterranean, for from the ports of Tripoli and Algiers, the Barbary pirates made themselves the terror of all sea-faring men and many a minor battle was fought between the Christian Greek pirates and these Muslim maritime predators. It was not simply, however, as sailors and traders that the Greeks excelled; their commercial acumen enabled them to operate on higher levels of commerce and industry, not only in the sea-girt islands of the Aegean but in some favoured areas of the Ottoman mainland.

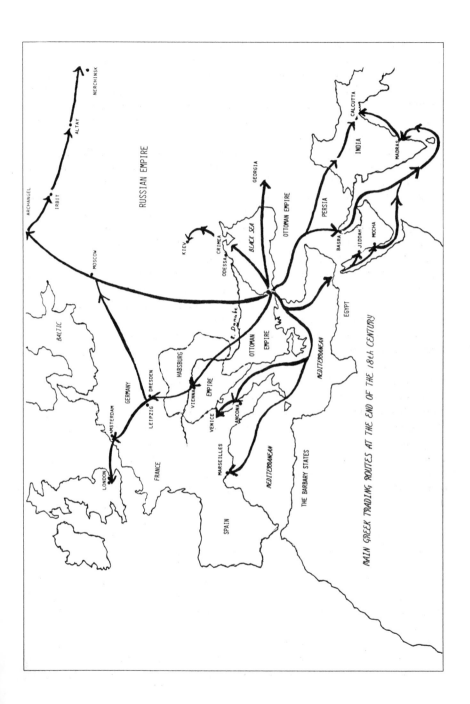

MAIN GREEK TRADING ROUTES AT THE END OF THE 18th CENTURY

Henry Holland, another English traveller, commented that where the obstacles to their progress were removed, the Greeks always showed themselves to be an active and enterprising people. "In various remote and mountainous regions of the Ottoman Empire e.g. the Mani and Agrapha, the writ of the Ottoman government scarcely ran while in others the Greek enjoyed a high degree of self-government often combined with tax privileges which at times amounted to virtual autonomy."[20]

The inland city of Joannina, surrounded by mountains in the depths of Epirus, became a centre of international trade, exploiting the cottons and cotton yarns of Thesally, the grain, timber, tobacco, wool and oil of Albania to Italy, Germany and Malta and importing the luxuries of Western Europe, making this city a sort of mart for books, which were diffused over other parts of Greece. The vast opportunities for commerce led to the formation of family firms like the one observed by Henry Holland in 1812 "of four brothers, one was settled at Joannina, another in Moscow, a third at Constantinople and the fourth in some part of Germany."[21] Trade linked this obscure Epirot town with the ancient capital of the Czars for the principal branches of several Joannina houses were established in Moscow and a large amount of Greek money was lodged in the security of Russian banks. Napoleon's occupation of the city produced tremors in far-off Epirus as Holland records: "We were in Joannina at the time the news of the burning of Moscow arrived; and living chiefly among merchants, could judge of the great sensation this event excited amongst them. The losses sustained by some individuals in the destruction of the magazines was very great."[22] The best Greek dwellings in the city differed little in outward appearance from those of the Turks. It was unwise for Ottoman subjects to live in what appeared to be opulent dwellings so the houses had few windows turned towards the street and those guarded by iron bars. Inside, however, Greek houses displayed greater signs of luxury, evidence of the civilizing effects of the habits of Western Europe acquired by much-travelled Greek merchants. Tables and chairs of European form, mirrors of Venetian or German manufacture graced the rooms but always a picture of the Virgin or a favourite saint with a votive lamp burning before it. The houses contained spacious courtyards with a flight of steps leading to a large wooden gallery from which entrance to the principal rooms were gained. This gallery was supported by a stone arcade which led to the entrance gate. At the end of the gallery was a raised kiosk which was, with the gallery, the usual residence of the family in summer. A small garden occupied one side of the court.

In 1795 Moritt observed that despite the spectacular advantages of Constantinople's position, the Turks there hardly engaged in any manufactures.[23] As with trade, so with manufacture, the Greeks stepped in where the Turks scorned to tread. The island of Tenos had a great trade in silk and the Tenians were knitters of silk stockings, gloves and other articles of haberdashery.[24] The outstanding example of Greek industrial initiative was Ambelakia, a mountain

6

village of Thesally, which became the centre of an international industry and trade. There were twenty four manufactories in the town where every year the inhabitants dyed over 2,000 bales of cotton, manufactured in the surrounding districts, and then exported them to Germany from where they were distributed to Pest, Vienna, Leipzig, Dresden, Anspach and Bayreuth. The Ambelakia merchants had factories in all those cities and they sold raw cotton there to German manufacturers. In the annals of European commerce there were, probably, few more extraordinary enterprises than this burgeoning commercial success, originating in an obscure Greek village. The company at Ambelakia had three principal directors, with associates at Vienna and inferior correspondents at Pest, Trieste, Leipzig, Salonica, Constantinople and Smyrna, but in every case the constitution of the company ruled that all these individuals should be chosen from the inhabitants of Ambelakia. In 1797 a French traveller, Felix Beaufour, said that "Ambelakia, by the activity of its inhabitants resembles a city of Holland rather than a Turkish village...it gives birth to an immense commerce that connects Germany to Greece by a thousand threads."[25]

Nearer to the centre of Turkish power was the soap manufactory run by Greeks at Haivali in north western Asia Minor. The Revd William Jowett of the Church Missionary Society observed in 1818 that Greeks so dominated Haivali that there were no Jews, no Mosques and not above ten Turks in the place.[26]

It was not, however, by the bread of commerce alone that the Greeks lived for in every place where they congregated some attempt was made to keep the language and traditions of their race alive by the foundation of schools. Schools of a kind existed throughout the period of Ottoman rule, imparting only a basic linguistic and religious knowledge. In the 18th and 19th centuries, however, more advanced academies were revived or founded in places like Chios, Smyrna and Haivali. In these there was an emphasis on the Greek classics, the rudiments of mathematics and even the natural sciences. Greek teachers in these schools were often graduates of European, in particular Italian, universities. Large numbers of books in Greek were printed, mainly in Venice, for Greek readers. At the beginning of the 18th century these books were mainly religious in character, but by its end they had become increasingly secular, purveying the wisdom of the European Enlightenment. The literary fare of Locke, Voltaire, Montesquieu, Beccaria and Rousseau could hardly fail to make the Greeks more restive under the barbarities of Ottoman rule. An instance of this was observed by Moritt in Constantinople in 1795: "The people here pay no regular taxes of any sort, the coffers of the Grand Signior being filled with presents and extortions of the Pashas and by seizing the confiscated property of the rich Greek or Armenian merchants when found out, which is no inconsiderable source of revenue."[27]

It was not only fiscal tyranny that the Turks inflicted on Greeks. At Kim Chowkee in Gujerat, Bishop Heber met two poor Greeks from Trebizond on a begging journey to redeem their families from slavery. As early as 1578, the leading Greek merchant of Constantinople, Michael Cantacuzenus was summarily hanged at the gates of his own home at Anchioli on the orders of the Sultan. In 1819, when Greeks in India were enjoying the full benefits of religious toleration under the rule of the East India Company, a Greek, Athanasios of Smyrna, "a young man of about four and twenty years of age, in deportment and appearance as handsome as a cedar of Libanus" was executed by the Turks for his adherence to his ancestral faith. The Turks were prepared to tolerate the practice of Christianity but relegated all Christians to a position of political and civic inferiority. Athanasios, the son of a boatman, served a Turkish master "who often proposed with great offers and temptations to elevate him from the degrading bondage of a Greek to the privileges of a Turk, which can be done only by taking the exterior mark of a disciple of Mahomet with the public renunciation of Christianity." Athanasios resisted for a time but, in a moment of weakness, succumbed and accepted Islam. His subsequent sense of guilt drove him to make a pilgrimage to Mount Athos, the centre of Greek monasticism. Returning home, he publicly declared his return to his ancestral faith. Turkish revenge was swift. He was imprisoned, tortured and even offered bribes to return to Islam, but he refused. "At last, a Turkish blacksmith was ordered by the captain of the guard to strike off his head, but as a last attempt to induce the sufferer to live a Turk, the executioner was desired to cut a little of the skin of his neck that he might feel the edge of the sword; this last attempt having failed of success, and Athanasios on his knees declaring with a calm and resigned countenance that he was born with Jesus and would die with Jesus, the horrid deed was finished by a single blow." The body lay guarded and exposed for three days, the breast and stomach towards the ground, the head placed between the legs. This account[28] comes from an Anglican missionary, the Revd Charles Williamson, chaplain to the Levant Company's Factory in Smyrna.

It is not surprising then that the commercial talents of the Greeks were, more and more, deployed outside the boundaries of the Ottoman Empire to avoid the harassment and cruelties of the Turkish authorities and this was one considerable reason for the Greek commercial presence in India.

References: Chapter One

1. *Istanbul*, M Pereira
2. *A Grand Tour: Letters and Journeys 1794-98*, JBS Moritt (The Century Lives and Letters), p190
3. *The Movement of Greek Independence 1770-1821*, Ed. Richard Clogg (London), XV
4. *The Perspective of the World*, Fernand Braudel; *Civilisation and Capitalism 15-18th Century*, (Fontana), Vol. 3 pp480-481
5. Clogg, op. cit. p28
6. *Le Port Franc d'Ancone*, Alberto Caracciolo (Paris 1965), p30
7. Braudel, op. cit. p481

8.   *Ibid.*
9.   Moritt, op. cit. p60
10. Braudel, op. cit. p457
11. *Ibid,* p461
12. *Ibid,* pp461-462
13. Clogg, op. cit. XVI
14. *Ibid,* p41
15. Moritt, op. cit. p215
16. *Mani,* P Leigh Fermor (John Murray 1958), p114
17. Clogg, op. cit. p31
18. *Ibid,* p32
19. P Leigh Fermor, op. cit. p114
20. Clogg, op. cit. XII
21. *Ibid,* p28
22. *Ibid,* p28
23. Moritt, op. cit. p76
24. *Ibid,* p215
25. Clogg, op. cit. p32
26. *Ibid,* pp78-80
27. Moritt, op. cit. p75
28. Clogg, op. cit. pp66-68

2
The Goal: India

Thou, by the Indian Ganges' side,
shouldst rubies find. (Andrew Marvell)

Between the 15th and 18th centuries the world of the Orient from Egypt to China embraced a single world economy composed of a network of long distance mercantile connections. It was totally dependent on monsoons and trade winds which enabled Arabs, Indians, Chinese and Europeans to traverse the Indian Ocean and the western Pacific in search of commerce. In this vast arena of trade, the sub-continent of India enjoyed a geographically central position between the Empire of Imperial China to the east and the power of the Ottoman Sultans in the west. Merchants from Gujerat and the Malabar and Coromandel coasts competed with Arab traders from the Red Sea, Persians from the Gulf and Chinese from Canton. "Everything that anybody could want could be found here: luxury goods alongside commonplace commodities, silk, spices, pepper, gold, silver, precious stones, pearls, opium, coffee, rice, indigo, cotton, saltpetre, teak (for shipbuilding), Persian horses, elephants from Ceylon, iron, steel, copper, pewter, shimmering fabrics for the rich and powerful, coarse cloth for the peasants of the spice islands or the black population of Monomotapa".[1]

During the course of this period it was clear that merchants from the western end of this vast area tended, by their enterprise, to outrival their Far Eastern competitors. A thriving trade was conducted by merchants of many races between the ports of Mocha, Jiddah and Basra on the one hand and those of both western India and Calcutta on the other. Mocha was the centre of a thriving coffee trade and with Jiddah became the leading ports of the Red Sea.[2] Year after year ships from India arrived at these ports with cargoes of spices from the East Indies and Bengal which were exchanged either for specie or the coffee berries of Arabia.[3] Among the textile goods exported from Bengal were khasseidas, woven by the Muslim women of Dacca, which were worn as turbans by the soldiers of the Sultan of Constantinople and the Pasha of Egypt.[4] Northwards from the Red Sea and Basra, other ships carried the produce of India to Egypt, Constantinople and eventually to the Mediterranean ports of Europe. Every year ships from Bengal laden with rice, gum-lac and cotton goods were sent to Basra, and returned laden with dried fruits, rose water and precious metals.[5]

This trade was stimulated by the presence in India, since the 14th century, of a native monetary economy developing into a primitive form of capitalism.

10

Chains of native moneylenders were ready, at a high rate of interest, to provide credit to European traders. The free English merchants and even the factors of the East India Company, who, in the early days, were allowed to trade privately, could only do so by applying to the shroffs or native bankers for credit. These men were often merchants on their own account who also controlled transport facilities. Some of them had princely fortunes like Virji Vora of Surat said in 1663 to possess eight million rupees and Abdul Ghafur who owned twenty ships each between 300 and 800 tons and a turnover reputed to be equivalent to that of the East India Company. The textile exports from India to Europe were wholly dependent on the financial intermediaries, the Banyans, in the 17th and 18th centuries. The French merchant, Tavernier, who traded extensively in India explains how he carried hardly any liquid money since it was easy to borrow from a native moneylender in Golconda and pay it back in Surat. This banyan network extended to all commercial vantage points in the Indian Ocean. The French economic historian, Fernand Braudel, says that in the face of this evidence we should "not consider the itinerant merchants of the Indian Ocean as minor figures: as in Europe, long distance trade lay at the heart of the most advanced capitalism in the Far East".[6]

Among the Levantine merchants who took advantage of the opportunities afforded by this trade, the most adventurous and the oldest group of foreigners in India were the Armenians. Once natives of an independent Christian Kingdom, they had been conquered by the Safavid rulers of Persia, one of whom, Shah Abbas, in 1604 transplanted 40,000 of them from Armenia to Persia. From their centres in this country Ispahan and New Julfa, Armenian merchants poured a steady stream of commercial activity into India. The Armenian merchant, Hovhannes, son of David, has left an account of an extraordinary commercial enterprise he was engaged in between 1682 and 1693. He started from Julfa, the Armenian suburb of Ispahan, and journeyed to Surat and from there across northern India, with long stops in Agra and Patna, till he crossed the Himalayas to arrive in Khatmandu. From there he journeyed to Lhasa where he spent five years without interruption before he retraced his steps to Julfa. During this long period he was not alone amongst foreigners, for he was received and assisted by other Armenian merchants, did business with them and associated himself with their affairs. The list of goods he handled were extraordinary: silver, gold, precious stones, musk, indigo and other dye stuffs, woollen and cotton cloth, candles, tea, and the scale of his trade was impressive, for on one occasion he sent two tons of indigo from northern India to Shiraz via Surat and on another, two hundred pounds of silver. On a third occasion he despatched ten pounds of gold obtained in Lhasa from other Armenians who had travelled as far as Sining on the Chinese frontier to trade silver for gold. The Armenians were not the only merchants trading with India; there were also Italians, Cypriots, Candians, Georgians and Greeks. It is almost certain that, apart from the Italians, all the

11

people referred to above were Greeks of the diaspora who are listed separately from those of the mainland of Greece.

We can trace the progress of Armenian trading activity in India by the building of their churches: Chinsura in 1695, Calcutta in 1724, Saidabad in 1758, Dacca in 1781. The oldest Armenian inscription on a tomb in Dacca is dated 1714.[7] There were about some three to four thousand Armenians in Bengal in 1757,[8] and from this community emerged some of the great merchant families in Bengal - the Arrakiels, the Pogoses, the Michaels and the Stephens. The records of the Customs House in Dacca in 1773 show that Armenian merchants were engaged in trading between Dacca, Sylhet and Chandpore in rough cloth and oil.[9] They also carried on an extensive trade in salt and betel nut and even held zamindaries.[10] In 1636 George Mandeville, the Chief of the Company's Dacca Factory emphasised the ill-consequences of Armenian competition on English trade in the city. That they constituted a powerful force appears from the fact that an important part of the city, 'Armanitola', was named after them. That they did not limit their trade to Bengal is attested by the fact that William Hickey, taking ship at Madras, met a little weazen-faced, elderly Armenian going on mercantile business to China. It is to this Armenian community of Bengal that some of the earliest Greek traders to India looked for patronage and assistance and paid for it "one arcot rupee for every bale of merchandise they received from Dacca, Sylhet, Bandana, Assam, Patra and Moorshedabad, whether it was sold in Calcutta or exported for the Turkish market".[11]

Originally, it was in connection with the Red Sea trade that the Greeks of the Ottoman Empire came to be associated with India. At the beginning of the 17th century there is evidence of the presence of Orthodox Christians on the sub-continent,[12] though the first Greek tombstones that have survived date from 1713 and 1728.[13] Central to the Levantine trade was the 'queen' of products, coffee from Mocha which, by the time of Charles II, was beginning to appear as an exotic drink in England. Its advent in that country seems to have a connection with Greeks. John Evelyn notes that in Oxford "There came in my tyme [1637] to that College [Balliol] one Nathaniel Conopios out of Greece, from Cyrill, the Patriach of Constantinople, who returning many years after, was made (as I understood) Bishop of Smyrna. He was the first I ever saw drink coffee, which custom came not into England till thirty years after".[14] In 1710 a German traveller in Cambridge, Zacharias Conrad von Uffenbach talks about "The Greek's Coffee House, so-called because the host is a born Greek."[15] Officially, trade in coffee and other Near Eastern products was a monopoly in the hands of the English Levant Company but this monopoly was breached by Greek traders to such an extent that it brought forth angry protests from English merchants to the English Consul at Smyrna in 1804: "If Englishmen are to enjoy no advantages over Ottomans in trading with their own country and if we are to meet with no support from their Worships, rather than be made the tools of Greeks to our own prejudice, we shall solicit to be freed from the restraints and shackles of the Company's Law".[16]

The first Greeks to engage actively in the Indian trade came from the Thracian cities of Adrianople and Philippopolis but more especially from the latter. This city is on the banks of the Maritsa River, surrounded by six hills which rise steeply from the Thracian plain to four hundred feet. In 341 B.C. Philip of Macedon, father of Alexander the Great, conquered this ancient city called Pulpadora and re-named it after himself. In Roman times it was officially called Trimontum because the Roman Army had fortified three of its six hills and it was the capital of Roman Thrace. After the break-up of the Roman Empire it was fought over by the tide of races that broke through the walls of the Roman frontiers. It was rebuilt by the Emperor Justinian and occupied during the Middle Ages by Greeks, Slavs, Bulgars and Crusaders, until it was taken by the Turks in 1364. Its population until recent times was a mixture of Greeks, Bulgarians and Turks. In 1885 it became part of the new state of Bulgaria and after the first World War its name was changed from Philippopolis to Plovdiv. It still retains memorials of its troubled past and former glories: parts of the Roman walls, the medieval ruins of Czar Ivan Arsen II's fortress, the Bachkovo monastery, 16th century mosques and 19th century churches. In the 18th century it was a flourishing city and a centre for the manufacture of rough, woollen cloths called in Turkish 'ambades'. The people of the district raised large quantities of sheep and goats and the peasant women worked their wool to produce the woollen cloths. Abbatzedes is the name given to the local people who stitch these cloths. A great deal of this commodity was exported from Philippopolis to India where one of its chief customers was the Mughal Army who used it for saddle bags and saddles for horses, elephants and camels. Sometimes it was embossed with gold and silver and used to deck palanquins and gun cases to protect them from the damp.[17] In 1724 up to 50,000 crowns worth of this cloth was being exported to India. About the middle of the 18th century the production of ambades had so expanded that the weavers formed their own guild. A contemporary Greek writer records that most of the citizens of Philippopolis "enriched their homes and families with Indian products in which Philippopolis is richer than any other city in Thrace".[18] To facilitate this trade Greek merchants from this city installed commercial agents in Constantinople[19] who were themselves often citizens of Philippopolis.

While the merchants of the Levant, Armenians, Greeks and Jews were spreading their tentacles onto the commerce of the Red Sea and the Indian sub-continent, the historically more significant advance of the Western European nations, particularly the English and the French, was also taking place. The success of the English East India Company from its foundation in the last years of the reign of Elizabeth to its stupendous military success at Plassey, is not the subject of this narrative but the consolidation of British commercial and imperial

13

power in India is the political background of the Greek commercial presence in India.

Trade drew the Greeks to India and in the last decades of the 18th century they profited from the British presence to anchor one end of their trading operations in Bengal and the other in Constantinople, a commercial cable which passed through the Red Sea and the Persian Gulf. By the early years of the 19th century, the increasing power, wealth and competence of English merchants of the Company began to make it more difficult for the Greeks and Armenians to retain a significant share of this international trade. By now, many Greek merchants, from Philippopolis, but also from other parts of Greece and Asia Minor, had settled in Bengal. They brought their families from Greece, built Orthodox churches in Calcutta and Dacca and even a school for Greek children in Calcutta. Unlike the majority of the English, most of them did not return home but were buried in Indian earth. Commenting on this fact, John Bebb, the Company's Resident in Dacca in 1788 said "From a country subject as this is to a far-distant nation there is a continual unavoidable drain to its prejudice. This drain is increased by these men [English merchants]. None of them ever make or propose an establishment in Bengal. Their fortune, as soon as they have acquired any, is removed to Europe and so much increases the drain to this country. Whatever they gain is gained from its bowels. No assistance, no relief do they yield in return. Did the Bengali or Armenian merchants possess the large property the foremost subscriber (amongst the English) is said to have acquired, he or his son would increase the establishment and the wealth would circulate in the country to its benefit". What is said of Bengalis and Armenians could equally be applied to Greeks.

By the beginning of the 19th century the role of Greek traders in India began to change. The East India Company established trading posts in some of the larger cities in Bengal which became the centres for markets and were the place of intersection of trade routes where it gathered the materials of the country for export overseas. Its servants were forbidden to trade with Europe but were allowed to engage in trade with Basra, Muscat and Suez and eastwards to Sumatra, Penang and China.[20] This trade depended upon an existing infrastructure of native trade - the task of transporting goods to the ports and inland centres, the organizing and financing of production and the handling of elementary exchange.[21] These activities were carried out by Indian merchants and some Europeans. Thus in the first decades of the 19th century the activity of Greek merchants in Bengal began to shift from engagement in the Red Sea/Levant trade to local and internal trade within the confines of territories under the control of the Company.

There is evidence of a number of Greek merchants and shopkeepers operating in the north western territories of Agra and Oudh. Some of them were country produce brokers, acting as agents for the big Calcutta and Bombay firms.

In Cawnpore, for instance, Greek merchants were the largest dealers[22] but they were also to be found in Delhi, Meerut, Agra, Fategarh, Lucknow, Muttra and Karnaul.

By far the greatest number of Greeks in India were to be found in Bengal. In Calcutta their presence has been dated to 1750[23] and their first place of settlement in the city was in Amratollah Street where they were preceded by the Armenians. Here they lived in the antique, shuttered houses and here they eventually built their church. According to one estimate there were in 1817 about thirty Greek households in the city.[24] It was, however, Dacca and its neighbouring port of Naraingunj that contained the major concentration of Greeks in Bengal. Lying north of the Burhi Ganga river, a channel of the Dhaleswari, Dacca was, in the 17th century the Mughal capital of Bengal. Most of its historic buildings - the Lal Bagh fort, the Burra and Chota Katras (caravanserais), the Husayni Dolan monuments of the Shia Muslims, the Hindu Dhakeswari Temple - date from this century which was the period of its greatest glory. It contained seven hundred mosques. The capital was removed to Murshidabad in 1704 but Dacca retained its economic importance.

The Greeks began to settle in the city about 1772[25] and by 1795 an official list of Greek merchants in Dacca[26] recorded thirty eight names, though the total Greek population must have been much larger if we take into consideration wives and children and the fact that many of these merchants are known to have employed other Greeks in subordinate capacities. From Dacca they traded with Sylhet, Bandana, Assam, Chittagong, Patna, Murshidabad and Calcutta.[27] The importance of Dacca lay principally in its industries and crafts. It was famous for the weaving of fine muslins, unique in their kind and because of the lightness of their texture poetically described as "woven wind", and for its exquisite embroideries. It specialized particularly in the export of khasseidas, fabrics made principally of English twist but embroidered with Moongur or Tussar silk and exported to Basra and Jiddah from where it was despatched to Egypt and Turkey.[28] Besides muslins and khasseidas, there were thirty six other kinds of cloth manufactured in the city. In 1838 the export merchants in cloth were mainly Hindus but also contained within their ranks a number of Greeks.[29] During the British period, the importance of Shah Bundar, Dacca's inland port during the Mughal period, declined and its place was taken by Naraingunj, ten miles south of Dacca, which became the chief trading station where the godowns were filled to bursting with bales of muslins and khasseidas in the heyday of its prosperity. From here, Greek merchants despatched their cloth by boat to Calcutta. From November to June they wafted down the Burhi Ganga, Dhaleswari, Sital-lakhya, Meghna and the Sunderbuns via Khulna. During the rainy season the shorter route through the Faridpur Creek was preferred.[30]

One of the oldest trades in India was the conveying of salt, for it was one of the few commodities which linked the cities to the peasants in the countryside.

It was taken from its place of manufacture down river to local centres from where it was distributed throughout the countryside by local dealers and travelling merchants using pack animals.[31] The importance of this trade was recognized by Warren Hastings who made salt a government monopoly in 1772.[32] Hastings established a new system with a civil officer in each agency or provincial division under the supervision of the Comptroller at Calcutta. The malangis or salt workers were placed under the agents from whom they received advances. They could not sell their salt to any other person. The agents stored the salt and sold it to wholesale dealers at a price fixed by the government every year. The difference between the price paid to the malangis and the price paid by the wholesale merchants was the cost of the duty. In 1784/5 Government income from salt amounted to Rs 6,257,470 but it declined in subsequent years to about Rs 4,676,870. The office of Comptroller was abolished in 1793 and the powers and duties of the Salt Department were transferred to the Board of Trade. Some Greek traders from Dacca and Naraingunj dealt extensively in this commodity,[33] bought it at a price fixed by the Government from the Company's agents in Chittagong and transferred it by water to Naraingunj.[34]

Another of the major imports of Dacca was chunam - lime made from burnt shells - which came from Sylhet. It had two principal uses. As a kind of loam or stucco it could be used as building material especially employed for fine polished plaster. Its alternative use curiously enough was as a kind of relish spread over betel leaves and called in the vernacular 'paan'. Some Greek merchants were deeply involved in the manufacture of chunam in Sylhet and its conveyance along the River Meghna to Naraingunj.

As the sons of Greek merchants grew to manhood in Bengal, not all of them were able to follow their fathers into trade. There is clear evidence that the volume of trade in Dacca had sharply decreased in the 1830s and that the once prosperous city was sinking into economic decline, badly bruised by the failure of its native cloth industry to compete with the cheaper products of the dark, satanic mills of Lancashire.[35] Bishop Heber in his travels through the district in 1824 observes that "Dacca is but a wreck of its ancient grandeur. Its trade reduced to a sixtieth part of what it was.... the cotton produced in the district is mostly sent to England raw and the manufacturers of England are preferred by the people of Dacca themselves for their cheapness."[36] It was the beginning of the end of the relative mercantile prosperity of the early Greeks, largely from Philippopolis, which had commenced in the middle of the 18th century. Some merchants continued to thrive, largely in the salt trade, but their numbers were reduced through the 1830s and 1840s and their sons began to look for employment elsewhere. Service with the Government as writers and clerks was a favoured alternative. Bishop Heber says, in 1824, that in Dacca "of Greeks the number is considerable and they are described as industrious and intelligent people, mixing more with the English than the rest (of Europeans) and filling many of the subaltern situations under government." He even notes that "the clerk at the English church (it happens singularly enough) is a Greek." The memory of this man has survived on the Dacca Greek Memorial which now stands in the grounds of the University:

> Sacred to the memory of Basil Demetrius
> Clerk of St. Thomas' Church, Dacca
> Born 5th September 1800.
> He faithfully served as Commissariat
> Assistant IX years,
> Writing Master and Teacher in the Dacca
> College IX years,
> Clerk in St. Thomas' Church, Dacca XL
> years.
> Blessed are the pure in heart for they
> shall see God. Mt. V, 8.
> MDCCCLX.[37]

Some of the more restless spirits at the end of the century even turned to the profession of arms and took service under Maratha chiefs and there is even a recorded case of a Greek pirate harassing the pilgrim traffic between India and Mecca. In this he was, in a way, true to his Hellenic origins for in the Mediterranean the professions of merchant and pirate amongst Greek mariners were easily interchanged. So these sons of Hellas took root in Hindustan and after life was over their bodies rested in Indian earth, far from the Aegean land that gave them birth and the murmur of the wine-dark sea.

References: Chapter Two

1. Braudel, op. cit. pp484-487
2. *Ibid*, pp478-480
3. *Economic Annals of Bengal*, JC Sinha (Macmillan 1927), pp75-76
4. *A Sketch of Topography and Statistics of Dacca*, James Taylor (Dacca 1840), p308
5. *The East India Company and the Economy of Bengal from 1704 to 1740*, Sakumar Bhattacharya (Calcutta 1969)
6. Braudel, op. cit. p125
7. Sinha, op. cit. pp67-68
8. *Ibid*, pp71-72
9. *Dacca, the Mughal Capital*, A Karim (Asiatic Society, Dacca), Appendix 10
10. *Dacca*, Ahmad Hassan Dani (Dacca 1962) p43
11. *Ecclesiastical Records and Memorials of Departed Friends and Relations of the Inhabitants of Calcutta*, Asiaticus (John Hawkesworth 1802)
12. *Greeks and Philhellenes in India during the Greek Revolution*, Spyros Loukatos (Athens 1965), Chapter 3 (no English translation)
13. Asiaticus, op. cit.
14. *The Diary of John Evelyn*, Worlds Classics Edition, p9

15. *Cambridge Commemorated*, L & H Fowler (CUP 1984), p146
16. Clogg, op. cit. p41
17. Braudel, op. cit. 9 513
18. Loukatos, op. cit. p20
19. *Ibid*, chapter 3
20. *India Britannica*, Geoffrey Moorhouse (Book Club Associates 1983) p37
21. Braudel, op. cit. p495
22. *Rulers, Townmen and Bazaars*, C A Bayly (CUP 1983), p434
23. *Selections from unpublished records for the years 1748-1767 inclusive, relative mainly to the social conditions of Bengal*, Rev. James Long (Calcutta 1869, reprinted Calcutta 1973)
24. Loukatos, op. cit. p329
25. Asiaticus, op. cit.
26. Bengal European Inhabitants 1783-1807 India Office Library & Records (I.O.R.)
27. Asiaticus, op. cit.
28. Taylor, op. cit. pp176-177
29. *Ibid*, p308
30. Bhattacharya, op. cit. p185
31. Bayly, op. cit. p153
32. Sinha, op. cit. p76
33. Taylor, op. cit. p44
34. Sinha, op. cit. pp217-218
35. Taylor, op. cit.
36. *Narrative of a Journey through the Upper Provinces of India*, Bishop R Heber (London 1828), Vol. 1 p140
37. Received from British High Commission, Dacca

3

Panaghiotis Alexios Argyree

Much have I travelled in the realms of Gold,
And many goodly states and Kingdoms seen.
(Keats)

Who was the first Greek merchant in India in modern times? The question cannot be answered with any certainty. That there were many humble Greek traders who came to India from the Levant in the course of the 18th century can be deduced from the conversation that Bishop Heber had with a Greek shopkeeper of Nasirabad, a Mr. Athanass, in 1825 who told him that members of his family had come out to India for two or three generations to make a living and had returned to spend the evening of their lives in their native country. All we can establish is that the earliest record of Greek merchants in India is to be found in the aisles of the Catholic Cathedral of the Virgin Mary of the Rosary in Murghihatta, Calcutta. Here there are two tombstones which contain the following inscriptions:

> Hic Jacet Nicholaus Christianitza, Natione Graecus, in Transilvania vir sincerae fidei Deum et in Homines, obiit aetatis suae anno XXXVII aerae Christianae MDCCXIII, XVIII Augusti Nacientes morimur. (18th August, 1713.)

> Hic Jacet Georgius Johannis Drascoelo, nationis Graecis ex Philippopole. Anno Domini MDCCXXVIII diue XX August. (20th August, 1728.)[1]

Two interesting facts may be gleaned from these monuments. The first is that both men belonged not to the population of mainland Greece but to the great diaspora which had spread over the Ottoman Empire and its European neighbours even as far as the rugged hills and woods of vampire-ridden Transylvania under Hapsburg rule. The second is that even at this early date we encounter the Thracian city of Philippopolis which more than any other sent its sons to trade in Bengal.

Though we may not be able to establish who was the first Greek merchant in Bengal there is no such difficulty in ascertaining who was the founder of the Greek mercantile community in Calcutta. All the authorities[2] agree that it was a Greek merchant from Philippopolis, Alexios Argyree. At this point we have to mention a serious difficulty which confronts the genealogist and historian. It was unusual in the 18th century for Greeks to bear true surnames. Instead, each man bore a patronymic which was not inherited by his sons. This makes the task of the genealogist in tracing descent a nightmare. In addition to this difficulty, it would appear that Greek contact with the English business world led many Greeks to anglicise their names so that, for instance, 'Jordanni' became 'Jordanny' and finally 'Jordan', and 'Christodolus' became 'Christopher'. It was also, sometimes, the practice of Greeks to reverse the order of their names so that 'Emmanuel Panioty' could become, in another context, 'Panioty Emmanuel'. To make matters worse English scribes often transcribed Greek names with bizarre inaccuracy. Most of these difficulties appear with the name of the founding father of the Greek community in Calcutta. The following list shows some of the variations of his name which appear in extant records:

Alexiou, son of Argeery or Argyree
Alexander Argeery or Argyree
Panaghiotis Hadji Alexiou
Hadjee Alexious Argyree
Chatze Alexious Argyree
Alexios Argyree
Alexander the Greek
Hadjee Alexee.

The term 'Hadji' and its Greek derivation 'Chatze' require explanation. The former term was an honorific title assumed by every Muslim who had completed the pilgrimage to Mecca. The Greeks, living as they did under Muslim rule, adopted this Islamic term and applied it to those Greeks who had visited the Christian Holy Places in Palestine.[3] In 1838, an English traveller, C. B. Elliot, describes a voyage from Smyrna to Beirut in a ship on which were "ten Greek hajees making a pilgrimage to Jerusalem." They amused their children by peering into Elliot's cabin and "pointing out a thousand wonders in every action and every article of the first Englishman they had seen". It would appear that when Argyree first arrived in India he used the name 'Alexander' and later reverted to the name of 'Alexios'. An anglicized version of his Greek name 'Panaghiotis' eventually became the surname of his descendants in India in the form of 'Panioty'. The word 'Panaghiotis' is derived from 'Panagia' the title used for the Virgin Mary in Greek.

The early details of Alexios Argyree's life, and indeed much of his subsequent career, are shrouded in silence. There is so much one would like to know but cannot. The date of his birth is unknown. He was born in Philippopolis and attended the Greek school in that city and then engaged in the local clothing trade - the export of rough, woollen cloths called 'ambades'.[4] After this a shutter of silence descends upon the years of his early manhood until we come across him in Calcutta in 1750.[5] We are told that he earned his living in Bengal principally as an interpreter[6] and in later life the East India Company certainly employed him as a skilled Arabic interpreter so that we are entitled to assume that he left his native city at a fairly early age to travel in the Levant where he acquired a knowledge of Arabic. We do not even know by what route he came to India. Since in later life he traded along the sea route between Calcutta and Basra, one could assume that he arrived in Bengal by sea from either Basra, Jiddah or Mocha. However, we cannot be sure of this because we know that one of his contemporaries, a Greek merchant from Argyree's native city of Philippopolis, who was the ancestor of the Athanass family of Calcutta and Meerut, entered the subcontinent by way of Persia and Afghanistan to settle in Calcutta as a merchant.

The city which Argyree came to in 1750 was already the greatest centre of trade in India. "A city of refuge for money from all over Bengal, Bihar and Orissa",[7] filled with rich Bengali and Up-Country bankers who recognized that British rule offered a respect and security for their money and property unknown in the rest of northern India. Forty thousand people lived in the settlement which was divided into an English town (not yet the neoclassical city of the 19th century) and a Black Town, already showing a disastrous lack of rational planning, crammed with humanity living in a dowdy patchwork quilt of lanes and gullies. Some fifty vessels a year made the tortuous and hazardous journey up the Hugli and with them brought the multifarious races of traders that were the true begetters of her wealth.

The settlement was governed by a President who presided over a council of nine members. In theory, its authority was derived from the imperial will of the Mughal Emperor in Delhi who had given the East India Company permission to trade in Bengal under certain conditions, but for all practical purposes the rule of the Company over Calcutta was absolute. It was not the Emperor in far away Delhi but the Nawab of Bengal, who had wrested de facto power in the weakening of the bonds of Empire after the reign of Aurangzeb, and whose power threatened the Company's trading powers in Bengal. In 1750, however, Nawab Alivardi Khan was an able ruler who had the wisdom not to push the English too hard and an uneasy equilibrium existed. The seat of the Company's government in Calcutta was ensconced behind the walls of Fort William and in 1742 the British had begun building the Maratha Ditch to protect the eastern side of the city against the depredations of those fearsome horsemen of central India who were beginning to terrorize parts of Bengal.

In this teeming hive of commerce, Alexander the Greek (Alexios Argyree) put ashore in 1750. Again, lack of information prevents much addition to this bare fact. He probably met other Greek merchants and did business with them and was in contact with the rich and prosperous Armenian community congregated around Amratollah Street with its heavy antique houses and its Church of St. Nazareth[8] built in 1724 under the auspices of the Armenian merchant Aga Nazar, raising its spire and solid piers over the roofs of the adjoining dwellings. Years later, in this very quarter, Alexander was to be the main agent in the building of a Greek Church and the sight of St. Nazareth probably provided the inspiration.

In 1750 Warren Hastings came out to Calcutta as a junior writer, lodged in Writers' Building, and it is an interesting coincidence that Alexander arrived in Calcutta in the same year, because in later years he had reason to be grateful to the great Governor for his interest in the proposal to build the Greek Church in Calcutta. In February 1755 the curtain lifts and we are given an interesting and fairly detailed picture of the commercial activities of Greek merchants which, in this case, ended in an unfortunate pecuniary loss for Alexander. He entered into an agreement with another Greek Merchant in Calcutta Dimitri Seapoy. 'Seapoy' sounds odd for a Greek name though 'Dimitri' puts the question of his origin beyond doubt and we are, in this instance, dependent on the clerks of the Company who transcribed the proceedings and probably misspelt an unfamiliar Greek name. Dimitri was clearly of greater financial standing than Alexander and was prepared to lend him 1,000 Arcot Rupees at the exorbitant rate of 20% for a voyage of commerce to Basra. In addition, he entrusted Alexander with a consignment of two bales containing three hundred pieces of sousies (silkcloth) for sale in that city. Presumably Alexander needed the loan to buy articles of export to trade on his own account. He sailed from Calcutta in the *Prince Edward*, reached Basra, sold the consignment of sousies at its estimated value and returned to Calcutta. In the interval Dimitri had died and his estate was unadministered. Despite frantic efforts on the part of Alexander to repay 3,400 rupees he owed to Dimitri he could find nobody who would accept responsibility for its receipt.

In the meantime the political situation in Bengal had taken a decided turn for the worse. In April 1756 the old Nawab, Alivardi Khan died and was succeeded by his grandson, Siraj-ud-Daula. The new Nawab, casting covetous eyes on the glittering wealth of Calcutta, picked a quarrel with the Company and attacked it. The inadequate defences of the city and the pusillanimity of the Governor, Roger Drake, led to the swift capture of Calcutta by the Nawab's forces. In the panic that preceded the event, Alexander deposited all his valuables including four large pearls belonging to his mother (value Rs 600) together with the Rs 3,400 belonging to Dimitri in Fort William for safe keeping. His confidence in the impregnability of the Fort was misplaced for, after a feeble defence, the citadel fell. What followed was the notorious 'Black Hole of Calcutta' and a stream of refugees poured out of the city downstream to Fulta. One of them was a Greek whose name was probably 'Dracoulis' but who suffered from the usual inability of English scribes to cope with Greek names and became listed as 'Draco Conlas'[9]. In November 1756 another Greek, Constantine, put in a bill to the Company for supplying the refugees with provisions. Six months later came the punitive expedition of Clive, the recapture of Calcutta and the ultimate victory of Plassey. The new Nawab, Mir Jaffar, was forced to pay compensation to the British to the tune of eleven and a half million rupees which was conveyed to the Calcutta Treasury in a fleet of boats.

The Company set up a Commission of thirteen Armenian merchants to take evidence from those who claimed to have suffered losses in the recent catastrophe. Alexander put in a claim for his lost possessions, including the money which he owed to the estate of Dimitri. Unfortunately, serious differences of opinion arose amongst the Armenian Commissioners so the President at Fort William dissolved the Commission and replaced it with a fresh body composed wholly of Englishmen. The new Commission was ordered to begin the work of taking evidence all over again. Alexander appeared before them and repeated his story. Had he boldly claimed that all the money he had lost belonged to him without qualification he would probably have been reimbursed in full. But he was truthful, thereby conclusively proving that honesty is not always the best policy. The Commissioners, with maddening legal propriety, told him that he had no right to claim the Rs 3,400 which he owed to Dimitri since he was neither the executor nor administrator of Seapoy's estate. Only a legally deputed person could make this claim. Alexander protested vigorously but the Commissioners were adamant and there the matter rested for the time being.

From 1757 to 1763 the curtain descends once again on his activities though we have a limited amount of evidence to form some reasonable conjectures. It would seem that he was once again engaged in trading ventures in the Levant and found time to make the pilgrimage to the Holy Places in Palestine because when he next appears in the annals of Calcutta he is known as Hadjee Alexios Argyree. In 1763, another Greek merchant, Nicholas Muscovite (he must have been one of the many Greek merchants who traded with Russia), arrived in Calcutta and was appointed administrator of Dimitri's estate. Going through the accounts he discovered Argyree's debt and immediately sued him in the Mayor's Court in Calcutta for its return. The Court refused to believe Argyree's version of the loss of the money and Nicholas obtained a Court decree requiring Argyree to pay the sum into Dimitri's estate. In desperation he petitioned the President of the Council, Henry Vansittart, for a reconsideration of the decision of the Commissioners of Restitution in 1757. With it he submitted a declaration by William Magee, Notary Public of Calcutta that the written account accompanying the petition was a true copy of the original statement of losses submitted to the Commissioners and acknowledged by Mr Culling Smith, the secretary to the Commission at that time. The Secretary to the Council, John Graham, wrote to the Commissioners to enquire if they possessed any record of Argyree's claim in 1757. The new secretary of the Commission, Thomas Cooke, replied pointing out that no claim had been received by anybody called Hadjee Alexios but a claim had been received by one, Alexander, a Greek, for Rs 3,400 belonging to Dimitri Seapoy. Since he had no legal authority to make such a claim, the Commissioners had deducted it from his account. The Council's final opinion on the matter was that Alexios Argyree had a just claim to compensation since he had been required by the Mayor's Court to repay the debt but unfortunately the petition had been made too late as the whole of the Compensation Fund had already been disbursed and therefore nothing could be done for him. The whole maddening business was enough to make anyone doubt the providence of God and the workings of British justice, but Argyree does not seem to have lost faith in either.[10]

Sometime after the failure of his petition in 1764, he returned to Philippopolis and was made a Master of the Guild of Ambade Makers in 1766. Shortly afterwards he returned to Calcutta to make it his permanent home. He never saw Philippopolis again. It is not possible to be certain about the number of children he had. His eldest son was Panagiotakes Alexiou but he had other sons as well, two of whom were probably Emmanuel and Constantine Panioty.

In the year 1770 Argyree performed a notable feat in diplomacy that deserves an honourable mention in the history of British commerce. The theatre in which this intervention took place was Egypt where for some years the English and French had been fierce rivals. The French mercantile presence in Cairo had been growing steadily since the middle of the 18th century. From this centre they were transporting to Europe the products of the Levant and the Indies in increasing quantities — coffee, incense, gum, aloes, senna, tamarind, saffron bulbs, myrrh, ostrich plumes, fabrics of all kinds and porcelain.[11] This Gallic activity was viewed with increasing suspicion by the East India Company, especially as it had not yet obtained official permission from the Beys of Egypt to trade with that country. In November 1768 Governor Verelst in Calcutta made representations to John Murray, the British Ambassador to Turkey, complaining of the difficulties British merchants encountered in the ports of Mocha, Jiddah and Basra and asking him to use his influence to alleviate them.[12]

To follow up this initiative, the Calcutta government decided to send an embassy to Egypt to petition the Beys for liberty for the English to trade with Suez. The man chosen to lead this delegation was a well-known figure in Calcutta, Captain Cudbert Thornhill. He had traded to almost every part of India and was particularly conversant with the Red Sea Ports, especially Jiddah, where he had assisted the British explorer of Abyssinia, Mr Bruce. Like Argyree he had been present in Calcutta at the time of Siraj-ud-Daula's invasion and had been one of the refugees who found sanctuary at Fulta. An English visitor in Calcutta, Thomas Twining, described him in later years when he had become Master Attendant of Calcutta as "a respectable-looking old gentleman, dressed in black, with a powdered long-tailed wig and a large cocked hat in his hand.... the Captain had already laid aside the imperious action of the quarter-deck and resumed his shore character in which, however, some professional consequence was visible, but associated with an air of sincerity and frankness, or resolution and intelligence that gave a just idea of his many excellent qualities."[13] Thornhill chose Argyree as his Arabic interpreter and the embassy sailed from Calcutta at the close of 1770 in Thornhill's ship, the *Alexander*.

On December 29th they met with a severe gale in the Bay of Bengal that dismasted the ship. So acute was the danger that the crew expected the vessel to founder. Argyree, as so many others have done in a moment of extreme peril, made a solemn vow to God that if his life was spared he would build a church in Calcutta where his Greek brethren could offer the Orthodox Liturgy. His prayers were apparently heard for the *Alexander*, albeit the worse for her experience, survived the gale and Thornhill put her into Madras for refitting. In 1771 the *Alexander* arrived in Mocha and took aboard a cargo of coffee for Pondicherry. Here Thornhill decided that the monsoon season was too far advanced for the *Alexander* to proceed to Jiddah. It was indicative of the trust he placed in the character and competence of Argyree that he decided to send him overland to Cairo to obtain the object of the embassy. Unfortunately, no details of this mission have been preserved except that it was successful and Argyree was able to return to Calcutta with his mission accomplished.[14]

In April 1772 Warren Hastings became Governor of Bengal and by this time the scope of Greek trading activities and the number of Greeks in Calcutta began to increase. In 1774 a letter was despatched by the leading Greek merchants to the Orthodox Archbishop of Sinai, Cyril I, asking for a second Orthodox priest to minister to their spiritual needs. The letter was signed by Chatzee Alexios Argyree and six other Greeks.[15] All the available evidence points to the fact that he was regarded by his compatriots as the founder of the Greek community and the leading Greek merchant in Calcutta. It is not surprising therefore that it was he who, on April 11th 1774, approached Hastings with a petition for permission to build a Greek Orthodox Church in Calcutta which was signed by all the Greek merchants:

To the Honourable Warren Hastings, Esq.

President of the Council of Fort William.

That your petitioners having resided in this settlement for many years without having a place of worship and as there has lately arrived a priest but as yet no place for assembling to pay their adoration to the Almighty, we, therefore, your petitioners, most humbly beg permission to erect a chapel for that purpose and further beg to allow us a privilege of the land rent where the said chapel is to be erected for which favour we shall always add our sincere prayers for the prosperity of the British Nation who are famed in all parts of the world for that toleration in permitting and indulging the individuals under them in their religious rights and for this and every other indulgence that we have received we hope we shall prove ourselves good subjects and worthy of your kind protection and shall as in duty bound ever pray.[16]

The permission was speedily granted and a subscription list was opened for the cost of the church's erection. In the interim, Argyree bought a small house adjoining the Portuguese Church of the Virgin Mary of the Rosary where Divine Service according to the Orthodox rites could be performed until the church was built. Death intervened before Argyree could accomplish his cherished ambition but before he died he was able by his exertions to add another Greek colony of merchants to the existing community in Calcutta.

About 1772 Alexios Argyree began to extend his commercial activities to Dacca. It is unfortunate that, just as at the beginning of his mercantile career, the details concerning this business venture have not survived. All we know is that he acquired a considerable amount of property in Dacca and Backergunj which he left to his sons and it was in the former place that he expired in 1777. Surprisingly, he does not seem to have died a rich man. His estate only realized 80,000 rupees, 20,000 of which went to defray his debts in Constantinople. His body was transferred to Calcutta and laid to rest among the community he founded. Over his tomb in the Greek Church the following epitaph in Greek was inscribed:

> This tombstone covers the body of Alexiou, son of Argyree,
> from the city of Philippopolis, a man of noble family
> and resourceful character, who, while leading the life
> of a merchant in Bengal was taken up to the Lord in the
> city of Dacca. He took the initiative in founding
> this church. His remains were translated here where
> he now lies. August 5, 1777.[17]

References: Chapter Three

1. Asiaticus, op. cit.
2. Asiaticus, Loukatos, Bengal Obituary, op. cit.
3. *Bengal Obituary*, Second BACSA reprint 1987, p313
4. Loukatos, op. cit. Chapter 3
5. Asiaticus, op. cit. and Rev. James Long, op. cit. The Bengal Obituary incorrectly states the date of his arrival in Calcutta as 1770.
6. Rev. J. Long, op. cit.
7. *The Men Who Ruled India*, P Mason (Guild Publishing, London 1985), p32
8. *Bengal Obituary*, p310
9. *Bengal Past and Present*, Article, Vol. 3Q
10. *Bengal Public Consultations*, Vol. VI, 106 I.O.R.
11. Braudel, op. cit. pp478-480
12. *Bengal Despatches* E/4/6/619 I.O.R.
13. *Calcutta in the 18th Century - impressions of travellers*, P Thankappan Nair (Calcutta 1984)
14. Asiaticus, op. cit.
15. Loukatos, op. cit. Chapter 3
16. *Press Lists Public Records*, Vol. VIII p403 I.O.R.
17. *Bengal Transcriptions of Tombs*, Vol. I I.O.R.

4

Alexander Panioty

I am acquainted with misfortune's fortune,
And better than herself her dowry know.   (Hilaire Belloc)

The Greek name of Alexios Argyree's eldest son was Panagiotakes Alexiou but amongst the English in Bengal he was known as Alexander Panioty. He was born in Philippopolis in 1750 shortly before his father left the city on his first journey to India. As is the case with his father, we know nothing about his early life except that he married a Greek girl in Philippopolis and in 1771 came out to Calcutta under the auspices of his father. It seems almost certain that he joined Argyree in Dacca almost immediately after his arrival and became involved in his father's commercial activities in that part of Bengal. In February 1776 at the instigation of Argyree, the Greek priest in Calcutta, Father Constantine Parthenios successfully petitioned the Governor in Council for permission for Greeks to trade and settle in Sylhet. The likelihood is that before his death in 1777 Argyree had begun a commercial venture in Sylhet in which his eldest son became deeply involved.

Like so many other Greek merchants in Bengal, Alexander Panioty became an extensive purchaser of salt from the East India Company which he imported from Chittagong to Naraingunj by river. In the Bangladesh District Records there are a number of letters from Company officials recording the sale of salt in Chittagong to him between 1783 and 1785. The following is a specimen:

Mr M. Day.   Salt Office.
Chief of Dacca.   Jan 4, 1785.
Sir,
   I have received enclosed from Mr Plowden your receipt of the 21 Dec, 1784, for 10,050 sicca rupees for salt sold to Alexander Panioty which sum you will be pleased to pay to Mr John Johnson, who will give you a receipt for the same and your receipt will be returned.
I am and ca.
Henry Vansittart.
Comptroller.[1]

Salt trading in Bengal could be a rough and risky business subject to the depredations of dacoits who operated in the Sunderbuns and the river leading to Dacca, and the illegal attempts by predatory zamindars to impose taxes on the cargoes of traders passing through their lands. Michael Andreou, a Greek merchant of Calcutta, suffered this outrage in 1786 when Raja Baidyanath of Dinajpur seized his salt boats because he refused to pay duty to the Raja as he possessed a perwana (a pass or permit) from the Company to allow free transit of his goods.[2]

It was no doubt experiences like this which led Michael Andreou and Alexander Panioty to join with other Greek merchants in 1792 to petition the Governor General, Lord Cornwallis, as follows:

Sir,

We humbly beg leave to inform you that there are a number of Greeks in Calcutta, Dacca and Naraingunj who are always constantly in our employ as Conductors of boats and agents in disposing of salt etc. at the different stations of trade, and their chief employment is transporting salt which we purchase at the Hon. Company's sales; of which commodity we purchase annually to the amount of ten lakhs of Sicca Rupees. As it is very necessary for these conductors, whose names are here undermentioned, who are obliged constantly to go from place to place with goods, to have some arms for defence, we humbly request you will do us the favour to procure the permission of the government for their carrying in their boat five or six muskets each for the defence of themselves, their people and the property they carry. We shall give security to the government if required that no improper use shall be made of their indulgence. Names of conductors: George Theokan, Dimitry Elijah, Nicolah Calonah, Athanass Dimitry, Michael John, Constantine Daniel, Stamaty John, Nicolah Constantine, Paully Stratty, Constantine Christodolus, Constantine Theodore, John Verdaloko, Anastas Constantine, Mafseel Constantine.

We have the honour to be, Sir, your most obedient servants:

Of Calcutta: Mavrody Kyriakos, Michael Andrew, Mixanly Ardeur, Nicolay Callonah, Sonozaor Nazoras, Shereen Abraham, Christodulo Nicolay.

Of Dacca: Panioty Alexander by his attorney, M. Kyriakos. Constantine Shaw by his attorney, M. Kyriakos.

Calcutta, 28 July, 1792[3]

Lord Cornwallis granted the petition. Encouraged by this success in August of the same year, Michael Andreou and Christodulo Nicolay put in further applications for muskets for the same purpose which were similarly granted. Michael Andreou stated that they were to be used specifically on his boats plying between Dacca and Chittagong.[4]

In 1788 Alexander Panioty's business affairs in Sylhet suffered a singular reverse which led to a considerable loss of money from which he never fully recovered. The whole matter comes to light in a number of letters of complaint from the Greek priest in Calcutta, Father Constantine Parthenios, to the Governor in Council and the reply made to these by Mr Willes, the Collector of Sylhet.

Evidently, bad feeling between Greek traders and English officials in Sylhet was of long standing, and the Greeks had petitioned the Council before 1788, complaining of various injustices inflicted on them by a former Collector, Mr Lindsay. On that occasion the Council sided with the Greeks and declared their hope that the Greeks would never again suffer oppression in that district.

Alexander Panioty had embarked upon the manufacture of chunam in Sylhet. He appointed as his agent another Greek, Paulee Straty, who had arrived in India in 1787, to look after his affairs there and to initiate the chunam manufacturing business. For this purpose, Straty rented a property from a local zamindar, Puroa Raja, at a place called Tehlee Khal and hired the services of natives to manufacture the chunam, coolies and other auxiliary workers who gathered at this place. At this point, Mr Willes, the Collector of Sylhet, erupted upon the scene with a cohort of sepoys, seized, dragged and bound Straty's employees and imprisoned them. They were told that they could only recover their liberty if they entered into an agreement not to do any further work for Straty. The Collector followed up this coup-de-main with a public notice that the manufacture of chunam was forbidden in his district and (so Parthenios says) he permitted some other Europeans to do so on his behalf. "It will be unnecessary for me to comment on the conduct of Mr Willes which I have here troubled your lordships with, and which is fully supported by the affidavits of the people immediately concerned and should your lordships be pleased to consider this as a case meriting your lordships' attention, it will, with many other circumstances of oppression, be more fully established by Mr Paulee Straty now on his way to Calcutta for that purpose".

The affidavits and dispositions which Father Parthenios refers to are indeed numerous but confusing though they bring to life in a vivid manner the uncertainties of commercial life in the Mofussil at the end of the 18th century, and it comes as a surprise to realise that when all this took place in Bengal the French Revolution had not begun its turbulent and bloody progress in Europe. Among the documents is a letter from Father Parthenios to Mr Willes which describes Alexander Panioty as "the chief merchant of my congregation", and says that unless the Collector remedies the grievances relating to the manufacture of chunam in Sylhet "Mr Panioty Alexander the proprietor will be most surely the loser of twelve thousand rupees which God forbid - it would be the immediate destruction of my congregation." Even allowing for clerical exaggeration, the statement draws attention to Alexander Panioty's central position in the local Greek community and to the fact that the activities of many other Greeks depended on his prosperity.

Another letter is from the Puroa Raja, Sree Ram Naum, the owner of Tehlee Khal, to Straty, giving him permission to bring stones from Puroa, cut wood and all that is requisite for the manufacture of chunam. He adds "My country is going to ruin from various causes, no aurangs or market places are being established nor do any traders appear. For this reason I gave you assurance of my protection". Tehlee Khal is described as "bounded to the north by the river Peeyaini, to the south by my territories, to the east by the banks of Tehlee Creek and the Ramana Creek and to the west by Chumareah Creek". The Greeks are to be charged Rs 16 rent per annum.

Other Indians who submitted affidavits were Gunisram Das who had been employed for the past ten months in the service of Alexander Panioty as a sircar. He says that Straty had sent several petitions in the Persian language to Mr Willes relating to the chunam affair and that Straty was employing about a hundred people in the chunam works. He also states that the Europeans permitted by the Collector to manufacture and trade in chunam are Messrs Robinson, Rait, Luke and Smith. One Thaik Nizamuddee of Ouchaal says he was employed by Alexander Panioty as a peon to take messages and letters from Dacca to Straty in Sylhet. He says he witnessed the arrest and confinement of the chunam workers by the sepoys.

The charges against Willes were serious for, if true, it meant that one of the Company's Collectors was conspiring with other non-official Europeans to corner the manufacture of chunam in the district and was using the Company's soldiers to eliminate other competitors. Not surprisingly, the Governor in Council sent copies of the affidavits and depositions to Mr Willes to answer. Needless to say, the Collector's reply is a complete refutation of the Greek charges. He denies any personal involvement in the trade of his district. He dismisses the affidavits as the work of a conspiring attorney-at-law in Calcutta, one Mr Raban. This was Thomas Raban who lived in a house at the corner of Tank Square and Lal Bazaar and is mentioned by William Hickey in his 'Memoirs'. Willes says, with commendable dignity, that he hopes the government will protect officers in the Mofussil from the mischievous and conniving designs of Calcutta attorneys. He explains that Tehlee Khal was part of a grant made by the Mughal government to the Company. It was abandoned by the ryots due to the depredations of the Cosseahs, the hill rajas (of whom the Puroa Raja is one). The only title the Cosseahs have to the property is forcible seizure and therefore there is great impropriety in recognizing Straty's renting of the land from the Puroa Raja. As a final barb he declares that Paulee Straty "is a very quarrelsome man frequently in dispute with the natives" and asks that he may be ordered to quit the district of Sylhet.

Things went badly for Alexander Panioty for the Governor General in Council upheld the Collector and ordered Straty to leave Sylhet but agreed that he should be given reasonable time to settle his affairs.[5] It is not possible to offer any opinion as to where justice lay in this case for the Council did not record the arguments and considerations that led to its decision. However, there was no doubt that for Alexander Panioty and the Greek Community in Bengal the prohibition to manufacture chunam in Sylhet was a serious financial blow from which Alexander himself never fully recovered. As for Paulee Straty, the fierce-tempered Greek, he disappears from history except for a grave and a tombstone in the Greek Churchyard in Calcutta,

'Sacred to the memory of Paubly Stratee, a native of Kydonia in Greece. Born 1758. Died in 1826'.[6]

In another document he is described as hailing from Mitylene on the island of Lesbos, opposite Kydonia which is on the mainland of Asia Minor. This fertile island produced a light red wine whose colour was said to be improved by the addition of elderberries and was reckoned by connoisseurs to be the finest in Greece. One wonders if he longed to taste it again in his hot and sweaty exile in Bengal.

In 1785 Warren Hastings handed over the reins of government to his successor and embarked for England. No sooner had he arrived than the ranks of his enemies began to close around him. By February 1788 they had so far succeeded in convincing public opinion that he was guilty of crimes against the people of Bengal and he was impeached by the House of Commons at the bar of the House of Lords for his high crimes and misdemeanours. But the great proconsul had also his friends and admirers, amongst whom was the Greek community of Bengal. He had been a good friend to them, given them permission to build their church in Calcutta and himself contributed Rs 2,000 to the subscription list for its erection and "thus set an example to the English to encourage the pious intentions of the Greeks".[7] On 13 December 1788 the merchants of the Greek community in Bengal sent a petition and address to the Honourable Court of Directors of the East India Company as a testimonial to the government of Warren Hastings which they, no doubt, hoped would be of some use to him in countering the accusations of Fox, Burke, Sheridan and his other Whig enemies.

The petitioners identified themselves as "the offspring of Hellas, called by Europeans, Greeks, now residing for commercial purposes in Calcutta and other places in the Kingdom of Bengal" and go on to pay tribute to Hastings for his efforts to encourage them to build their church in Calcutta in which they "considering themselves lawful subjects of his Most High, Powerful and Sacred Majesty, the King of Great Britain" offer up daily prayers for his "permanence, prosperity and happiness". The concluding paragraphs are like a Thucydidean panegyric to Hastings which is surely extraordinary in the annals of British Imperialism, especially considering that the Greeks had nothing to gain from the praise of the seemingly discredited and powerless Governor General:

"We take the liberty of testifying and declaring by this humble representation his Christian and universal character, his beneficent and charitable disposition to all mankind, his just and impartial love of all the native inhabitants, whether high or low, of this kingdom and his fervent zeal for the prosperity of this country in general and of every individual in it, manifesting to all and every one

31

of them marks of paternal affection and stretching forth his hand to those whom he found in indigent circumstances and destitute of the necessities of life. He was a zealous patron for the dispensation of justice to every individual and of a faithful balance of equity. In a word, he was enriched with all human and moral indowments and famous not only for his moral and political virtues but worthy of praise and to be highly spoken of for his desire to preserve and improve the literature of this country, all of which excellencies will render him admired and immortal throughout the universal world".[8]

The address is followed by the signatures of two Greek Orthodox priests (Constantine Parthenios, Rector, Greek Church, Calcutta, and Nathaniel Cyphano, priest and monk of the convent of Mount Sinai) and of seventy Greek merchants. Apart from its intrinsic interest it is also a valuable document for the historian of the Greek community in Bengal. At the head of the list of merchants is Alexander Panioty who signs himself 'Panageotes Alexios'.

After the signing of the Hastings Petition the trail turns cold. In 1802 we discover that Alexander is living in Dacca "the survivor of misfortunes ..... his descent from Argyree, his zeal in the days of his prosperity to forward the pious wishes of his father and his having lost a most amiable wife in 1798 are all the circumstances that have come to my knowledge concerning him" says a contemporary observer[9] who calls himself 'Asiaticus'. One brief inconsequential glimpse we have of him, in those dark days, is in the will of a French tailor of Calcutta, Jacques Fleury, who died in 1806. One of his debtors was Mr Panioty (Rs 50).[10] Alexander's daughter, Sultana, married John Perroux, Head Assistant of the Salt Office in Calcutta. Perhaps he had professional dealings with Alexander as a purchaser of salt from the government. John was the son of André Perroux, a Savoyard who arrived in India in 1777 and was steward to Messrs Barber and Palmer, Cositollah Street. John and Sultana had three daughters and a son. Two of the girls, Julia and Louisa, died in 1811 and were buried in the Greek Cemetery. The third daughter, Cecilia, married Edward Smithson Brown in Calcutta in 1816. Sultana's tomb was in the Greek Churchyard, Calcutta with the following inscription:

> Sacred to the memory of Sultana, the wife of John Perroux of Calcutta and daughter of Alexander Panioty of Dacca who was suddenly snatched from this transitory world beloved by all who knew her on the 2nd Nov, 1816, in the 24th year of her age.[11]

Her daughters and her father-in-law were also buried in the Greek churchyard:

> André Perroux, native of Savoy, died July 31, 1805, aged 56 years. Also Julia died 1811 (8 months) and Louisa died 1811 (3 months), daughters of Jno and Sa Perroux.

The East India and Bengal Directories from 1790 to 1818 do not include Alexander Panioty's name among the small number of important Greek merchants even though Father Parthenios had referred to him in 1788 as "the chief merchant of my congregation". This seems to be evidence of the fact that his losses over the chunam business in Sylhet had been considerable and pushed him into a commercial backwater. However, he seems to have recovered somewhat for in the Bengal Directory of 1818 he suddenly surfaces at Naraingunj and is thereafter mentioned as trading in Dacca until 1821. From 1810 onwards he threw himself into the project of building a Greek Orthodox church in Dacca, petitioning the Archbishop of Sinai to send out a priest from St. Catherine's Monastery in Sinai to serve the spiritual needs of the Dacca Greeks. His endeavours were successful and the inauguration of the Church took place on November 3rd, 1812.[12] In this respect he had dutifully followed the footsteps of his father as a champion of the Greek faith in Bengal. He was buried inside the church which he had founded below a memorial tablet inscribed in both Greek and English. The latter inscription reads:

Sacred to the memory of Panioty Alexander Esquire who departed this life the 10th of January, 1821, O.S., aged 69 years 10 months.

A translation of the Greek inscription is as follows:

I was called Panaiotes and my father was Alexios. Philippopolis was my native land. Now your native land is the abode of the Blessed One, rejoicing with others. The tomb inside the Holy Church, which in your devotion you built, holds your body. Farewell, you had a great heart and soul, O memorable man! Galanos says that he lived for seventy years less two months and departed this life on 10th Jan., 1821.[13]

References: Chapter Four

1. *Bangladesh District Records,* Dacca District (Univ. of Dacca 1981), Vol. 1 1784-1787, Ed. Sirajul Islam, p102 et al.
2. Board of Revenue Proceedings 7 June, 1786, F 229, quoted in *The Salt Industry of Bengal, 1757-1800,* Balai Barui (Calcutta 1985)
3. *Press Lists Public Records* Vol. XIV p27 I.O.R
4. *Ibid,* p35 I.O.R
5. *Ibid,* Vol. XII pp426, 477-479
6. *Bengal Transcriptions of Tombs,* Vol. 1
7. *Bengal Obituary,* p313
8. *Press Lists Public Records,* Vol. XII p465 I.O.R
9. Asiaticus, op. cit.
10. Will sworn 20/11/1806 I.O.R
11. *Bengal Obituary,* p313
12. Loukatos, op. cit. Chapter 3
13. From unclassified material in the Library of the Society of Genealogists, London. They appear to be notes collected about 1923 by the Education Department in India to record British and European monumental inscriptions.

5

The Greek Orthodox
Church in Bengal

And therefore have I sailed the seas and come
to the holy city of Byzantium. (W. B. Yeats)

The Greek Orthodox Church can claim to be the mother church of Eastern Europe to whose missionaries, in the early centuries of Christianity, the Slavs of the Balkans and the great plains of Russia owe their Christian heritage. After its official breach with Rome in the 11th century and, especially after the conquest of the Byzantine Empire by the Turks, its missionary operations were circumscribed and Greek priests were not often seen outside the Levant. It is, therefore, surprising to find a Greek priest in Wisbech, Cambridgeshire, in Elizabethan England in 1586. We hear about him from an autobiographical account of a hunted Jesuit priest, William Weston, who was detained at Wisbech at the Queen's pleasure. This Greek Papa was a native of the island of Patmos (revered as the last home of the Apostle, St. John). He came to England, relying on letters of recommendation which the English Ambassador to Turkey had given him in Constantinople. He was on a begging mission, collecting alms for the release of Greek captives of the Turks, and was invited by the Vicar of Wisbech, Matthew Champion, to address the people of the parish. He wore ordinary threadbare clothes and knew just enough Latin and Italian to explain himself through an interpreter. He had with him letters patent from the two Patriarchs of Constantinople and Alexandria, written on parchment in most clear and elegant Greek characters, both endorsed by the pendant seals of the two Sees - the former of white wax, carrying the effigy of the Blessed Virgin and the latter was of black and carried the likeness of St. Mark.[1] It was this Metropolitan See of Constantinople which, in the late 18th and early 19th centuries, was involved in a bizarre missionary rivalry with another ancient See, a closer neighbour of Alexandria's, the Archbishopric of Sinai, for the pastoral care of the Greeks of Bengal.

Sometime about the year 1760, a dusty, travel-stained Armenian merchant from India reached the goal of his pilgrimage, the great monastery of St. Catherine, set in the fastness of the Sinai Desert. Built, so tradition has it, on the site of the apparition of the Burning Bush to Moses, it was one of the holy places of Christian pilgrimage in the Middle East. Cut off from its mother-church of Constantinople by the conquering waves of Islam, it lay like a wrecked galleon, full of sacred treasures, in its splendid isolation. In the monastery church the golden foliage of the candelabra formed a dense forest through which could be glimpsed the rich, dark hues of ikons hung in a long row along the north and south walls of the basilica. This venerable church was attached to a monastery in which the holy liturgy of the Greek Orthodox Church was lovingly performed, day in and day out, by monks who had abandoned the cares of the secular world and, like Elijah, longed only to hear "the still, small voice of God". The monastery was the centre of the Archbishop of Sinai, who normally resided in Alexandria. Many years later, in 1844, it became famous when the German scholar, Tischendorf, discovered the fourth century Codex Sinaiticus in the monastery, picking out forty leaves from a basket of papers intended for lighting the oven.

Our anonymous Armenian merchant, after slaking his spiritual thirst at the shrine of St. Catherine, sought an interview with Cyril, Archbishop of Sinai. He spoke of large numbers of Eastern Christians, Armenians and Greeks, who lived and traded in India with not a single priest to look after their spiritual needs so that these men and their families were left to the wiles of the ubiquitous Jesuits who were endeavouring, not without some success, to bring them into the fold of Rome. He begged the Archbishop to take pity on these isolated sons of Eastern Christendom and to send them some learned priests.

The Patriarch of Jerusalem, Dositheos, to whom we are indebted for this rare nugget of information, rather unkindly commented on his fellow bishop "but neither the Patriarch nor those around him were interested but only bothered about oppression and plunder and not about what the Catholic Church had received and handed down".[2] It would seem that he did Cyril an injustice because in 1769 we hear of a Greek priest, Nicophorus, from the monastery of Sinai occasionally performing the Greek liturgy in Calcutta though, as yet, there was no Greek Church nor settled place of worship in the city.[3] In 1771 Alexios Argyree made his ambassadorial journey from Calcutta to Egypt and while he was there he made contact with the Archbishop Cyril in Alexandria. Full of enthusiasm, after the recent vow he had taken, he sought to interest the Archbishop in his project to build a Greek Church in Calcutta. It seems he was successful for shortly after his return and his appeal to Hastings to allow the building of his dream church, Nicophorus left Calcutta and was replaced by a younger priest from Mount Sinai who arrived in the city on October 11, 1772. It would seem that for some unknown reason a coolness had developed between Nicophorus and the Greek merchants and the Archbishop had probably decided that the difficulties of the Bengal Mission could only be handled by a younger man who possessed greater administrative authority. The new priest was Ananias, the Chancellor of the monastery of St. Catherine.

By 1774 Ananias was celebrating the liturgy in the small house in Amratollah Street which Argyree had purchased. As a further step towards the consolidation of their religious status, the Greeks, inspired by Argyree and Ananias, formed a society officially known as 'The Orthodox Brotherhood of the Greeks in Calcutta' and they declared the Crown of England as their protector.[4]

In February 1774 Argyree and other Greek merchants of Calcutta wrote a letter to the monastery asking for a second priest to be sent out to help Ananias and for ikons to be acquired from Crete for their new projected place of worship.

In 1775 the Archbishop of Sinai sent out to Calcutta, Father Constantine Parthenios, a monk of Mount Sinai and a native of Corfu. He was a man of enormous charm, good looks and intelligence and he became a well-known and popular figure in Calcutta, not only among the Greeks but in the wider European community. 'Asiaticus' describes him as "a gentleman polite and communicative and one who is unquestionably the most enlightened person under the English government of all descendants of Hellas". Zoffany took him as the model of Christ in his painting of the Last Supper which hangs in the Church of St. John in Calcutta. Not only as a priest but as a correspondent and diplomat he served the Calcutta Greeks well, penning urbane letters in English to the Council on behalf of their commercial concerns. On his arrival, he immediately threw himself with enthusiasm into the plans of Argyree and became the most energetic collector of donations for the projected Greek church, successfully approaching the Governor General and other members of the English community for donations. Soon afterwards there arrived a letter from the Archbishop addressed to Georgios Baraktaroglou (Argyree by now had transferred his commercial activities to Dacca) and the Greek merchants of Calcutta, expressing his joy at the proper establishment of Orthodox ritual in Bengal.[5]

In 1777 two prominent Greeks departed from the Bengal scene: Argyree died in Dacca and the Chancellor Ananias left Calcutta and returned to Sinai. In his place two other monks arrived in Calcutta, Nathaniel of Syphnos and Damian. With them they brought a precious cargo of ikons from Crete. It is perhaps difficult for Western Europeans to understand the significance of this event and the joy it aroused in the hearts of the Greek community. Ikons (the painted images of Christ, the Virgin Mary and the Saints) are an integral part of the worship, theology and religious culture of the Orthodox Church. They are a Hellenic refutation of Semitic and Islamic puritanism, which refuses to picture the concept of a totally transcendent God, and an affirmation of the doctrine of the Incarnation that "The Word became flesh". The Greek Orthodox Church still commemorates the restoration of ikons after the Iconoclast Controversy by the Empress Irene on the First Sunday in Lent. In church the ikons, gleaming like an open casket of gems, are displayed on the iconastasis, the screen which separates nave from sanctuary and are a focal point of worship during the liturgy. The priest burns incense before them and reads a prayer of intercession. "Gleaming smokily in the concavity of their churches and presiding as familiar lares in every house, from Trebizond to Corfu and from Macedonia to Cyprus, icons were the arms-parlant, the shields, devices, helmets, crowns, crests, supporters and the stiff swirl of mantelling of the King and Queen, the warriors and the magicians of a lost Arthurian Byzantine Olympus to which they would come back one day".[6] After the fall of Constantinople in 1453, Crete, under the protection of Venetian arms, became the main centre of Greek ikon painting. "Cretan icons, glowing on slabs of olive, walnut, hard-pine, poplar and plane, travelled all over the archipelago and the mainland to Venice..... and to Russia..... the Cretan technique was the strongest strain in the iconography of occupied Greece".[7] It is not surprising therefore that the Calcutta Greeks specified that the ikons they wanted should come from Crete and should have hailed their arrival with such enthusiasm.

In June 1780 the foundation stone of the Greek Orthodox Church was laid at 7 Amratollah Street and on August 6, 1782, the church was consecrated and dedicated to the Transformation of Our Blessed Redeemer. It bore in front the following inscription:

1780
The Temple of the Lord
The Holy Transfiguration.
1781

This dedication owes its importance in the Orthodox cycle of feasts to the fact that it demonstrates vividly the dogma of the two natures of Christ, divine and human. The liturgy on that memorable day was celebrated by Nathaniel of Syphnos and Constantine Parthenios and we can easily reconstruct the scene. Compared with churches in the cities of the Levant, the Calcutta church was a relatively humble affair but it corresponded to the main architectural features of other Greek Orthodox churches - in the plan of the Greek Cross, with a domed ceiling, the iconastasis separating the nave from the sanctuary, the symbolic Holy of Holies derived from the Temple ritual of Judaism and the chandelier with wax lights suspended from the ceiling. We can imagine the two bearded priests, richly robed, accompanied by young boys in surplices carrying wax tapers. Before the consecration a curtain is drawn before the altar behind which the priests pray that the bread and wine might be sanctified through the power of God. Then they re-appear to the congregation, bid peace to the people and bless them and then one of them delivers a sermon. Underneath their rich robes they wear their black habits and on their heads black hats covered with a veil to symbolise the truth that the wearer is under the influence of the Gospel. For Greeks the saintly idiom "is their own, the language as it were, that their great-grandfathers spoke in happier days. It is a family affair and Our Lord and Our Lady and their enormous saintly retinue have long since become honorary fellow countrymen".[8] That the Church was the object of Turkish ferocity made it the outward symbol and talisman of Greek survival. The cost of erecting the Greek Church in Calcutta was estimated at Rs 30,000.

In 1782 Nathaniel of Syphnos wrote to the monastery of Sinai for permission to celebrate mixed marriages between Greek Orthodox persons and partners from some other Christian faith. It was indeed a problem for the Greeks, living as they did in a society where most other Europeans were either Anglicans,

Protestants or Roman Catholics. To a very large extent the Greek families in Bengal intermarried with each other but there were an increasing number of mixed marriages and in the years ahead the phenomenon was to increase. The Bengal Directories of the early years of the 19th century record the following mixed marriages:

Jan. 26 1808. Ducas, Helen of Calc m. John Pierson Knott, Lt, Madras Establishment. Widower.

Aug. 21, 1810. Athanas. Miss of Calc m. Hodgkinson R. Lieut. Madras Native Infantry.

Nov 11, 1811. Archangelou, Mary m. Chisell. L. 2nd Bn. 4th Bengal Native Infantry.

Sept 26, 1816. Athanas, Sophia m. Ensign C.J. Crane, 4th Bengal Native Infantry.

Jan 20, 1820. Joaquin Foscholo m. Mmme L'Aunette Benville.

Sept 9, 1823. Elias, Jos m. Jebb, Miss eldest daughter of late N. Jebb.

Dec 23, 1825. Mr Geo Kalonas m. Miss Louisa Battaye.

It would appear from the above that young military gentlemen found Greek girls attractive. Another somewhat later tribute to a mixed marriage was recorded on one of the tombstones in the Greek churchyard:

Sacred to the memory of Eliza Georgiana, the beloved wife of Charles Brownfield. She departed this life on Saturday the 7th May 1842, aged 27 years and 7 days. An affectionate wife, a fond mother and a sincere friend.

The verses that follow somehow break through the stilted tones of funerary verse to suggest a genuine love and deep sorrow:

Dear wife that never made thy husband weep
Till now; thou sleepst the last dreamless sleep,
Thine image like the moon in winter's night
Shall shed on life's dim close a sacred light;
But never more, may this sad heart receive
The bliss thy loving smile alone could give.[9]

Permission to conduct mixed marriages was granted to Nathaniel by the Archbishop of Sinai.

There was another side to the question of mixed marriages which involved peculiar difficulties. In the 18th century European women as a rule did not come out to India and it was therefore fairly common for European men to live with native women. At first this problem did not seem to affect the Greeks to the same extent as other Europeans. Argyree and many of the early Greek merchants brought their Greek wives and children with them from Europe. Nevertheless there were marriages between Greeks and native women and the Greek Church in Bengal had worked out a strategy to deal with this problem. About 1802 Asiaticus wrote "The Greeks in Bengal would admit proselytes, were they not apprehensive of vagrant Indians throwing themselves on the charity of their community, the aggregate fund of which is too small for the purposes of extensive benevolence, or even the administration of relief to any but the indigent of their own circumscribed society, and then the distribution is made with a frugal hand. However they admit proselytes in the following cases: if a Greek wishes to marry a native woman, she is at first baptized and their progeny educated conformable to the rites of the Greek Church: several native orphans and forlorn youth of both sexes (perhaps fifty) serving in Greek families have been baptized and educated at the expense of their masters; there are several of this description now in Bengal who understand the ancient Greek and read and write the modern language with facility".

One unusual example of this parental solicitude was the case of a merchant from Philippopolis, whose precise name is not known, but who arrived in India circa 1750 by the overland route through Persia and Afghanistan. We do not know the name of his wife but he had a son, John Athanass, born in 1753 in Calcutta. After trading in the city for several years, sometime before 1788 he decided to return to his native place in the Balkans but before leaving he made a careful and generous provision for his son. Surprisingly he did not leave him in the care of Greek friends but in the charge of some Protestant missionaries in Calcutta, and deposited a considerable sum of money with his agent for his son's education and maintenance. The missionaries did their work well for John Athanass grew up to be a successful and prosperous merchant of Calcutta. When he came of age the capital sum of his father's investment devolved upon him and became the foundation of his future wealth. He did not forget his father but corresponded with him and when he died in 1835 left a sum of money to one of his father's relations in Philippopolis.

Shortly after 1782 an unfortunate quarrel erupted between the Greek merchants and their ecclesiastical patrons in Sinai. Religious quarrels often produce an intensity of feeling which put other quarrels in the shade because they engage the deepest and most heartfelt passions of men and women. To the outsider they often appear either unedifying, ridiculous or amusing and certainly some entertainment can be derived from these Hellenic chronicles of Barchester. It seems that the dispute centred around the pecuniary demands made on the Greek community by the monastery which were hotly resisted by the merchants. In this quarrel, Nathaniel of Syphnos drew on himself the anger of his monastic brethren by supporting the stand made by his congregation. By 1792 the monastery had had enough of its recalcitrant clients and their rebellious brother, and was determined to restore proper discipline. Another monk, Dionysios of Moudana, was sent out to replace Nathaniel. When he arrived in Calcutta he wrote a slashing letter to the Archbishop of Sinai which was highly critical of his predecessor. Archbishop Constantius of Sinai (who had replaced Cyril) ordered Nathaniel to hand over immediately his authority as Rector of the Church to

Dionysios and reduced the former to the status of a simple monk. The merchants replied by refusing to recognize Dionysios as Rector and a fierce contest began which lasted twenty-five years. The merchants continued to accept Nathaniel as their pastor; the monastery refused to recognize his ministry in Calcutta and ordered him back. Encouraged by the support and friendship of his congregation, Nathaniel refused to obey. Poor Dionysios was left in lonely occupation of the Church supported by his ecclesiastical superiors but shunned like a leper by the majority of his congregation. One of them, Demetrios Galanos of Athens, described him as "the cause of dishonour to our nation".[10]

About the end of the century the main emphasis of Greek commercial activity was shifting from Calcutta to Dacca and the Greeks in the latter city were beginning to outnumber their brethren in Calcutta. In 1795 the name of Nathaniel turns up in a list of Greek inhabitants in Dacca[11] and Asiaticus describes him as "Mr Nathaniel, a native of Syphnos, who performs Divine Service in a temporary structure, sometimes at Dacca and sometimes at Narayangunj". Nathaniel seems to have tired of the clerical battle in Calcutta, leaving Parthenios to contest Dionysios' official claim to the Rectorship of the Church there. In 1792 the Dacca Greeks, who had hitherto used the Portuguese cemetery at Tizgong, acquired a burial ground of their own purchased by Coja Simon, a Greek merchant from Caesaria.

Back in Calcutta, in 1802 Asiaticus notes that the officiating clergymen are Dionysios and Paessios from Salonica - the latter having been sent out by Sinai as a reinforcement to the beleagured Dionysios. Parthenios, however, continued to reside in the city, a pillar of strength to the merchants but he died in 1803 deeply mourned by the Bengal Greeks. In his will[12] he left a small legacy to his god-child, Helen Ducas, the daughter of a Greek from Corfu, Alexander Ducas. In it he also says that his years in Bengal were full of suffering and vexation. Did he remember at the end of his life, with an exile's aching affection, his distant and lovely Ionian homeland? Nathaniel of Syphnos survived him by seven years, dying in Dacca amongst the families he had elected to serve in his lonely, rebellious way. He was lovingly commemorated by his parishioners as follows in a Greek inscription (Dacca Memorial, South wall, 3rd tablet from left):

To the memory of Father Nathaniel
A holy and saintly Christian minister
in his speech and in his life,
a second Thomas,
a priest without compare who
contentedly resided in Dacca,
Coming from his native land of Syphnos
where he was born in 1736.
He departed this life in Dacca on March 12, 1810.
Happy was he, venerated with
great respect and honour.

The Bengal Greeks were now without any effective priests - none in Dacca and the rejected Dionysios in Calcutta. Sinai had tried to strengthen the position of the latter by sending another monk to replace Constantine Parthenios. This man, oddly enough, was also called Parthenios with the addition of the patronymic Hagiomauritou but he died on his way out to Bengal. The merchants now made a daring and cunning move clearly inspired by the Machiavellian principle of 'Divide and Rule'. They despatched a letter to Sinai on December 13th, 1811, outlining the perilous spiritual situation they were in - no baptisms, no marriages, no funerary rites, no eucharist in the absence of any acceptable priest. They begged the monastery to take pity on them and send out two priests - a superior for Calcutta and another for Dacca. Foreseeing the possibility of a refusal or an ultimatum couched in terms which they would have found difficult to accept, they sent another letter to the Patriarch of Constantinople, Jeremias IV, asking for a priest from the Metropolitan See to be sent out to them. What so far had been little more than a local conflict now had the dramatic possibility of becoming a titanic ecclesiastical quarrel between two ancient Sees. The letter to Sinai was signed by twenty nine Greek merchants most of whom were based in Dacca but some in Calcutta. At the head of the list was Panagiotes Alexiou (Alexander Panioty) and in it was also included the signatures of two of his sons, Joannes and Konstantinos.

The double-letter tactic seemed to have worked, for in 1812 both Constantinople and Sinai reacted favourably. The latter, probably pressured by the likelihood that the former would intrude into what they considered their own ecclesiastical preserve, sent out to Calcutta one of their best men, the Archimandrite Benjamin. He arrived with a letter from the monastery to the Greeks reminding them of the great burden it had undertaken in the past with regard to the Bengal Mission and demanded, as an indispensable condition of its continued support, the payment of the Archimandrite's expenses, the recognition of the rights of the monastery in the matter of baptisms, marriages, funerals and other religious celebrations and the doubling of the original annual contribution to the monastery by the Greeks. It seems that the Calcutta congregation accepted these conditions and their new pastor, Benjamin, made a very favourable impression on them.

In the meantime, the Patriarch of Constantinople had been no less active. He sent out to India one of his priests, Gregory of Syphnos, who reached Calcutta in April 1812. Sizing up the situation and realising that Sinai had forestalled Constantinople in Calcutta and that the largest congregation of Greeks was in Dacca, he contacted Alexander Panioty who eagerly invited him to join them and was met with a splendid reception when he arrived in Dacca in May. He seems to have been exactly the right sort of pastor the Dacca Greeks wanted. Since Alexander Panioty had already built a church in Dacca, Gregory was at once plunged into the preparations for its official opening. The church was consecrated on November 3, 1812, and Gregory performed the first liturgy and delivered a sermon in which he stressed the significance of the event.

The Monastery of Sinai was furious when they heard that an interloper from Constantinople had installed himself in Dacca and it sent strict instructions to its priest, Benjamin, in Calcutta to have no dealings with Gregory and to avoid, in any way, recognizing his unlawful occupation of the Dacca parish. Despite these injunctions, it is pleasant to record that Benjamin appears to have ignored them and there was a friendly co-operation between both priests in their ministry.

In the middle of 1817, after five years of parochial work in Dacca, Gregory of Syphnos left to return to Constantinople. The Patriarch Jeremias was clearly pleased with the work he had accomplished in Dacca and impressed with the possibilities of the Bengal Mission. He began to contemplate the idea of a new Orthodox Bishopric of Bengal with Gregory as the first Bishop. It was not to be, for at this critical moment he died and his successor, Gregory V, was soon to be embroiled in the storms of the Greek Revolution against the Turks during which, innocent though he was of any revolutionary activity or even sympathy with the rebels, he was brutally killed by the Turks in revenge for Greek atrocities on the Morean mainland against their countrymen. No Orthodox Bishopric of Bengal ever emerged nor did the Metropolitan See of Constantinople send another priest to replace Gregory of Syphnos in Dacca. The battle of the Sees in Bengal was over and the monks of Sinai were left, once more, in exclusive possession of the field.

On July 21, 1817 Sinai sent Ambrosius Ghimouschanales, one of their monks, to Dacca and the rift between the Dacca Greeks and the monastery was finally healed. Ambrosius in Dacca and Benjamin in Calcutta settled down to a long and uninterrupted ministry which lasted right through the twenties when the flames of insurrection tore through Greece, and Turkish tyranny was devoured on the Greek mainland in their fury. On May 11, 1832 the monastery replaced Ambrosius by the Chancellor Ananias of Serroi who was, by all accounts, an outstanding priest who consolidated the administrative and pastoral work accomplished by his predecessors in Dacca.[14] The storm was over and calm waters lay ahead.

During these years two English visitors to Dacca left their brief impressions of the Greek parish. In 1824 the newly appointed Anglican Bishop of Calcutta, the deservedly popular Reginald Heber, began a long exhausting visitation of his far-flung diocese. Early in his travels he visited Dacca and paid a courtesy call on the Nawab who mentioned that the Greek priest, Ambrosius, whom he praised as "a very worthy, well informed man" was anxious to be introduced to the Bishop. At a later date in the Nawab's palace this introduction was effected to the mutual satisfaction of both men. Already in 1824 Heber notes the decline of Dacca's prosperity as a trading centre: "The European houses are mostly small and poor, compared with those in Calcutta and such as are out of town are so surrounded by jungle and ruins as to give the idea of desolation and unhealthiness".[15]

42

Sixteen years later, a similar unfavourable impression was recorded by another English visitor, Lt. Col. CJC Davidson of the Bengal Engineers. The clerk of the Greek church told him that there were few European-born Greeks left in the city for most of them had not lived long. Davidson grimly comments "Anyone could point out the cause of the speedy death of the priests, as their house stands in a close, confined alley surmounted by foetid drains which are never cleared". Davidson met the Parish Priest "a remarkably handsome Papa who has his dwelling in a small lower roomed house in the area of the church". This priest was Gabriel who had replaced Ambrosius and was himself replaced by Joseph of Zakynthos in 1841.

The colonel was not particularly impressed either by the humble Greek Church. "I paid a morning visit to the Greek chapel which contains but little worthy of note. It has, however, a spire surmounted by a cross.... the church is a room about thirty feet long by about twenty feet wide. It has no railed-in altar or elevated space but the floor is all on one level. The large wax candles stood on each side of the centre of the eastern end of the room.... on the floor below.... a dark stone with an English and Greek inscription to the memory of a Greek gentleman" (this would be Alexander Panioty's tomb).

Davidson, a true Victorian whose tastes probably veered towards the 'realistic' in painting, showed little appreciation of the icons in the church as his bald, rather philistine description of them reveals: "Over the centre was a picture of the Virgin Mary gazing at an infant Jesus, apparently at least thirteen years of age, lying on a bed, and to the right but a little to the rear, stood Joseph. On the left hand of this altar was a full length portrait of the Virgin Mary, between seven and eight feet high, looking five and thirty years of age. On my right, as my cicerone stated, was the picture of Jesus Christ himself and round the walls of the room, each with a suitable Greek inscription, were paintings of the angel Gabriel, the apostles and divers Greek saints, all surrounded by flying angels in each of their corners in the style of the 12th century. They were painted on wood and copper, neatly executed in oil miniature style with a fine varnish and had been procured from Greece about five years ago. In addition to this was a fine print of the Last Supper after a Raffaelle which I should rather have seen in my own portfolio."[16]

In 1829 poor old Dionysios of Moudania, also known as Dionysios George died in Calcutta, a relic of old controversies. His tombstone in the Greek Churchyard in Calcutta reads:

Sacred to the memory of the Revd Dioniscious
George who departed this life 23 June 1829
after being about forty years minister of the
Greek Church in the city".

The inscription tactfully omits the fact that for the whole period of his tenure he was not recognized as such by the majority of his congregation and errs on the liberal side because his stay in Calcutta was not above thirty seven years. Beneath the inscription is the following verse:

> He was indeed a simple hearted man,
> May we like him do all the good we can,
> One who knew his worth this stone doth raise,
> In token of his well deserved praise.

One can imagine him in his last years as an old gentleman smiling vaguely, anxious to please, pottering around Amratollah Street, a Hellenic Mr Harding with all the storms of life long since abated.

The number of Greek Orthodox worshippers in Bengal between 1800 and 1820 is difficult to assess with accuracy for the information is somewhat conflicting. Loukatos says that there were about one hundred and twenty families, mostly in Dacca but some in Calcutta and of these about thirty households from Philippopolis. 'Asiaticus', writing about 1802 reckons there are about forty "native Greeks" in Calcutta but he probably means 'Greek families'. These all contributed to the upkeep of the Church whose revenue was enhanced by the rent of four houses contiguous to the Church "the bequest of pious Greeks on their demise". The Calcutta Church in the twentieth century has been moved from its original site on two occasions. Amratollah Street had become in the early part of this century one of the busiest centres in the city and the noise of traffic made it difficult to hold church services. In February 1923 it was moved from 7 Amratollah Street to Russa Road, Kalighat, where a new church was built whose foundation stone was laid on 3 November 1925. Since Indian Independence it has moved again to a new site in Ashutosh Mukharji Road. In 1847 the Greek Church in Dacca collapsed and was never rebuilt.[18] It had not lasted a century; so transient was the work of the merchant from Philippopolis.

There is much evidence to suggest that the Orthodox Church in Bengal with its slender resources was fighting a losing battle in trying to maintain the spiritual allegiance of expatriate Greeks and there was a steady drain to the Roman Catholic and Anglican Churches. The Greek shopkeeper of Nasirabad, Mr. Athanass in 1825 told Bishop Heber that he usually attended the worship of the Church of England and presented himself before the prelate to ask for a blessing since Heber was the only Christian bishop he had seen since he had left Smyrna sixteen years previously. His reverence for the episcopal office was such that he would not sit down in the same room as Heber.[19] Under these circumstances it is easy to understand the transition from Greek Orthodoxy to other forms of episcopal religion.

References: Chapter Five

1. *William Weston*, Philip Caraman (Longmans 1955)
2. Loukatos, op. cit. p16 Note 1
3. Asiaticus, op. cit. Chapter 3
4. Calcutta Directory 1856
5. Loukatos, op. cit. Chapter 3
6. *Mani*, P Leigh Fermor (John Murray 1958) p243
7. *Ibid*, pp233-234
8. *Ibid*, p220
9. *Bengal Obituary*, p313
10. Loukatos, op. cit. Chapter 3
11. Bengal European Inhabitants. 1783-1807 I.O.R
12. Bengal Wills 1803 I.O.R
13. Loukatos, op. cit. pp94-96
14. *Ibid*, Chapter 3
15. R. Heber, op. cit. Vol. 1 p92
16. *Diary of Travels and Adventures in Upper India*, Lt. Col. CJC Davidson (London 1843)
17. Indian Monumental Inscriptions, Vol. 1 I.O.R
18. A H Dani, op. cit. p44
19. *Narrative of a Journey through the Upper Provinces of India from Calcutta to Bombay, 1824-25* Second Edition, R. Heber (John Murray, London, 1828) Vol. II Chapter XXIII p450

6

The Mavericks

Part A - The Athenian Brahmin

I am he that aspired to know (R. Browning)

One of the great intellectual triumphs of the European expansion to the East in the 18th century was the discovery of the literature, philosophy and history of the ancient Sanskrit civilization of India. As early as the 16th century isolated Europeans began to make contact with the hitherto totally unknown languages of the sub-continent. One of the first of these was an English Jesuit, Father Thomas Stevens, who reached Goa in 1579 and, in the pursuit of his missionary work, began a serious study of Marathi and other languages of the Deccan. He was succeeded by a Florentine merchant, Filippo Sasetti, who lived in Goa from 1583-1588, studied Sanskrit texts on medicine and folklore and seems to have been the first person to have observed a relationship between Sanskrit and European languages.

Following in the wake of these pioneers came a number of Frenchmen and Germans who through their observations and studies began to make Europeans aware of the riches of Oriental literature - Francois Bernier, a French merchant who, in the late 17th century, lived for twelve years at the court of the Great Mughal; Anquetil Duperron who in 1801 published a translation of the Upanishads; the German priest Roth (1610-1688) who produced the first Sanskrit/Latin grammar; the Dutch preacher Abraham Roger who seems to have been the first European to have discovered the Vedas in 1663 and the German Jesuits Hanxledon and Wessdin who achieved the first solid and definitive work of Sanskrit scholarship.

By the end of the 18th century the British conquest of Bengal and the enlightened patronage of Warren Hastings gave British scholars an unique opportunity of furthering the quest. Nathaniel Brassey Halhed, a Persian and Bengali scholar, published in 1776 'A Code of Gentoo Law on the Ordination of Pundits' and in 1778 'A Bengali Grammar'. Charles Wilkins (1749-1836) was the first Englishman to learn Sanskrit and translated the Bhagavad Gita. The one who made the greatest mark on Sanskrit studies, however, was Sir William Jones, a first-class scholar who explored every aspect of ancient Indian learning and in 1784 founded the Asiatic Society of Bengal which did so much to further the cause of Sanskrit studies. A contemporary of his, Henry Thomas Colebrook (1765-1837) became an even greater Sanskrit scholar who produced the first learned account of the ancient Vedas.[1]

Almost exactly contemporary with Colebrook's scholastic career was that of a relatively unknown Greek scholar, Demetrios Galanos from Athens. It is one of the minor mysteries of history that the achievement of this man in the field of Sanskrit studies, recognised by German and Italian experts, should remain almost unknown in Britain and is never referred to in English works on the subject. Apart from random references to him by British contemporaries in Bengal, it would seem the only serious consideration of his work in the English language is an article in a learned publication 'The Transactions of the Third International Congress for the History of Religions' by a Greek diplomat John Gennadius which was published in Oxford in 1908.[2] Galanos was a man of extreme modesty and a retiring disposition. Though he was one of the earliest and ablest pioneers of Indology he laid no claim to literary achievement and published nothing in his lifetime. The only critical reference to his work came from a 19th century English scholar in India, a Mr Clark, secretary to the Asiatic Society, who, commenting on the manuscripts of Galanos' translation of the Gita, said "In reading the translation I felt as if one soul had been parted in twain and set at the two ends of the world, in Greece and India, each one meditating on the same great philosophical issues". The silence of English scholars on his work was not paralleled in Germany where distinguished Indologists recognised the power and originality of his labours. One of the greatest of German scholars, Professor Theodore Benfey, reviewing Galanos' 'Prodromos' in the 'Gottingirche gelehite Anzeigen' in 1846 said that his versions of Sanskrit texts made clear many passages formerly inexplicable and which were riddles for former translators, and so rendered possible not only the correction of corrupt texts but the explanation of many points of Indian mythology and religion hitherto not understood. This was due to his unrivalled knowledge of the language and peoples of India but more especially to the fact that he won the intimate friendship and confidence of Brahmins as no other European before him had done and thus obtained much that was jealously preserved by oral tradition. Several of his translations were never attempted before in any European language while of others the original texts were not even known to exist. In 1841 the Ephore of the National Library of Greece, G. Kozakis Typaldos, assisted by the Keeper of Printed Books, G. Apostolides, commenced editing and publishing, with the assistance of European Indologists, a series of Galanos' papers which in 1853 were published in seven octavo volumes.[3]

Galanos was born in Athens in 1760 the second son of fairly affluent Greek parents under Ottoman rule. His elder brother died in childhood and the third and youngest son looked after the family estates and named his son Pantaleon after his grandfather. At this time Athens possessed a high school which was conducted under the patronage and direction of a Greek nobleman, Joannes Benizelos. He was not only a patron of learning but a patriot and selfless philanthropist who dedicated his life to the cause of Greek learning and to the assistance of those unfortunate Greeks who had become victims of Turkish tyranny. In the Ottoman dungeons of the city were incarcerated many Greek prisoners living in conditions of the utmost squalor. Little care was taken of them and in these grim surroundings they were allowed to rot, forgotten by the outside world but not by Benizelos. He obtained from the Turkish authorities permission to visit these men. Prison regulations absolutely forbade gifts to prisoners so Benizelos entered the prison wearing clean underwear and then exchanged it for the vermin-infested garments of some unfortunate inmate.

It was under the direction of this noble patriot that Galanos began his studies in Greek. He gave early indication of his aptitude for letters, possessing an enquiring, reflective and critical mind. By the age of fourteen he had acquired all the rudimentary learning that the high school of Athens, limited by the restrictions of Ottoman rule, could afford. With the encouragement of Benizelos, his parents sent him to Missolonghi where an academy existed under the direction of a Greek scholar, Panagiotes Palamas. He did not stay long but transferred his studies to Patmos whose fame as a centre of Greek learning was enhanced by the presence of a very learned monk, Daniel Kerameus.

His progress as a scholar was so rapid that his uncle Gregory, Bishop of Caesarea, got to hear of it from his teachers and in 1781 urged his nephew to come to Constantinople. After six years of study at Patmos Galanos left the island and arrived in the great city. His uncle tried to persuade him to take Holy Orders, for with episcopal patronage behind him and the undoubted intellectual talents that he possessed, he would almost certainly have attained the office of a Bishop in the Orthodox Church. Galanos refused because his ambition was to devote his life entirely to the study of Greek literature and philosophy and his strong sense of religion led him to doubt whether he could combine the pursuit of scholarship with the vocation of a dedicated priest. Having made this important decision he remained in Constantinople pursuing his studies and eking out a living by giving lessons in Greek.[4]

In 1781 the Greek Church of the Transfiguration had been consecrated and the Greek Community in Calcutta was growing apace. Constantine Pantazes, the Epirot, was the leading Greek merchant in Calcutta and had provided money to establish a Greek school there for the children of the community to ensure that they were educated in their native language and culture. The first teachers at the school were the Greek chaplains of the Calcutta community, but by 1782 Pantazes had decided that the school required a lay teacher of greater ability. He wrote to his agent in Constantinople, Mandrazoglou, to ask him if he could procure the services of a suitable man. The latter contacted Bishop Gregoris of Caesarea who suggested Demetrios Galanos who accepted the appointment.[5] It would be interesting to know why he did so. If his sole aim was to study Greek literature and philosophy he could have done this far more easily in Constantinople than in distant Calcutta. His ready acceptance of this unusual assignment suggests that he must already have been inspired with a desire to study the culture of ancient India. Where this inspiration came from we do not know and our ignorance is frustrating.

It was typical of the unworldliness of the man and his total freedom from pecuniary ambition that before he left Constantinople he remitted to poor relations of his in Athens the small amount of money he had saved, leaving himself only enough funds to enable him to make the journey to India. He must have taken the trouble to inform himself of the ecclesiastical position of the Calcutta Greeks, for he left Constantinople to travel to the Monastery of St. Catherine at Sinai whose community had so far provided the priests who looked after the spiritual welfare of the Calcutta Greeks. From Sinai he travelled overland to Basra where he took ship for Bengal, arriving in Calcutta in 1786.[6]

In that year two other distinguished visitors landed there also. Lord Cornwallis came out to replace Warren Hastings as Governor General and to begin his momentous tenure of power. He was not, like his predecessors, a man who had risen from the ranks of the East India Company's administration but an aristocratic soldier who had had the misfortune of commanding the British forces in America against the rebellious colonists and having to surrender to George Washington at Yorktown. He was to make his name in India as the author of the Permanent Settlement of Revenue in Bengal. The other visitor was Thomas Daniell, an innkeeper's son, who had mastered the art of landscape painting. He brought with him his nephew William and for the first few months of their stay in the city they secured a precarious living by odd jobs of repairing and cleaning oil paintings. But not for long, for Thomas began drawing twelve views of the city which he engraved and sold as acquatints. These compositions were an instant success and the Daniells were launched on their careers as landscape artists whose paintings helped to mould the British visual conception of India. Some three years before Galanos, Henry Colebrook arrived in Bengal. He was to become perhaps the greatest British Sanskrit scholar and his work as an Indologist was almost exactly contemporary with that of his Greek counterpart though they do not appear to have known of each other's labours. It was Colebrook's interest in mathematics and astronomy that led him to begin his study of Sanskrit. He soon tired of the restless social life of Calcutta and was relieved to be appointed Assistant Collector of Revenue at Tirhut.

Galanos took up residence in the house of Constantine Pantazes in Calcutta and began his work teaching at the Greek school. He seems to have involved himself at once in the affairs of the community since we find his name on the Hastings Petition of 1788.[7] His signature is in the thirteenth place out of seventy signatures, just above those of the sons of Alexander Panioty. The signatures above his are the names of senior Greek merchants who had been in India for a relatively long time. This fact shows that, though he was a newcomer to Calcutta and not a merchant, he already occupied a respected position in the community. In his leisure from his pedagogical duties he began to acquire rapidly an excellent knowledge of English, Persian, Hindustani and Sanskrit. His mastery of Hindustani was such that it was said that he could converse easily and fluently with Hindus of every caste. In his relations with the pandits whose acquaintance he sought, he was greatly assisted by the ascetic life he led, his known commitment to his own religion and his firm moral outlook. He was accepted by Hindus almost as one of themselves and not simply as a learned sahib.

By 1792, after six years teaching in Calcutta, his desire to deepen his knowledge of Sanskrit and explore the ancient Indian texts led him to resign his position as teacher in the Greek school. He decided to go and live in Benares, the ancient holy city of the Hindus where he believed that he would be able to make contact with the most notable Brahmin scholars of his day. To further this aim he made up his mind to live the life of a Brahmin. He began to adopt the dress and diet of the priestly caste and conformed himself outwardly to all its complicated external rituals and regulations and continued this way of life for forty years until the time of his death.[8] He did this, however, without in any way abandoning his belief in Greek Orthodoxy and the Christian Revelation. He did not display the somewhat extreme enthusiasm for Indian religions which is related of 'Hindu' Stuart. Major General Charles Stuart, who came out to India as a very young man, soon fell completely under the spell of Hinduism. He bathed daily in the river according to Hindu custom, built a Hindu temple at Saugor, possessed a collection of Hindu household gods and when he died in 1828 had the model of a Hindu temple erected over his remains in the South Park Street Cemetery with effigies of Hindu deities prominently displayed.[9] Despite his respect and love of ancient Indian culture, Galanos was too aware of Hindu faults and too embedded in his Christian faith to go to these lengths. His adoption of the Brahmin way of life was a means to an end - to win the confidence of his Brahmin friends and thus to glean a harvest of knowledge. He was not the first European to do so. He had been preceded by an Italian Jesuit, Roberto De Nobili, who adopted the Brahmin way of life in order to evangalize Hindus in the early 17th century in the south of India. He is said to have made some 100,000 converts. Before he left Calcutta Galanos arranged with a Greek friend, probably his patron Constantine Pantazes, to remit annually to him a small amount of his scanty savings so that he could maintain a frugal life in Benares.

When Galanos arrived in the holy city of Benares in 1792 it contained some fourteen hundred Hindu temples and twenty thousand Brahmins. Its streets were thronged with pilgrims swarming up and down its ghats leading down to the sacred river Ganges along which the city stretches for three miles, rising gracefully tier by tier. It was a very ancient city, reputedly founded by Kasi Raja about 1200 B.C., hence its alternative name 'Kassi', often used by Galanos in his correspondence. Its proximity to the sacred Ganges, its fame as a centre of pilgrimage and as the place where all Hindus would wish to be cremated had been established for thousands of years. At the southern extremity of the city was the famous Durga Temple where sacrifices were offered to the Goddess Durga-Kali every Tuesday. The temple itself swarmed with a tribe of reddish-brown monkeys occupying every nook and cranny of the sacred edifice and overflowing into the streets and bazaars nearby. A late Victorian Protestant missionary, the Revd W. Urwick, visiting Benares, acidly commented: "Hinduism, instead of tracing men to monkeys like Darwinism raises monkeys to be gods, a step higher than men".[10]

The Dasasamed Ghat was one of the five celebrated places of pilgrimage in the city, where crowds of sadhus with their long shaggy locks reaching down to the ground performed their sacred ablutions and imposed severe penances upon their bodies. Nearby at the Burning Ghat the corpses of Hindus lay with wood stacked around them ready for cremation or already burning, sending their acrid fumes into the hot Indian sky. In Galanos' day suttee was still practised here. Further along the river was the famous Well of Salvation in which devotees washed themselves from hand to foot, sipping the foetid water from their cupped hands believing that it was filled with the sweat of Vishnu which infallibly washed away all sin. Near the well is the temple of Ganesh, the god of Wisdom, whose elephant-headed, three-eyed effigy was smothered in red paint. At the feet of the god crouched the figure of a rat. At the other end of the city was the famous Kotwal Temple housing the presiding deity of the city symbolised by a huge truncheon of stone called 'dandpan' and attracting the usual crowd of worshippers. Here priests with rods of peacock feathers inflicted vicarious punishment on the backs of worshippers. But the chief temple of the city was the Golden Temple, dedicated to the god Bisheshwar or Shiva. Within its courts lay a forest of linga, the squat conical representations of the male organ of generation, smeared with oil and paint and be-garlanded with flowers. The temple was graced with a fifty foot golden tower which glinted in the rays of the sun.

Benares was also the scene of other rival faiths. Towering over the city, a challenge and affront to Hindu orthodoxy, were the slender minarets of the Mosque of Aurangzeb the bigoted Mughal persecutor of Hindus and the fanatical son of Islam. Approached by a long broad flight of steps, its main aesthetic glory was its beautiful minarets inside the chief of which was a narrow winding staircase leading to the place where the voice of the muezzin pronounced the sole existence of Allah in this city of many gods. It was also a cradle of Buddhism where Gautama, after six years solitude and asceticism at Gaya, settled at Sarnath four miles north-west of the city. Here were to be found two large stupas built by King Asoka in 250 B.C., the Dhamek, a solid round tower ninety-three feet in diameter and one hundred and eight feet in height, and Lori's Leap, a mound of solid brickwork seventy-four feet high. In Galanos' time, however, their ruins were the only memory of Buddhism left in the city.

In 1802 his residence in Benares was quaintly noted by 'Asiaticus' who says that "Demetrios Galanos from Athens must be particularized as a man whose accomplishments and skill as a grammarian have rendered him highly respectable and the delight of the Grecians. This gentleman is now pursuing his studies in the Sanskrit language at the Oxford of the East". When Asiaticus wrote this he must already have been there for about ten years. However, in a list of Greek inhabitants of Dacca compiled by the government in 1795, his name unaccountably appears and the number of his years of residence in India is given as five.[11] The latter piece of information is undoubtedly incorrect as he is known to have arrived in India in 1786. Perhaps he was visiting Dacca from Benares when the census took place.

Over his long period of residence in the holy city a silence rests as he quietly pursued his lonely studies. The silence is broken by Bishop Reginald Heber who, in his account of his travels in northern India in 1824, gives a brief but illuminating description of his activities. "Benares being in many respects the commercial, and in all, the ecclesiastical metropolis of India, I was not surprised to find persons from all parts of the Peninsula residing there. But I was astonished to hear of the numbers of Persians, Turks, Tartars and even Europeans who are to be met with. Among them is a Greek, a well informed and well mannered man, who has fixed himself here for many years, living on his means, whatever they are, and professing to study the Sanscrit. I heard a good deal about him afterwards in Allahabad, and was much struck by the singularity and mystery of his character and situation. He is a very good scholar in the ancient language of his country, and speaks good English, French and Italian. His manners are those of a gentleman and he lives like a person at ease. He has little intercourse with the English but is on friendly terms with the principal Hindoo families. He was once an object of suspicion to the government but after watching him a long time they saw nothing in his conduct to confirm their suspicions and during Lord Hastings' first Pindari War, he voluntarily gave, on different occasions, information of much importance. So few Europeans, however, who can help it, reside in India that it seems strange that any man should prefer it as a residence, without some stronger motive than a fondness for Sanscrit literature, more particularly since he does not appear to meditate any work on the subject. He was a partner in a Greek House in Calcutta, but is now said to have retired from business. There is also a Russian here, who by natural affinity, lives much with the Greek. He is, however, a trader and has apparently moved in a much humbler rank of society than his friend".[12]

If Heber, with his scholarly tastes, could not appreciate Galanos' desire to live in Benares solely for the purpose of studying Sanskrit texts, we can appreciate the bemusement of the police spies set to watch him. No doubt, his association with a Russian also raised the suspicions of the government at a time when Russian advances in Central Asia were beginning to disturb the Company. We know the name of this man from an inscription in the Greek Church in Calcutta probably commemorating his death: "The stranger, Demetrios Galanos, the Athenian to the stranger, Peter Federof, the Russian". It is interesting that Heber, despite his apparent interest in Galanos, never considered it worthwhile to mention his name and he shows the usual disdain of the British upper class for men of trade. His description of Galanos as having previously engaged in commerce in Calcutta is not strictly correct as there is no doubt that he was a teacher at the Greek school but he may have, through Constantine Pantazes, invested some of his savings in trading ventures. Galanos certainly maintained contact with his mercantile compatriots in Calcutta and Dacca and it was he who composed the epitaph on the memorial to Alexander Panioty over his grave in the Greek Church in Dacca because its concluding words are "Galanos says that he lived for seventy years less two months and departed this life on 10th Jan, 1821". In the early years of his stay in Benares, Henry Colebrook was stationed not far away at Mirzapur from where he was able, like Galanos, to consult the pandits of the city. It was at Mirzapur that he made the progress which was to gain him the reputation of the most learned of British Indologists. In 1801 he was appointed to the Court of Appeal in Calcutta and a little later a professor of Hindu Law and Sanskrit at Wellesley's College in Fort William. It was here that he compiled a Sanskrit Grammar, and in 1806 became President of the Asiatic Society. He left India in 1814 while Galanos was still toiling away at his Indian texts in Benares and was to do so for another nineteen years. Colebrook was five years younger than Galanos but lived to almost exactly the same age - the former died in 1837 at 72 years of age, the latter in 1833 aged 73.

During his long residence in the city Galanos never lost his interest in the affairs of the Greek Orthodox Church and of his native country. When the monastery of Sinai deposed Nathaniel of Syphnos as the Rector of the Calcutta Church and replaced him with Dionysios George of Moudania, Galanos joined his fellow Greeks in siding with the former, and dismissing the latter as "the cause of dishonour to our nation". On the other hand he had a high opinion of Nathaniel as "a splendid example of learning and virtue". When Sinai in 1812 sent out the Archimandrite Benjamin to Calcutta, Galanos immediately expressed his respect for the new pastor. Just before his death he likewise praised the Chancellor, Ananias of Serroi, who replaced Benjamin, for his piety, patriotism and merit.[13] He was particularly close to the Archimandrite Gregory of Syphnos who was sent by the See of Constantinople to be the parish priest of Dacca in 1812 and corresponded with him regularly. When the latter was returning to Constantinople from Calcutta in 1817, Galanos wrote to him with playful erudition "I pray both the Ocean Lord, Poseidon and the Indian Varuna to give thee fair voyage, going and returning". His attachment to his native land and the pride he felt in its liberation from Turkish rule prompted him to send a copy of one of his Indian translations, through the Archbishop of Athens, Neophytus, to Capodistrias, first Corfiot President of Independent Greece with the following inscription: "To the Eminent Signor Joannes Capodistrias, President and Governor of Greece, Demetrius Galanos, the Athenian, sends as a present from India, this excellent manual of Zagganatha, the Brahmin, translated into Greek for the benefit of the young philologists of the Greek race. From the Holy City of Kassis, also known as Benares". Despite his devotion to the cause of Indian literature he was critical enough to observe the faults of contemporary Indian religion. These he attributed to the historical fact that Indians had laboured from time immemorial from three fatal circumstances. They had never, like the Greeks, known liberty, for the whole peninsula had been repeatedly overrun and subjugated by alien conquerors. This political thraldom had been aggravated by an all-pervading sacerdotalism and they were further handicapped by a complex system of caste.[14]

When he reached the biblical limit of three score and ten his thoughts began to return to his native city and he planned to return to Athens to die. Not anxious to make the arduous return journey on his own he wrote to his nephew Pantaleon in Athens persuading him to come out to India to act as his escort. Pantaleon made arrangements to travel to India with Ananias of Serroi, the priest whom the Sinai community was sending out to Bengal to take over the parish of Dacca and the overall supervision of the Greek Church in Bengal. When Pantaleon arrived in Calcutta in 1832 Galanos wrote to him from Benares urging him "to all the respect you show to me, show as much and more to my very good friend Constantine Pantazes, for he is my alter ego" and to "go to the house of my other friend, Manolakes Athanasiou to greet him and kiss his right hand".[15] This letter, with its manifestations of friendship and regard for his old acquaintances, was probably the last he wrote. Pantaleon was making arrangements to travel up to Benares when he heard in Calcutta that his uncle had died after a brief illness on May 3rd, 1833.

He was buried in the English Cemetery at Benares, with the following inscription in English:

Sacred
to the Memory of Demetrius Galanos
An Athenian who died at Benares
in the East Indies on the 3rd of May 1833
Aged 72 years.[16]

There was also on his tomb a longer inscription in Greek which may be translated:

Demetrius Galanos from Greece has died in the land of India. Being a devotee of the arts and learning he became illustrious by name and reputation. Having departed this troublesome life, he has gone to an everlasting life without pain.

Accordingly, his nephew, Pantaleon, for courtesy's sake, sets up this monument to his everlasting memory.[17]

There is a third inscription on the tomb in Persian characters:
Manifold griefs! Demetrios Galanos has gone away into Paradise from this world! Besides themselves with grief, people cried out 'Alas! He who rivalled Plato in eloquence has departed.[18]

Gennadius says that his bosom friend and Master, Satoul Singh, inscribed for him the following epitaph in Hindi:
Woe, a hundred times woe! Demetrius Galanos has left this world to reside in eternal abodes to the sound of Earthly tears and wailing. I have cried out, ah me! by grief demented. He is gone, alas, the Plato of this age.[19]

This inscription seems to be the same as the one in Persian characters but translated differently.

He made his will in October, 1832, and put his signature to it only three days before his death. He nominated Constantine Pantazes as his executor. He left small legacies to Brahmin friends and to his Hindu servant but the rest of his estate (£3,000) was to be equally divided between his nephew and the new University of Athens to which he also bequeathed his Sanskrit library, papers and manuscripts. These remain his final lasting monument. They can be roughly divided into two groups: 1) translations from Hindustani and Sanskrit into Greek; 2) drafts of several vocabularies and dictionaries: Pali-Greek-Persian-Hindi-Greek-English and Sanskrit/Greek. In the last named (which is still unpublished) were recorded for the first time many words culled from Sanskrit sources.

The contents of the seven volumes of his work published in Athens in 1853 can be briefly described as follows:
Vol. I 'Forerunner of the Indian Translations of Demetrios Galanos the Athenian' (The Prodromos) consists of five of the minor Sanskrit pieces rendered into Greek: a) Ethical sentences and allegories of Batrihari the King, b) Councils concerning the vanity of the world, by the same, c) Political, economic and moral precepts culled from various poets, d) synopsis of sentences and precepts of Sanakea, moralist and philosopher, e) Zagannatha Panditaraza's allegories, examples and similies.
Vol. II contains the Balabharata or Synopsis of the Mahabharata.
Vol. III comprises the Gita which Galanos called 'Thespesion Melos' a name adopted by Schlegel in his edition of the poem.
Vol. IV Kalidasa's Ragha Vamsa.
Vol. V Itihasa - Samutchchaya.
Vol. VI Hitopadesa.
Vol. VII The Durga.

His Bhagavata Purana and a few other translations remain unpublished.[20] The most recent study of his work is no later than 1913 - 'L'Opera di Demetrio Galanos' by P.E. Pavolini, Florence.

His biographer, John Gennadius, makes the following comment on his work in general "Even a casual reader would be struck by the great value of the notes constituting a veritable store-house of Indian lore. They interpret allegories, supply historical data, elucidate mythological traditions, explain the names and attributes of Indian deities, give parallel passages from Greek philosophers, account for obscure beliefs and popular sayings. Even the terminology of botany and zoology in India is made clear and of several passages he gives also a paraphrase, thus investing in a beautiful and lucid Greek form many a mystical passage of Oriental phraseology".[21]

One can conclude this description with the praise of a modern Greek author for Demetrios Galanos: " Distinguished for virtue, wisdom and learning he did credit to the Greek name in India and through his translations of Indian writings into Greek he established himself as the greatest of Indian-speaking modern Greeks, setting once more on a firm foundation the ancient cultural and political relations between Greece and India. Because of this he gained the reputation of a modern Pythagoras or Plato and was considered equal to Adam Koraes (a great Greek educator), a second Koraes for India and the East".[22]

Part B - The Mercenaries

A name disinherited, a broken sword;
Wounds unrenowned; battle beneath no Lord;
Strong blows, but on the void, and toil without reward.

(Hilaire Belloc)

Among the Greeks who went out to India there were some who became bored with the hard, often humdrum, life of the trader and whose adventurous spirits were drawn to the profession of arms. In the turmoil of late 18th century India when the once mighty Mughal Empire had broken under the pressure of native military adventurers and Europeans hungry for trading advantages, there was ample opportunity for the mercenary soldier to ply his ruthless craft. In the Dacca List of Greek traders in 1795 we come across one such person, Angelo Vetelk. He arrived in India in 1788 and like many of his young compatriots found his way to Dacca where he became a junior working for senior Greek merchants like

Alexander Panioty. What happened to him after 1795 we can only discover through a later administrative record of 1808 which tells us that he was then resident at Patna "formerly a lieutenant in the Maratha service". Sometime after 1795 he had exchanged his bales of merchandise and his ledgers for a soldier's sword in the service of some Maratha prince.

A non-merchant Greek about whose military activities we have more knowledge was an individual who arrived in Calcutta from Constantinople in 1790 and who called himself Count Alexander Gika. He was a member of one of the famous Phanariot noble families of the Ottoman Empire. They derived their name from the 'phanari' or lighthouse in Constantinople, near which the Ecumenical Patriarchate, the spiritual headquarters of Orthodox Christianity, was situated and around which revolved the financial and intellectual life of the Greeks of the city. They were the descendants of the Greek families who were prominent in the city when it fell to the Sultan's armies in 1453. Many of them intermarried with Italians, Albanians and other Christian peoples and sometimes even their names were not Greek but they were always Orthodox in religion and entirely Hellenized. The Gikas (or Ghikas) were Southern Albanian in origin but completely Greek in culture.

The enemies of the Phanariots would have described them as the quislings of their race who worked wholeheartedly with the Ottoman tyrant to uphold his Empire so long as they could share its political perquisites. Their defenders could, at least, claim that they were born survivors, determined, even at the nadir of Greek fortunes, to retain for themselves and thereby for their race, some part of the enormous imperial power wielded by the Turks. They were men of good education and courtly manners but their lives were spent in degrading oriental intrigues, imitating the vices of the seraglio, living dangerously near to deposition, disgrace and sudden death but driven by a voracious ambition to clutch at the power, dignity and wealth which could be achieved only through the favour of the Sultan. In this they were entirely successful.

They were the nearest approximation to a noblesse de robe in the Ottoman Empire and provided it with skilled diplomats and negotiators. In particular they assumed the office of interpreter to high Turkish dignitaries, a function which enabled them to act as de facto governors of many Aegean islands and to exert an influence on the very texture of Turkish diplomacy. An Alexander Ghika was Porte Dragoman in 1739 and at the siege of Belgrade was the intermediary in negotiation between the Grand Vizier and the Austrian General. Their greatest success, however, was to monopolize the rule of the two Danubian Principalities of Moldavia and Wallachia (the modern Rumania). The Vaiwordes or supreme rulers of these under Ottoman rule were always Phanariots. They were solemnly invested with their office in the Patriarchal Church with many of the prayers and ceremonies formerly associated with the Byzantine Emperors, even to the retention of the exalted title of 'God's Annointed'.

At Jassy and Bucharest, their provincial capitals, they maintained an archaic pomp, surrounded themselves with their Phanariot relatives and exercised an almost unlimited power over their Rumanian subjects in the name of the Sultan. Their office was obtained by intrigue and sustained by the wiles of their trusted agents in Constantinople who had not only to sweeten Turkish officials with timely bribes but also to fend off the plots of other Phanariot families eager to replace those who enjoyed the immediate fruits of office. It was from this strange, talented yet debased nobility that Alexander Gika came and one wonders why he exchanged the glittering prospects and sordid dangers of Phanariot life in Constantinople for the very different uncertainties of life in British Bengal.

On his arrival in Calcutta Gika took up residence at 19 Dhuramtollah Street and is recorded as living there in 1794 "of no particular occupation".[23] On January 22nd, 1796, he wrote the following letter to the Governor General, Sir John Shore:

'Hon'ble Sir,

I have just been informed that the Government of Calcutta has forbid all Europeans who are not in the service of King or Company to go to, or remain in any of the Company's provinces and that you have ordered your Residents at the Native Courts not to protect any European without your express orders.

I find myself under the necessity of humbly representing to you, Honourable Sir, that I take frequent journeys into the interior part of Hindoostan, and that I frequently find occasion to retire some time to Futtyghur [Fategarh] or elsewhere, for my private affairs or on account of my health, with an intention of undertaking fresh voyages of discovery; as my conduct has always been such as never to incur the displeasure of your Government, I take the liberty humbly to beseech you to exempt me from this order, by permitting me to have free egress and regress and to be allowed to remain in the English provinces or in those of the Nawab Viziers as I have hitherto done.

But if the Government do not judge proper to grant me this indulgence, it will not only be my first duty to obey the letter of their orders but I am likewise ready to quit this country or go to Calcutta or to Europe on the receipt of your orders.

After a long and disastrous voyage I arrived here the day before yesterday. My intention was to go to Futtyghur to pass the rest of the winter there, and to take care of M. Launay, my secretary, who is extremely ill, intending to return here after his recovery but the aforesaid orders of the government prevent me and I am obliged to remain here at the peril of my life. If my humble request can be granted I humbly beg you will, as soon as may be convenient, make me acquainted with your orders. I have the honour to be most respectfully,

Honourable Sir,

Your most humble and obedient servant,

A. C. Gika.

(A true translation. Signed L. M. Lawden)'[24]

Internal evidence suggests that this letter was written from Cawnpore and it reveals some interesting aspects of the writer's character. The diplomacy and wiles of the Phanariot are manifested in the excessive humility of the phraseology but also in the boldness of his approach. The letter is deliberately vague as to Gika's intentions in the Up Country territory. What exactly were his 'private affairs' and what precisely were 'the fresh voyages of discovery' that he was contemplating? Subsequent knowledge of his career makes one suspect that he was conducting negotiations with a Maratha prince with a view to obtaining a military commission for himself and his 'secretary' in that potentate's service and he did not think it wise to reveal this to the Government.

Gika's 'secretary' Launay is an intriguing character. In later years his close association with his master led him to adopt his name and habitually refer to himself as 'D'Launay Gika' or 'L. Gika'. Could he have been a Frenchman of the same name, referred to by William Hickey in his Memoirs as the secretary of Admiral De Suffren in command of the French Fleet in the Indian Ocean in 1782?

Gika's diplomacy was successful and a letter from the Public Department signed by its secretary, J. R. Harrington, granted him and Launay passports to Cawnpore and Fatehgarh with permission to travel freely within the Company's territories so long as they did not take up permanent residence in any place.[25] Sometime afterwards, in 1796 or 1797, they accepted military commissions from a Maratha chief, Raja Ambajee Ingliah. In doing so, they were following the example of a great many other European adventurers amongst whom were the famous cavalrymen James Skinner and William Gardner, the former serving Daulat Rao Scindia of Gwalior and the latter Malhar Rao Holkar of Indore. However, their timing was dangerous for the moment was rapidly approaching when the Company would be forced to confront the power of the Maratha Confederacy on fields of battle. An inconclusive engagement (the First Maratha War) had ended in a treaty in 1782 but the storm clouds were already gathering in Central India as the century drew to a close.

Aurangzeb, the persecuting Mughal Emperor, had unwittingly put claws into the Maratha people of the Deccan. Under the leadership of the great warrior Shivaji (1627-1680) they had successfully harried the imperial armies. After Shivaji's death his power eventually passed to Brahmin ministers who, in 1720, became the hereditary rulers of the Peshwa dynasty established at Poona. From here they dominated the Maratha Confederacy which whittled away the might of the Mughals until their Empire became little more than the city of Delhi and its environs. By the end of the 18th century, the power of the Peshwas had also deteriorated so that the great Maratha generals Scindia of Gwalior, Holkar of Indore, the Gaekwar of Baroda and Bhonsla of Nagpur had become princes in their own right, struggling amongst themselves and against the Peshwa to obtain paramount power in Central India.

The task of establishing stable government in the territories they dominated was not one in which these princes excelled. Their chief aim was to collect as much tax as they could from the defenceless peasants. The repeated passage of their armies over a war-torn countryside made this more and more difficult so that they raised the collection of taxes to the status of a military operation. Troops were habitually used to extract tribute from poverty-stricken ryots and the soldiers rarely collected only what was strictly due to the prince. Peace between rulers brought no comfort to the tillers of the soil for when the official exactions ceased, unofficial ones took their place, operated by gangs of disbanded soldiery who owed formal allegiance to no chief. Thomas Munro, one of the Company's most distinguished Civil Servants, described the situation vividly: "A mutinous unpaid army was turned loose during the sowing season to collect their pay from the villages. They drove off and sold the cattle, extorted money by torture from every man who fell into their hands and plundered the houses and shops of those who fled".[26]

The Maratha armies were a formidable fighting force, probably the most efficient native armies in India at this time. A contemporary Maratha observer, Pandarung Hari, gives us the following generalized description: "A Maratha Army consists in general of horse and foot of every neighbouring nation, religion and costume. Few of the men in the same line, either cavalry or infantry, have weapons of a like form. Some are armed with sword and shield, others with matchlocks and muskets. Some carry bows and arrows, others spears, lances or war rockets. Many are expert with the battleaxe but the sabre is indispensable to all. The men in armour, of whom there are many to make up the variety, cut a very curious appearance. A helmet covers not only the head and ears, but protects the shoulders... our cavalry are a strange rabble, mounted on tall and short horses of every colour and kind. Saddles are always slipping off for want of girths; strings fastened to any old pieces of iron by way of bits supplied the bridles; old turbans served for martingales and tent ropes for cruppers".[27] To inject discipline and technical efficiency into this motley crowd the Maratha princes had recourse to the employment of European officers, mostly French and British, who transformed this splendid human material into a military instrument of deadly power. It was in this context that Gika and Launay were now operating.

The new Governor General, the Marquis of Wellesley, was determined to challenge the power of the Company's principal native rivals - Tipoo Sultan of Mysore and the Maratha Confederacy. In the fourth Mysore War of 1799 Tipoo was slain and his fortress of Seringapatan taken. It was now the turn of the Marathas to cross swords with the Company. What followed was the second Maratha War, 1803-1805.

The military complexity of this war was such that an attempt must be made to simplify the movements of the armies involved as a background to the understanding of the story of Gika and Launay. The theatre of the war covered roughly a long portion of Central India which ran from Delhi in the north to Poona in the south. Along it were two axes of power - one passing through Indore was controlled by Jaswant Rao Holkar, and the other, to the east of the first, ran through Gwalior and Berar and was dominated by Daulat Rao Scindia. Both these potentates were able and ambitious men who wanted sole domination of the Maratha Confederacy. Each was aware of the British threat but they could not bring themselves to trust one another and combine against the armies of the Company. The opening stages of the conflict were fought between the armies of Holkar and Scindia, each ruler trying to eliminate his rival and so dominate Central India. The other Maratha Princes - the Gaekwar of Baroda, the Raja of Berar and less powerful potentates like Gika's employer, Ambajee Ingliah, sat menacingly on the side lines, watching and waiting to see how this inter-Maratha conflict would resolve itself, before they adopted any distinct military posture.

In the opening battles, first Holkar and then Scindia obtained victories, but the former subsequently moved his army south to attack the Peshwa, Baji Rao. His forces captured Poona, drove the Peshwa out, and replaced him with a puppet ruler, Amrit Rao. In the north, Scindia held Delhi and the person of the powerless Mughal Emperor.

Towards the end of 1802 the Marquis of Wellesley decided that the time was ripe to break the threatening power of the Marathas and to utilize, if possible, the mutual rivalry of Holkar and Scindia. In the north, at Cawnpore, a British Army was concentrated under the command of Lord Lake; in the south, at Mysore, Arthur Wellesley was poised ready to strike northwards into the Deccan. On 21 December 1802, the Marquis of Wellesley, in a secret letter to his military commanders, noted that there was a considerable number of Europeans in the employment of Maratha chiefs and that they must not be permitted to continue their service. It had been noticed that the Maratha forces, particularly their infantry, had shown a vastly improved performance in bearing and discipline as a result of the work of European instructors. Therefore, these men must be informed that they should resign their commissions during the period of hostilities between the Company and the Marathas. If they did so, they must be supported for the duration of the war at public expense. A declaration to this effect was made known. Many of these European officers, including James Skinner, William Gardner, Gika and Launay, immediately resigned.

Wellesley followed this declaration with the Treaty of Bassein, 31 December 1802, between the British and the deposed Peshwa who became a British client and was promised restoration to the throne of Poona. Daulat Rao Scindia now perceived that the real threat to his power came from the British. He won the alliance of the Raja of Berar and tried to persuade Holkar to join an anti-British coalition. Jaswant Rao, however, refused the offer and withdrew his forces northwards to Indore, leaving Scindia and Berar to cope with the British. Arthur Wellesley captured Poona in May and Ahmednagar in June 1803 and in September smashed the forces of Scindia and Berar at the famous Battle of Assaye. He followed this up with a further victory at Argaum and by the end of the year captured Scindia's fortress of Gawilgarh.

In the north, Lake was also delivering hammer blows on Scindia's armies. He captured in rapid succession Aligarh, Delhi and Agra and inflicted on his opponent a severe defeat at the battle of Laswari on November 1st, 1803. Daulat Rao had had enough and made peace with the British on December 15, 1803. Jaswant Rao now, belatedly, showed his hand. In 1804 he advanced on Delhi but, after a minor success, was defeated by Lake at Fatehgarh. By 1805 he was beginning to feel the effects of British military power and in desperation advanced into the Punjab, hoping to win the support of the Sikhs. In this he failed and surrendered to the British at Amritsar in December 1805 and in January 1806 concluded peace.

Gika, who had resigned his commission with Ambajee Ingliah at the end of 1802, now claimed compensation from the Government for himself and his two subordinates, Major Launay and Captain Moreira. The Marquis of Wellesley's original promise of reimbursement from public funds had been expressed in general terms and vague language leaving a great deal to interpretation. Gika thus found himself locked in verbal battle with the Council, demanding far more than it was prepared to concede.

His claims were presented to the Government in a letter dated 12 November 1805, though it would appear that the correspondence had begun sometime in 1804. From this letter the following facts emerge - the Government had paid him the sum of Rs 17,000 in compensation for his loss of service with Ambajee Ingliah and a similar amount was paid to his colleagues, Launay and Moreira. These sums were intended as a final payment for loss of employment after December 1803 but it is not clear on what criteria this calculation was based. In fact the Government stated that it had some doubts as to whether the officers concerned were entitled to this compensation because at the time of their resignation, Ambajee was formally an ally of the British and his treacherous dealings with Scindia were not detected until after their resignations. However, the Government magnanimously conceded that in a broader sense, it might be considered that Ambajee was part of a general Maratha threat, so the compensation had been paid.

Gika was not satisfied with this answer and continued to press his claims and those of his colleagues for a great deal more. He mentions in passing that Launay and Moreira were "now in a very deplorable condition" as a result of their noble sacrifice. With his subtle Phanariot sense of what was due to him he argued that because Ambajee was in reality a confederate of Scindia's before December 1802, he and his colleagues ought to be paid a sum which was calculated from the moment of their resignation to the end of hostilities with Scindia (December 1803). Furthermore, since the latter had been secretly allied with Holkar, it was only just that the compensation should have included the period of hostilities with this ally up to January 1806.

This was not Gika's only complaint. He claimed that during his time with Ambajee he had performed several valuable services for the British Government for which, in justice, he should have been suitably rewarded. He says that when he resigned the Maratha service he made his way to Arthur Wellesley's camp, and there he was encouraged to believe that the Government was deeply grateful to him and would show its gratitude in a pecuniary manner. One dearly wishes that this meeting between the Phanariot nobleman and the future victor of Waterloo had been chronicled in more detail. Gika explains that he commanded a brigade of eight battalions of Maratha Infantry, two of which were led by Major Launay and Captain Moreira. From his description of subsequent events it would appear that he was operating north of Jubbulpore on the eastern flank of Scindia's forces. Here he received a request from a Company Officer, Colonel Cunningham, at Etawah, to recover a string of Company horses seized by Maratha bandits. Gika claims that he responded immediately, sent two of his battalions with artillery support, scattered the bandits and recovered the Sirkar's property. On another occasion, at Bellary, he persuaded an assembly of Maratha chiefs not to attack the British forces. He makes the additional claim that he persuaded 'Meer Khan', the companion of Holkar, to desert his master and come over to the British. If this man was 'Amir Khan', and if Gika was telling the truth, then it would have been a most valuable contribution to the Company's campaign against Holkar. Amir Khan was a Rohilla chief who was a close associate of Jaswant Rao but he does not seem to have deserted the latter, and was with him until the termination of hostilities. Gika asks for all these services to be taken into account, especially as he has expended considerable sums of money in their execution.

The Government, however, would have none of this. In a letter dated 31 May 1806 from the Council and signed by G. H. Harlow, G. Udny, I. Lumsden, it completely refuted Gika's claims. The Council denied that Jaswant Rao Holkar was confederate with Daulat Rao Scindia and therefore rejected the idea of paying the officers compensation until the cessation of hostilities with the former. More unkindly, it bluntly stated that Gika's services to the Government were not such as to justify any special reward and that, on his resignation from Maratha service, he could not be said to have automatically entered that of the Company's. The correspondence continued for some time with Gika getting more and more desperate at the obduracy of the Council: "Good God! What is my crime? How undeservedly I suffer! I must confess that I expected honours and rewards which I so nobly earned and which I thought due to me from justice as well as gratitude, instead of which I received some frigid repulsive civilities not very pleasant to the sensibility of a gallant mind". With that cry of outraged dignity, the correspondence on his side came to an end. The Phanariot and his friends were never re-imbursed by the Government to the extent that they expected. Their claims were finally rejected by the Council on April 29, 1809.[28] It is interesting to compare the settlement that Gika and his friends received from the government with two very similar cases of British officers. Colonel James Redhead Shippard, like Gika, joined the service of Ambajee Ingliah about 1799 and raised five battalions with 500 cavalry and 25 guns. He left Ambajee's service in 1801, settled in Cawnpore and received a pension of Rs 1,000 per month. Captain Richard Collins left the Maratha service about the same time and also settled in Cawnpore with a pension for life of Rs 180 per month.

What happened to Gika after that is not known but in 1810 he is noted as 'being resident Up Country'. His companion in arms Major D'Launay Gika died on September 13, 1818,[29] and on August 26 1834 his widow, Helen, married Mr C. Gomez of the Company's Lithographic press.[30]

Gika was not the only Greek to be involved in the second Maratha War as a mercenary soldier. One other was Adam George from Georgia who was probably the son of a Greek merchant, Simeon George, who arrived in India in 1787, signed the Hastings Petition in 1788 and was in business in Calcutta at Crooked Lane in 1811. The Greek connection with Georgia was ancient. It was the land of the Prometheus myth and the legendary home of the Golden Fleece sought by Jason and the Argonauts, and Greek settlers from Miletus founded towns in the western part of the country from about 600 B.C. onwards. The Georgians embraced Christianity in 337 A.D. but throughout its history this Christian Kingdom was involved in conflicts with the Muslim Persians and Turks until, in 1801, through conquest it became part of the dominions of the Czars of Russia. The Georgians had their own national church which maintained close connections with the Greek Orthodox Church and many Greek merchants settled in this remote Central Asian territory.

Adam George enlisted in a regiment of Hindustani Cavalry commanded by Colonel Robert Bruce about 1791. This must have been either the 1st Bengal Native Cavalry (the Oudh Cavalry) raised in 1776 or the 2nd Bengal Native Cavalry (the Kandahar Horse) raised in 1778. His rank is described at 'Naik Rissaldar'. The term 'rissaldar' was originally used in Upper India to designate the commander of a corps of Hindustani Horse and the word 'naik' as meaning a native captain or headman of some sort.[31] In the later military terminology of the Company's Armies, rissaldar meant a Viceroy's Commissioned Officer of Cavalry and a naik a corporal of Infantry but in this context 'Naik Rissaldar' probably meant the commander of a troop of cavalry, and as such Adam George served for five years and three months and then transferred to the service of Daulat Rao Scindia. He became an officer in General de Boigne's Regiment of Cavalry.

Benoit de Boigne was a Savoyard, born in 1751, who served as an officer in the Irish Brigade of the French Army and then transferred to the Russian service. As a captain in Czarina Catherine's army he was made responsible for training Greek levies and shared the fate of many an unfortunate Greek by becoming a prisoner of the Turks at Tenedos. He was released from Ottoman captivity on Chios through the intervention of Lord Algernon Percy and eventually made his way to India where he was commissioned as an ensign in the 6th

Madras Native Infantry in 1778. In 1782 he resigned his commission and came to Calcutta where he became a close friend of Warren Hastings. In 1784 he took service under Mahadaji Scindia, the father of Daulat Rao, trained his infantry battalions and defeated his enemies - the Rajput chiefs and Holkar - to make his master the paramount Maratha chief in Central India. De Boigne resigned his command in 1796 and when the second Maratha War began he was back in his native Savoy. Adam George must have joined de Boigne's Cavalry either just as the General was about to leave India or soon afterwards and he served upwards of six years with this unit.

He then became second in command of a force of Najeebs at Ajmer. They were a Maratha Corps of Infantry, armed with sabre and matchlock, having some semblance of European discipline. He was with this unit when he heard of Wellesley's proclamation warning European officers in the Maratha service to resign their commissions which he did almost immediately.

He retired to Farukkabad, where in 1805 he was treated for painful eyes by the Civil Surgeon, Mr Reilly. Oddly enough he does not seem to have applied for any compensation until December 24, 1813. Now resident at Fategarh, he presented a petition to the Earl of Moira, Governor General, for a pension which he was granted at Rs 120 a month, commencing on April 1, 1813. His petition mentions that he had "a large infant family"[32]

In the Military Burial Ground at Bhowanipore there was a tombstone with the following inscription:

To the Memory of Elizabeth Sarah George
the beloved wife of Adam George,
and eldest daughter of the late Wm and
Sarah Peat, died 22nd July 1839,
aged 20 years, 7 months and 8 days.
Believer shrink not from thy body's doom,
For Christ thy Saviour slumbered in the tomb,
Take courage then and faith shall comfort give,
Sure as he died so sure thy soul shall live.[33]

Her father, William Peat, was a Master in the Company's Bengal Marine. Adam George must have married this young girl when he was an elderly gentleman and one can surmise that he did so to provide a stepmother for his "large infant family". The date of his death, like so much else about this mercenary soldier, is unknown.

Part C - The Patriotic Pirate

That talkative, bald-headed seaman came
(Twelve patient comrades sweating at the oar)
From Troy's doom-crimson shore,
And with great lies about his wooden horse
Set the crew laughing and forgot his course.

(J. E. Flecker)

In December 1828 an elderly Greek gentleman, calling himself Captain Nicholas Kephalas, arrived in Port Louis on Mauritius, the island in the Indian Ocean which before 1810 had belonged to France but was now under British rule. In Greece the War of Independence was still raging against the Turks and Kephalas proclaimed to anybody who cared to listen that he was an envoy of the Greek Government who had been deputed to wage war on the Turks at sea. Somewhere in Port Louis he was able to purchase a brig which he suitably renamed 'The Hellas' and hoisted the flag of the insurgent Greeks and the Union Jack. He had no authority to fly the latter flag but Captain Nicholas Kephalas was not a man to show any over-zealous respect for authority unless it suited his purpose. Soon he was frequenting the taverns of the port, engaging sailors in nautical gossip and attempting to recruit them in his project of attacking Turkish commerce in the Indian Ocean, the Red Sea and the Persian Gulf. He persuaded a large number to sign up, including a half-pay lieutenant in the Royal Navy who had formerly served in the Bombay Marine, Samuel Lingard, whom he appointed the Sailing Master of 'The Hellas' and promoted to the rank of Captain in the Greek Navy.

With its makeshift crew 'The Hellas' set sail from Port Louis and in January 1829 arrived at Mahé in the Seychelles, taking on stores and recruiting a further eighteen sailors from different vessels in the harbour, the vast majority of them British subjects. They seem to have been a motley disreputable crowd and amongst them were Peter Jones, alias William Jones, a native of Madagascar, baptized at Edinburgh, who was engaged as ship's steward, William Williams alias Fitzgerald, a deserter from H.M.S. Helicon, and two of his shipmates, Monks and Adams. Altogether the crew numbered sixty-one and the state of discipline was extremely lax as they had no confidence in, or respect for, their officers. Within a few weeks 'The Hellas' set sail northwards heading for the Straits of Bab-el-Mandeb and for unsuspecting Turkish and Arab vessels who were destined to be her victims.

However strange her adventure or the credentials of her captain, 'The Hellas' was in a great historical tradition which went back to the 16th century Portuguese conquistadors. The Iberian races had, throughout the later Middle Ages, waged a war of reconquest against Islam and, step by step, driven the

Muslims out of the Iberian peninsula. When the great Portuguese captains and explorers like Da Gama and Albuquerque sailed to India in search of Christians and spices they were also consciously seeking to continue the crusade against Islam. They were, in fact, making a gigantic flanking attack on the Muslim world, taking it in the rear and inflicting considerable damage on its trade, military installations and amour propre. Some such idea also occurred to Kephalas - to aid his countrymen battling against Turkish and Egyptian armies in the Morea by mounting a maritime operation against Turkish shipping far from the battlefront. To what degree patriotism, desire for private profit and just pure love of adventure were blended in his motivation would be difficult to determine. The preparations for the voyage and the recruitment of his crew had a distinctly raffish flavour, reminding one of the way Squire Trelawney fitted out 'The Hispaniola' at Bristol in preparation for its voyage to Treasure Island.

While 'The Hellas' was ploughing northward through the Arabian Sea, in Surat on the west coast of India, a vakeel or lawyer, one Jamudin from the district of Tyabjee, was also setting out on a voyage to the Red Sea. Jamudin, a good Muslim, was bound for the Holy City of Mecca to perform the haj or pilgrimage which is one of the basic requirements of Islam. He had gathered his numerous family and his servants together and chartered a buggalow to take them to the port of Jiddah from where they could continue their journey to Mecca. A buggalow (also known as a buglar) was the name commonly given on the West Coast of India to Arab vessels built of teak, and they were to be found in large numbers plying between India, the Red Sea and the Persian Gulf. By the mercy of Allah things had gone well for Jamudin, the sea journey almost completed and Jiddah only a day's sailing away. On March 27, 1829, as the pilgrims were joyfully anticipating their arrival in Arabia, a sail was sighted, and as time passed, took the menacing form of a large ship bearing down on them. 'The Hellas' was about to claim its first victim.

One can imagine the scene: the alarmed jabbering of Arab seamen, the shrill cries of Indian women, the raucous commands from 'The Hellas' as the sailors boarded the buggalow. Its male occupants were taken aboard, stripped and searched. The booty included bags of incense, a great pile of richly embroidered clothes, including a 'tartan shawl,' and a small arsenal of weapons: sabres, shields and richly mounted pistols. The luckless passengers and crew were put ashore in a remote spot north of Mocha from where they made their way to the city and reported the incident to the Turkish Governor, Syed Abdulla Dooregh.

In the meantime 'The Hellas', taking the buggalow in tow, anchored off a village near Mocha and seven of its crew went ashore to buy fresh fish. Kephalas proved a careless tactician to behave in so carefree a manner in the close vicinity of his piratical activity. Nemesis followed hard upon as the energetic Turkish Governor, informed by the villagers, brought up a large armed party with pieces of artillery. He opened fire on the ship and Kephalas put quickly out to sea abandoning the sailors ashore and the buggalow which fell into the hands of Syed Abdulla.

'The Hellas' moved south and within the Straits of Bab-el-Mandeb encountered an Arab vessel from Cutch, carrying yet another group of pilgrims to Mecca - forty males (described as 'fakeers'), and ten or twelve women. Once again the ship was plundered of wearing apparel, matchlocks, spears, swords, creases (daggers), one barrel of gunpowder, cartridges for the matchlocks and two hundred dollars, and the victims allowed to proceed to Mocha. There, in a state of shock, they reported the incident, claiming that they had been attacked by *two* ships, one having three masts and the other two. The robbing of harmless pilgrims is hardly the sort of exploit one can commend, but it must be remembered that the conduct of both sides in the Greek War of Independence went far beyond the bounds of civilized behaviour and the Turks were guilty of the slaughter of innumerable Greek civilians and the desecration of many Orthodox places of worship. Wars are always ugly and religious wars particularly so.

The detailed itinerary of 'The Hellas' after this incident has not survived but eventually she steered through the Straits of Hormuz into the Persian Gulf to the port of Bandar Abbas from where Kephalas was planning to travel to Ispahan in Persia on his way to Russia, leaving 'The Hellas' under the command of Samuel Lingard. Something happened to make him change his mind so he took his ship out of the Gulf and sailed southwards along the west coast of India and finally put in at Goa.

In the meantime, the piratical activities of 'The Hellas' had become known to the Government of Bombay which began to piece together information coming in from a variety of sources to form an irritating and alarming picture. The British Residency in Mocha reported the anger of Syed Abdulla who was convinced that she must be a British ship since she was flying the Union Flag when he encountered her near Mocha, and in June 1829 Captain Pottinger, the Resident in Cutch, informed the Governor of Bombay of the incident in the Straits of Bab-el-Mandeb. In both cases most of the victims were Indians, subjects of the Bombay Government, who were entitled to its protection. The Portuguese Governor of Daman reported the presence of 'The Hellas' in Bandar Abbas and the news that Kephalas had been planning a journey to Russia, which must have raised eyebrows in Bombay, given the lingering suspicion of British Indian administrators about the Czar's political ambitions in the Middle East. The Bombay Government began an inquiry into the background of Kephalas and discovered that in 1827 he had been a guest of the British Resident in Mocha, Major Bagnold, under the name of 'Chiefala' (the Italian form of his Greek name), and he had claimed that he was a British subject on his way to Calcutta. The Resident, in an effort to exculpate himself, explained that, though his guest was an enthusiastic supporter of the Greek cause, his advanced age (he was sixty three at this time), and confined circumstances, prevented any suspicion that he was likely to engage in any bellicose activity. Kephalas left Mocha on 'The Carnatic' in the company of the French Vice-Consul, M. D'Armandy, "an honourable and humane man though more of a soldier than a diplomatist". Poor M. D'Armandy, returning to Mocha in 1829 after the piratical operation of 'The Hellas' off Jiddah, was immediately arrested by Syed Abdulla on the suspicion that he was hand in glove with Kephalas. Major Bagnold opined that the Turkish Governor knew that the Frenchman was innocent of this charge but he was putting pressure on the French and the British to assist him in suppressing the activities of 'The Hellas'. Kephalas had managed to make himself the epi-centre of a minor earthquake in international relations in the Red Sea.

Now in possession of the facts, the Bombay Government contacted the Portuguese authorities in Goa giving them a full report on the illegal actions of the Greek ship with a request that Kephalas and his crew should be handed over to face charges of piracy in the Vice Admiralty Court in Bombay. The Bombay Navy was ordered to take action against 'The Hellas' if she tried to resume her former adventures. But Kephalas was in luck, for the Goan authorities, while anxious to please the Bombay Government, showed a considerable respect and admiration for this Greek sailor who eloquently defended his actions as the work of a patriot who was in honour bound to assist his suffering countrymen by waging war against their cruel oppressors. He was allowed to strip 'The Hellas', pay off her crew and slip quietly away, to the extreme annoyance of the British.

However, Samuel Lingard was not so fortunate as his employer. He transferred from 'The Hellas' to another ship, but on December 2, 1829, was wrecked on the Kathiawar coast, arrested in Cutch and sent to Bombay where his status as a half-pay lieutenant in the Royal Navy and his former employment in the Bombay Marine was discovered. When questioned he tried to justify himself on the grounds that he was now a captain in the Greek Navy under the command of 'Commodore' Kephalas who, he claimed, was also a captain in the Russian Navy and had friendly contacts with the Abysinnians. The Bombay Administration's record of this matter does not relate what ultimately happened to Lingard.[34]

Who was this Greek, Kephalas, an elderly pirate who claimed to be a British subject, a commodore in the Greek Service, a captain in the Russian Navy with friendly contacts with the Czar's Imperial Government and the Abysinnians? He seems to belong to the realm of fiction rather than to the sober pages of history. He would, undoubtedly, have found a kindred spirit in Basil Seal, Evelyn Waugh's engaging ruffian, but one might well question whether in real life his claims could possibly measure up to the truth. Incredible as it may seem, the answer is mostly in the affirmative. Kephalas was a fantastic character whose exploits were so bizarre that historians have had great difficulty in assessing the true nature of the man, and even the details of his fabulous exploits are a matter of controversy.

In June 1975 battle was joined by two Greek historians, Vassos Tsimbidaros and Kyriakos H. Metaxas, over the life and career of Kephalas in the pages of the

London 'Greek Gazette'.[35] The former maintained that he was a crafty, fraudulent adventurer and the latter that he was, on the contrary, a great and selfless patriot. Metaxas was clearly a more careful historian and discovered in his opponent's work many serious errors of fact so that his account of Kephalas' activities must be treated with far greater respect. However, a lingering doubt remains, because in recounting the exploits of 'The Hellas', Tsimbidaros seems to come nearer the truth than Metaxas. The former gives a much condensed version of the events already related which is in broad agreement with British contemporary records except that he makes the gross mistake of confusing Goa with Madagascar and talks of Kephalas "building a small fleet". The latter, however, affirms that Kephalas fought "corsair sea battles in the Red Sea and the Persian Gulf against Turkish vessels, immobilising in the meantime large enemy forces, which otherwise may have gone to Greece". This ambitious claim does not seem to square with the information gathered by the Bombay Government. Nevertheless, in the following brief description of some of Kephalas' activities I am indebted to Metaxas' account though I have supplemented it a little from other sources and kept a watchful eye on 'the information' provided by Tsimbidaros.

Nicholas Kephalas was born in Zante or Zakynthos in the Ionian Islands in 1763 which was then part of the Venetian Maritime Empire, a beautiful spot which the Venetians called 'fior di Levante', with a wealth of sumptuous baroque palazzini and churches, most of which were tragically destroyed by an earthquake in 1953. Its cultural traditions were Italian rather than Greek or Turkish, and this may account for the fact that Kephalas often assumed the Italianate form of his name 'Chiefala'. It already had in 1763 past associations with England for it was the main source of the currants which went into plum puddings. In later years it came under British rule and it still contains a melancholy reminder of those days in the British Cemetery, full of the graves of soldiers who formed part of its garrison.

When he was about twenty five years old, like many of his countrymen, Kephalas adopted a sailor's life and for the next thirty years he traversed the maritime highways, particularly in the Mediterranean, Aegean and Black Seas, acquainting himself with several countries so that, besides Greek, he became fluent in Italian, French and English. It may be that during this early period of his life he visited Russia and obtained some sort of rank in the Russian Navy. But Kephalas was not amongst the ordinary run of seamen. He had a hunger for maritime knowledge of every kind which he combined with a vision of how this knowledge could assist his fellow countrymen. He retained in his fertile mind masses of maritime information, some of it culled from French, Italian and English sources but much of it based on his own experience. In 1817 he gave to the world the fruits of his labours and published in Vienna his 'Maritime Guide' and his 'Maritime Law', the latter being the first book on this subject written in

Greek. In order to finance publication he had to sell his ship 'The Ypomoni'. He followed this with the further publication of 'Charts of the Black Sea and the Mediterranean Sea', devised and drawn by himself in the light of his own observations on voyages. In the following year he brought out his 'Chart of the Mediterranean and the Aegean Sea' which he dedicated to the Ionian Government who declined the dedication and returned the copies of the books he had sent.

The apparent churlishness of the British-controlled Ionian Government can be explained by Kephalas' conduct some years previously. In 1809, during the Napoleonic War, the British had captured the Ionian Islands from the French, with the exceptions of Corfu and Paxos, and were imposing a strict blockade on the former. In the spring of 1810 the people of Paxos revolted against the French, so Kephalas, who was in Santa, took a galliot, 'The Santa Hellena' with 20 guns and a crew of 75, to Paxos to aid the islanders, flying the British flag. By the time he got there, the Paxian revolt had collapsed and the British Naval Commander in the Ionian Islands, who cannot have been pleased at the uncalled for incursion of a Greek ship, flying the British flag but acting on its own initiative, ordered Kephalas to retire. Tsimbidaros claims that before leaving Paxos he purloined the contents of the local treasury, but there does not appear to be any evidence to sustain this accusation. Disgruntled, Kephalas returned to his native island. In August 1812 he set out from there in his polacca 'Saint Spyridion' carrying a cargo to Constantinople. He did not obtain clearance from the British Military Authorities and though the precise reason for this omission is not clear, his subsequent conduct was distinctly suspicious for, once clear of the Ionian Sea, he hoisted the French Tricolour. Forced by a mistral wind to take refuge in Castellorizo, Kephalas presented himself at Constantinople and reported his circumstances to the British Consul. In the meantime, his ship was taken as a prize by the Turkish authorities and sold in Smyrna. Kephalas seemed to think that the British Military Government of the Ionian Islands owed him compensation so he bombarded it with petitions, but in 1815, in his absence, a British Tribunal sentenced him to perpetual banishment and, if he was apprehended, to hard labour for life. Clearly it felt that he was a dangerous character and this explains the curt rejection of the dedication of his books which, no doubt, he penned as a peace offering.

It is difficult to keep track of Kephalas' movements but some time after the publication of his books in Vienna and Paris he travelled from Odessa to London where, in a written declaration to his countrymen, he promised to give them further proofs of his devotion to their maritime welfare in the shape of two projected works, one on the method of constructing different kinds of ships and the other, a general gazetteer "of every known place on earth, an absolutely essential aid to travellers by land or sea". "When I return from London, as soon as Divine Providence shall deign to move the stout-hearted English to look favourably upon me, so as to bring my business to a successful conclusion then, my beloved countrymen, I promise you that without fail I shall fulfil my obligation to the Divinity by publishing these same books, as I desire to do with all my heart. May your good wishes help me on the way."[36]

When the Greek War of Independence broke out in 1821, Kephalas was working for an English shipowner, Mr Rich, and the news reached him at Mosul. Fired with enthusiasm, this extraordinary man abandoned his employment immediately and travelled to Persia where he obtained the ear of the Crown Prince and through him was able to convince the Shah that it was in his interests to launch a war against Turkey, and obtained from him letters to a number of heads of state in Europe. His mission came to a sudden end with the untimely assassination of the Crown Prince. In July 1822 Kephalas turned up in Portugal where his eloquence persuaded Dom Miguel of Braganza, the younger brother of the King, to accept the crown of Greece, subject to the approval of the Great Powers and on condition that he would provide military aid to the Greeks. In November 1822 he sailed from Lisbon to Greece on board 'The Scipion' with a legion of German volunteers who hoped to join in the struggle against the Turks. The Revolutionary Greek Government was desperately short of money so he volunteered to go to India to raise funds for it. This is interesting evidence of the fact that the presence of a Greek community in Bengal was well known to contemporary Greeks.

He travelled via Tripolizza, Nafplion, Syros and Alexandria to Cairo and there, in September 1823, he paid a courtesy call to Mehmet Ali, the Pasha of Egypt, whose sympathy he tried to enlist for the Greek cause without much success and whose views he reported to the Greek Government. Tsimbidaros has a fascinating picture of him dressed in opulent clothes at the court of the Pasha trying to persuade him that he was an expert in gold-mining who was capable of discovering and exploiting some veins of gold ore in Egypt, as yet undiscovered but mentioned by an ancient Greek authority. Apparently Mehmet Ali was taken in and provided the Greek with a large sum of money for this purpose. Kephalas and the money promptly disappeared. Again, there are no solid grounds for accepting the veracity of this story.

In 1824 Kephalas reached Calcutta where he contacted the Greek merchants, Constantine Pantazes, Peter Protopapas and other members of the Greek community there and then moved on to Dacca to meet the Paniotys, Ducases, Lucases and other Greek families in the city. He even journeyed to Benares where he met Demetrios Galanos - probably the only Greek that the latter encountered there. With their help his visit was a great success and he managed to raise the considerable sum of Rs 25,385 for the Greek cause. After a five month voyage around the Cape of Good Hope he was able to deliver this money through the bankers Fletcher, Alexander and Co. to the Greek Deputies in London. Later, in 1826, he published a book in Italian at Livorno describing his voyage to India which contained a description of Benares and of the politics, religion and costumes of the Indian peoples together with a geographical map of India.[37] This now rare book has never been translated into English.

One would have imagined that having travelled half way round the world he would have spent some time recuperating in London but he was relentless in the pursuit of his country's welfare. In March 1825 he took himself to Rome and managed to obtain an audience with Pope Leo XII on May 24 when he presented the Holy Father with a memorandum in which he attempted to distinguish the Greek Revolution from all the other Liberal revolts that had broken out in Europe soon after the war with Napoleon had concluded. He was aware of the fact that the Great Powers were highly alarmed at these events which had disturbed Spain, Naples, Piedmont, Portugal and the German States and had even begun to unsettle the Spanish possessions in Central and South America. Their tone was anti-monarchical and anti-clerical and in Italy was dominated by the Secret Society of the Carbonari which was extremely hostile to the Papacy and was therefore regarded with intense suspicion by the Pontiff. Kephalas was at pains to point out that the Greek Revolution had very little in common with these other Liberal uprisings, for its aim was to set up a Christian Monarchical state which would protect the religion of its people. He held out the bait that it would probably resume contacts with the Papacy which had been in abeyance since the 15th century. He hoped that if he could obtain the Pope's support, this would influence other Catholic monarchs to favour the Greeks. This Roman initiative and the contents of the memorandum were the responsibility of Kephalas alone, though the Greek Government was aware of it. On August 22 and 23 the Greek Deputies in London published a complete disclaimer of Kephalas' memorandum and other foreign journals retailed this information. The Papal Nuncio in Corfu forwarded to Rome information about him which probably included the fact that he had been banished from the Ionian Islands. Leo XII had no wish to annoy the Greek Government so Kephalas was expelled from Rome in September 1825.

In March 1826 he was back in London burning with indignation against the Greek Deputies as the following report from 'The Times' shows only too clearly: "A Greek called Nicolo Chiafala has just published in London, in the shape of a letter to the Lord Mayor, more serious accusations against his countrymen than have appeared in 'The Austrian Observer' [The Austrian Government was strongly opposed to the Greek Revolt.] He charges the Government with rapacity, venality and corruption. He announces his despair of their cause, unless the governments of Europe step in between them and the Mussulman Scimitar; and he crowns all by a narrative of an act of oppression, injustice and ingratitude towards himself which, if it did not produce, could not fail to aggravate his other complaints. According to this statement Captain Nicolo Chiafala had been so ardent a friend of Greek liberty that he had traversed half the world to procure it funds and friends. In 1823 he left Tripolizza and proceeded to Calcutta in the East Indies where he obtained subscriptions to the amount of Rs 25,000. This sum was placed at the disposal of the Greek Government, with an understanding or stipulation that the expenses of Captain Chiafala's journey (amounting to 3501) should be paid out of it before its appropriation. It was, however, withdrawn without this deduction, and the Captain has been left to starvation, or to the success of a petition to that very government which he now denounces. The Greek Deputies who here manage the loan which has been raised on the credulity of John Bull, and which has rather injured than assisted the cause of Greek freedom, refuse to pay his claims and have only afforded him a pittance to enable him to return home. We know nothing about the facts of the case, and cannot decide on such an ex parte statement; but if they are as the author of the letter represents them, the conduct of the Greek Government and their London Deputies cannot be too strongly reprobated".[38]

However, Kephalas distinguished between what he regarded as the iniquities of the leaders of the Revolution and the cause itself. The Sultan's failure to win any substantial military successes against the Greeks led him to call in the Pasha of Egypt, Mehmet Ali, who sent a powerful army and navy under his son Ibrahim to the Morea to subdue the Greek rebels who had unfortunately begun to quarrel amongst themselves. Soon Ibrahim began to achieve the military success which had been denied the Turks. Kephalas did everything in his limited power to elicit support in Europe against him and begged the feuding Greek factions to unite in face of this dangerous foe. When Missolonghi fell on April 26 he could stand the suspense no longer and left London to travel to Greece via Livorno and obtained from the Greek Government Letters of Marque to fight the Turks as a privateer. What followed in the Indian Ocean, Red Sea and Persian Gulf has been described at the beginning of this account though it is worth noting that he was telling the truth when he claimed to be acting with the knowledge of the Greek Government and that he was a British subject because as a native of Zante he could claim this status ever since the declaration of the British Protectorate over the Ionian Islands.

In 1833 Kephalas' dream came true for Greece became at last a sovereign Kingdom. In the year before Queen Victoria's coronation he surfaced once again in London and presented a documented lawsuit against certain British officials to Her Majesty's Government which was transmitted by the Foreign Secretary, Lord Palmerston, to the Advocate General. His case was rejected and he moved to Paris where he printed a pamphlet in French and Greek containing letters of protest against the injustices he had suffered to numerous celebrities which included the Archbishop of Canterbury.

From Paris Kephalas left for the wild Balkan Kingdom of Serbia, nominally part of the Ottoman Empire but in reality governed by its own King. Two rival dynasties, the Karageorgevics and the Obrenovics, vied for this honour and the Kingdom was rent by the fratricidal struggles of these two families.

74

Kephalas was welcomed by the current reigning King, Milosh Obrenovic, and lived for some time in Serbia under his protection. But in 1839 it was the turn of the Karageorgevics and Milosh was deposed and Kephalas hurriedly removed himself to Athens. Not one to retire contentedly into a modest seclusion he printed an appeal to King Otho of Greece, outlining his services to the nation and declaring his pecuniary needs. The King was sufficiently impressed to grant him two thousand drachmas from his private purse.

Some years later he was to be found in Adrianople and Constantinople offering his services to the old enemy, the Turkish Government, to dredge the port of Ainos at the mouth of the river Evros but, despite some preliminary interest, the Turks rejected his scheme. One cannot help being impressed by the audacious cheek of the Captain who was wanted in both the Ionian Islands and Bombay to face serious criminal charges and yet turned up in London to petition the Government against the conduct of British officials. Had the Turkish authorities in Constantinople known that the man who was applying to carry out an engineering project in their empire was the same person who had committed acts of piracy in their territorial waters some years before, Kephalas would have been in serious trouble.

In 1843 he left Constantinople to sail to Crete from where he addressed a letter to the General Assembly of Greece in which, amongst other things, he advised them "to ban all foreign parties so that Greek will only be Greek, and to consider as an enemy of the country and the nation, anyone who is attached to or supported by a foreign party." From Crete this indefatigable traveller sailed to the Holy Land to make the pilgrimage to Jerusalem and here he stayed six months but the wander-lust would not leave him and he began to plan, at the age of eighty, what would have been the greatest of his journeys. Inspired perhaps by memories of the sun-kissed, palm-fringed beaches, the baroque mansions and churches of Goa and the remarkable tolerance of the Portuguese Government some fifteen years before, he decided to revisit the city, negotiating the caravan routes across the Levant on the back of a mule. Fate was unkind to the old man - a fall resulting in severe injuries forced him to abandon this project almost as soon as it was begun. Painfully he retraced his steps through Beirut, Alexandretta, Mersin, Cyprus and Samos to Constantinople which he reached in 1845. Here he published the last of his books explaining why he had failed to obtain the contract for dredging the Ainos.

The last act of his life was played out in the ancient city of Salonica where he was befriended by Archbishop Hieronymos who gave him a room in the episcopal palace and, when he died in 1850, an imposing funeral and a tomb in the Cathedral. His possessions amounted to nothing more than an old trunk filled with copies of his books and a lifetime's correspondence. Was he a patriot? There can be no possible doubt about that. Was he something of a rogue? Probably, but there is no law of human nature which decrees that an individual must be either one or the other. Whatever his failings, in the words of Hamlet "He was a man, take him for all in all".

References: Chapter Six

1. *Indian Asia*, Philip Rawson (Elsevier, Phaidon 1977), pp32-38
2. *Demetrios Galanos, the Greek Indologist*, J. Gennadius in *Transactions of the Third International Congress for the History of Religions* (Clarendon Press, Oxford 1908). A copy is in the Bodleian Library, Oxford.
3. *Ibid.*
4. *Ibid.*
5. Loukatos, op. cit. Chapter 3
6. Gennadius, op. cit.
7. Press Lists Public Records Vol. XII p465 I.O.R.
8. Gennadius, op. cit.
9. T. Wilkinson, op. cit. p84.
10. *India One Hundred Years Ago*, Revd. W Urwick p134
11. Bengal European Inhabitants. 1783-1807 I.O.R
12. *Bishop Heber In Northern India*, selections from Heber's Journal ed. MA Laird (CUP 1971) p153
13. Loukatos, op. cit. Chapter 3
14. Gennadius, op. cit.
15. Loukatos, op. cit. Chapter 3
16. Gennadius, op. cit.
17. Bengal Transcriptions of Tombs Vol. I
18. *Ibid.*
19. Gennadius, op. cit.
20. *Ibid.*
21. *Ibid.*
22. Loukatos, op. cit. Chapter 3
23. Bengal Past and Present Vol. LIII, part 1
24. Bengal Consultations Z/P/4/39 I.O.R.
25. *Ibid.*
26. *An Assemblage of Indian Army Soldiers and Uniforms,* ed. Michael Glover (Perpetua Press 1973) p4
27. *A Squire of Hindoostan,* Narindar Saroop (Palit and Palit, New Delhi 1983) p39
28. Boards Collections: F/4/95, F/4/211, F/4/308, F/4/472, F/4/4722 I.O.R.
29. East India Directory, 1819
30. East India Register, 1835
31. *Hobson Jobson*, H. Yule and AC Burnell (Routledge and Keegan Paul) Reissued 1968 under *Ressaldar* and *Naik*
32. Boards Collections: F/4/472 I.O.R.
33. Bengal Obituary p255
34. Boards Collections: F/4/1266, Coll 50905 I.O.R.
35. *The Greek Gazette,* (London, June 1975) Vol.9 No.94
36. *The Greek Merchant Marine,* ed. Stelios A Papadopoulos (National Bank of Greece) pp184-185

37. *Descrizione della Citta di Benares nell', India dell indiano politersmo, sua culto, e costumi di guei popoli: fatta dal vaggiatore cap - Greco di Zante, nel sua viaggio nell' anno 1824, dal medisimo publicata, e corredata d'una carta Geografica dell' indie da esso disegrata, Livorno, Dai torchi in Glauco Masi, 1826*

38. Loukatos, op. cit. pp118-119

7

The Greek Community
in Bengal. 1774-1857

The merchant to secure his treasure,
Conveys it in a borrowed name.   (Alexander Pope)

The historian of the early Greek community in Bengal finds his path beset with gargantuan difficulties, some of which have been described in an earlier chapter. The records he has to depend on are largely those of the British Administration in India which were not overly concerned with foreign nationals from an obscure corner of Europe, conducting forms of trade which were not of great economic importance to the operations of the East India Company. He who would find a Greek presence in Bengal must dig hard and patiently in the records, searching for the proverbial needle in a haystack. The patronymics he discovers easily change form from one context to another and he has to employ the skills of a detective to establish whether he is dealing with the same man whose name has been spelled differently or another whose name bears some resemblance to that of the first. Often enough, the result is inconclusive. This frustration grows as he discovers that a large proportion of the names he has garnered remain only items in a bare list without the flesh of recorded incident to give life to his narrative. So many names are mentioned only once and then disappear into the limbo of the unchronicled dead.

The procedure adopted in this chapter is to describe and attempt some analysis of the contents of six basic documents which provide us with the names of early Greek merchants and within this documentary framework fit such other facts which have come to light and thus assemble painfully, as far as one can, the pieces of this historical jigsaw.

The earliest of these documents (Document A) is dated Feb 21, 1774. It is a letter addressed to the Archbishop of Sinai and is signed by seven Greek merchants of Calcutta, in the following order:

Georgios Baraktaroglou
Chatzee Alexios Argyree
Argyrees Angelee
Georgios Monolakee Arikoglou
Constantinos Georgiou
Theocharees Georgiou
Michalees Andreou[1].

They were merchants engaged in the export and import trade in Calcutta. Alexios Argyree from Philippopolis we have already met in Chapter 3, he who became the leader and true founder of the Greek merchant community in Calcutta. Constantinos Georgiou came from Constantinople and Baraktaroglou and Arikoglou almost certainly hailed from the same city or the mainland of Asia Minor because of the typically Turkish termination of their names. Michalees Andreou came from the Peloponnesus and Argyrees Angelee probably from Philippopolis. These were the founding fathers of the community though Baraktaroglou, Angelee and Arikoglou are never mentioned in subsequent records. Shortly after the despatch of this letter, Alexios Argyree shifted his commercial activities to Dacca and henceforth Greek trading in Bengal moved around two poles - Calcutta and Dacca.

The next document (Document B) is of vital importance[2]. It is the petition of 13 December 1788 (see Chapter 4) signed by sixty-nine Greek merchants in Bengal to the Court of Directors of the East India Company as a testimonial to Warren Hastings. Its interest to the historian lies especially in the fact that each of these merchants appends, after his signature, his place of origin. An analysis of these place names provides the following information:

From:-				
Philippopolis	25		Thrace	25
Caesaria	9	⎫		
Trebizond	2	⎪		
Smyrna	1	⎪		
Bythynia	1	⎬	Asia Minor	16
Brusa or Prusa	1	⎪		
Magnesia	1	⎪		
Constantinople	1	⎭		
Georgia	2		Russian Empire	2
Arta	1	⎫		
Athens	1	⎪	Mainland Greece	7
Pelopponese	1	⎬		
Thessaly	4	⎭		
Corfu	1	⎫	Ionian Islands	2
Cephalonia	1	⎭		
Nio	5	⎫		
Metyline (Lesbos)	2	⎪		
Rhodes	2	⎪		
Crete	2	⎬	Aegean Islands	15
Irineus (Erini)	2	⎪		
Nasiras	1	⎪		
Lamos (Lemnos?)	1	⎭		
Albania	1		Albania	1
Calcutta	1		Calcutta	1
Total:				**69**

One other merchant is described as 'a Sclavonian'.

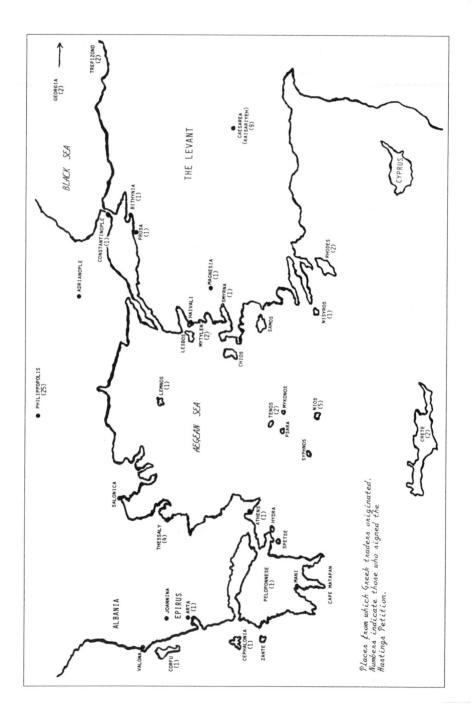

GEORGIA (2)
TREPIZOND (2)
BLACK SEA
BITHYNIA (1)
CONSTANTINOPLE (1)
PRUSA (1)
ADRIANOPLE
THE LEVANT
CAESAREA (KAISARIYEH) (9)
CYPRUS
MAGNESIA (1)
SMYRNA (1)
RHODES (2)
HAIVALI
NISYROS (1)
LESBOS
MYTYLENE (2)
SAMOS
CHIOS
PHILIPPOPOLIS (25)
LEMNOS (1)
AEGEAN SEA
TENOS (2)
MYKONOS
NIOS (5)
PSARA
SYPHNOS
CRETE (2)
SALONICA
ATHENS (1)
HYDRA
THESSALY (4)
SPETSE
ALBANIA
JOANNINA
EPIRUS
ARTA (1)
PELOPONNESE (1)
MANI
CAPE MATAPAN
VALONA
CORFU (1)
CEPHALONIA (1)
ZANTE (1)

*Places from which Greek traders originated.
Numbers indicate those who signed the
Hastings Petition.*

What is notable is the very high proportion of merchants from the Thracian city of Philippopolis whose citizens were foremost, from the beginning of the 18th century at least, in trading with India. Alexander Panioty (who signed himself Panageotes Alexios) was at the head of the petition as he had already at this date established himself as the chief merchant of the Greek community and he was resident in Dacca. There are two merchants from Document A, both resident in Calcutta, who signed this document: Theodore Charis (Theocharees Georgiou) from Arta in seventh place, and Michaelees Andreou from the Peloponnese in the thirty-third place. About thirty-two signatories never seem to appear again in extant records. Did they return home or continue their activities in Bengal but in so humble a capacity that no record of their work or death has survived? The above analysis of places of origin must lead us to treat with reserve the remark of 'Asiaticus' in 1802 that "few of the Greek islanders came to Bengal and at this very day the Turkish Greeks prevail in Calcutta". Except for the Ionians and Georgians (only four on the list) all these merchants were subjects of the Ottoman Empire but of this number only nineteen out of sixty-nine hailed from Asiatic Turkey and no less than seventeen came from the islands of the Aegean and Ionian seas. The predominance of the citizens of Philippopolis, a European city, has already been noted - about 35 percent of the total.

Our third source of information (Document C) is the Bengal Directories of 1790 and 1792 which contain a stark list of Greek merchants in Bengal. Six are noted: Mavrody Kyriakos, Shereen Abraham, Michael Andrew, John Demetrius, George Leonidas and Theochary Godeela. Two of these, Theochary Godeela from Arta and Michael Andrew from the Peloponese, appear in both A and B documents and the other four are only in document B. Mavrody Kyriakos (Marodes Thireacos) who is there described as the Warden of the Greek Church in Calcutta and as hailing from Philippopolis, Shereen Abraham from Caesaria, John Demetrius from Metyline and George Leonidas from Smyrna. It is significant that Alexander Panioty is not mentioned in Document C. We do not know on what principle the compilers of the Bengal Directory selected these names but it is likely that they were those of the most prosperous Greek merchants and all of them were resident in Calcutta. The omission of Alexander Panioty's name fits in with the known fact of his considerable losses in chunam manufacture in Sylhet and the resulting curtailment of his commercial activity.

The fourth document (Document D) is a petition to the Governor General, Lord Cornwallis, in 1792 asking for permission to arm certain Greek conductors to protect their boats plying between Dacca and Chittagong and the stations in between and engaged chiefly in the salt trade. Nine merchants signed the petition, seven from Calcutta and two from Dacca. Of the former, Mavrody Kyriakos, Michael Andrew and Shereen Abraham are names that occur in the B and C documents, and two others, Nicolay Collonah and Christodulo Nicolay appear only in the B document. The two Dacca signatories Alexander Panioty (Panioty

Alexander) and Constantine Shaw (Constantine Shahiny) were both from Philippopolis, and their assent is given through their attorney, Mavrody Kyriakos. The petition also contains the names of seventeen other Greeks[3] for whom the firearm licences were required. Of these, ten can be certainly traced to Dacca, two others may belong to Dacca and the remaining five cannot be ascribed to any particular place. It would seem from this evidence that though the greater number of the more prosperous merchants were still to be found in Calcutta, the younger Greeks were beginning to drift towards Dacca to find employment in the more adventurous but humbler occupation of conductors of boats.

The fifth document (Document E) is a list of Greek merchants living in Dacca in 1795 compiled by the Civil Administration[4]. There are thirty-eight names and in each case the number of years of residence in Bengal is stated. Alexander Panioty is mentioned first in the list with a period of twenty-four years residence. Two others, Alexander Kyriakos from Philippopolis and Michael Polity from Constantinople, equal this total but Constantine Shahiny (Constantine Shaw), also from Philippopolis, is the oldest inhabitant with thirty-six years residence. Seven have resided between ten to twenty years and twenty-seven under ten years, while eighteen of these names also occur in the B document. The impression gained from this evidence is that the Greek settlement in Dacca was growing, attracting the younger immigrants and surpassing in numbers the community in Calcutta.

The sixth and last document (Document F) is another petition to the Archbishop of Sinai, dated December 13, 1811.[5] Again Alexander Panioty headed the list of signatories, evidence of the fact that he had by this time recovered from his losses twenty years previously. The second place is occupied by Theocharees Georgiou (Theodore Charis) a veteran merchant of Calcutta, whose name occurs in Documents A, B and C. Taking the list as a whole, of the thirty names, seventeen can definitely be identified as residents of Dacca (ten of these occur in the B list), two are certainly from Calcutta and there is doubt about the remaining eleven. Once more the evidence reinforces the impression of the burgeoning growth of Dacca as a Greek settlement at the start of the 19th century.

To these early days of adventure belong two tombstones formerly in the Greek Churchyard in Calcutta:

Here lies the servant of God, Georgios Leontiou from the city of Smyrna who died on 8 January, 1792.

O Man, see and understand that death will surely come. Therefore on this tablet it is recorded that Soteerios, whose native city was Philippopolis and whose father was Sogios pursued a commercial calling in this life and died while returning from Patna 17 May 1793[6]

The only volumes of the Bengal Directory and the East India Directory from 1792 to 1817 available in the India Office Records do not contain the name of a single Greek merchant in either Calcutta or Dacca. This does not mean that they did not exist, but that the compilers of these publications did not consider any Greek merchant important enough for inclusion. This interpretation is supported by the comment of 'Asiaticus' (circa 1802) that the Greeks "are almost all poor as the branches of trade they engage in are of little importance" and he dismisses the Dacca community with the contemptuous description of "a few peddling Greeks".

This situation began to change about the year 1818 with the arrival in Calcutta of a Greek merchant who had been trading in Agra since about 1795. His name was Constantine Pantazes (also spelt Pandazee and Pandajee), and he was of Epirot origin but emigrated from his native land to Adrianople from where, about 1795, he left with his family for India. He eschewed Calcutta with its settled Greek community and began operating in the humble capacity of an up-country trader at Agra where he is listed as a merchant from 1795 to 1817. In 1818 he probably, as a result of his commercial success, set up business in Calcutta in Amratollah Street[9] where Argyree's Greek Church was situated. Evidently he prospered, for he is listed year after year in the Bengal Directory as the first named Greek merchant of Calcutta from 1818 to 1842, the year of his death. His commercial activity must have included trade with the Levant, for he and his partner, Soterios Antoniou, retained an agent in Constantinople, a merchant from Philippopolis called Mandrazoglou.

Since Argyree's day no single merchant in Calcutta had emerged as the clear and undisputed leader of the Greek community in that city. From 1818 to 1847 Constantine Pantazes filled this role and corresponded with the Patriarch of Constantinople and the Archbishop of Sinai on its behalf and was recognized by the former prelate as "The Honoured Trustee....of our beloved and most dear children in the Lord who live in the city of Calcutta". He died a wealthy and respected figure and his tombstone was erected in the Greek churchyard:

Sacred to the memory of Constantine Pandazy, Esq, Greek
Merchant, died at Calcutta 29 March 1842, in the 72nd
year of his age. He was humane, meek and liberal both
in prosperity and adversity and his chief aim was to do
good and to avoid offending God and man.[8]

One of the most important contributions which he made to the Calcutta community was the founding of a Greek school. He was conscious of the fact that the Calcutta Greeks were a relatively small body, working in an overwhelmingly alien environment, subjected not only to the influences of the indigenous culture but also to the official regime of the British. This consideration and the intermarriage of Greeks with European women from other communities, and occasionally with Indian women, meant that the children of these unions might lose their Greek character and the cultural heritage of Hellenism. To combat this he provided the money for the establishment of a Greek school in Calcutta, and arranged for the despatch of the distinguished Athenian teacher, Demetrius Galanos, from Constantinople.[9]

In this work Pantazes was ably seconded by another Epirot merchant, Peter Protopapas, who arrived in India sometime between 1818 and 1821. Among the early Greek merchants of Bengal he is unique in that we know his precise place of origin, which was the village of Coucoulias in the district of Zagora in Epirus, a considerable port with a shipyard for the construction of merchantmen used in the Mediterranean and Black Sea trade.[10] Like Pantazes he was an enthusiast for Greek learning and culture and threw himself into the affairs of the Greek School in Calcutta, which functioned as an extension of the Greek Church, and whose first teachers were Orthodox priests and later the laymen, Demetrius Galanos and Petros from Kapesodos who arrived in India in 1792. Protopapas' interest in Greek education was not confined to Calcutta, for he did not forget the schools of his native Epirus and despatched in instalments the sum of 40,000gr for their maintenance. It is sad to relate that this money never reached its intended recipients, being seized and misappropriated by one of the nobles of Coucoulias.[11]

Significantly, these two great benefactors of Hellenic learning in Calcutta were both Epirots. Epirus, and particularly the town of Joannina, had from the beginning of the 18th century established itself as a centre of Greek intellectual activity. Henry Holland in 1812 says that "the extensive traffic of the Greeks of Joannina is a means of tendering this city as a sort of mart for books, which are brought hither from the continent when printed, and from this point diffused over other parts of Greece".[12] Another English traveller, William Martin Leake, affirms that "The Greek spoken at Joannina is of a more polished kind than is usually heard in any part of Greece proper; its phrases are more Hellenic, and its construction more grammatical. This is a natural consequence of the schools long established here, and the residence of many merchants and others who have travelled and dwelt in civilized Europe".[13]

When, in the early years of the 19th century, the Philiki Etairia, the Secret Society which did so much to spread ideas of Greek nationalism was formed, it was the Epirot merchants Nicolaos Skouphas and Athanasios Tsakaloff who were amongst its founders. Not surprisingly, therefore, it was the two Epirots, Pantazes and Protopapas, who organised the Calcutta Greeks to help their long-oppressed countrymen when the tocsin of revolt sounded in the Greek War of Independence. The Bengal Greeks sent considerable sums of money to help their embattled compatriots and a Philhellenic Society was formed in Calcutta whose members included large numbers of distinguished British residents like Bishop Reginald Heber, the leading Chinese merchants and even the sons of Tipoo Sultan who played a conspicuous role in the social life of Calcutta. There were four of them, Moizuddin, Sultan Sahib, Gulam Mohammed and the eldest, Fateh

Hyder who lived in the Bara Mahal, now the Tollygunge Club. In 1806 they had been removed to Calcutta by the British who suspected their complicity in the Vellore Mutiny. Indicative of the deep feeling roused in liberal and radical circles by the Greek War of Independence was the fact that the famous young Eurasian intellectual Henry Vivian De Rozio, teacher at the Hindu College and editor of several Bengali newspapers, composed a poem celebrating the Battle of Navarino at which Admiral Codrington crushed the Egyptian-Turkish Navy and thus virtually ensured the liberation of the Greeks. By their efforts the Greeks of Bengal were able to remit the sum of £2,200 to Greece through the agency of the London Greek Committee. This was indicative of the intense interest which the Bengal Greeks took in the affairs of their Fathers and was the topic of Heber's up-country conversation with the Greek shopkeeper, Mr. Athanass in 1825. "He was very anxious to have news from Greece and I felt sorry that I had nothing good to tell him".

Two other Calcutta Greek merchants in the first half of the 19th century were John Lucas who traded from 1818 to 1854, first at Armenian Street and then at Portuguese Church Lane, and John Athanass from 1821 to 1835 at Gooriamal's Lane. The latter was the son of a Greek merchant from Philippopolis, the provision for whose education and upbringing by Protestant missionaries has already been described in Chapter 5. With this unusual background and his subsequent conversion to the Baptist Faith he remained rather apart from the rest of the Calcutta Greek Community. His signature does not appear on the Hastings Petition in 1788, though he was thirty-five years old at that time and already an established merchant of Calcutta, and when he died in 1835 he was not buried in the Greek Churchyard but in the South Park Street Cemetery under the following monumental inscription:

> Sacred to the memory of John Athanass Esq., who departed this life on 1 September 1835, aged 82 years. Despising ostentation and happy in retirement the world knew him but little and appreciated him less, yet the poor whom the world neglects will bless him for those simple provisions, which his charity bequeathed to all their wants. But it was in his family where all his affections centred, that his real virtues were displayed. Purity, veracity and piety evinced the goodness of heart and the sincerity of his faith, and led his children to award this testimonial, and to love the Father and revere the Christian."

His wife's monumental inscription was to be found in the North Park Street Cemetery:

> Sacred to the memory of Mrs. Hannah Athanass, lady of the late John Athanass Esq., who departed this life on 18th August 1837, aged 67 years. Her ways were ways of pleasantness and all her paths were peace.[14]

John and Hannah had three daughters, all of whom married military men. The second of the marriages of two of these girls have already been recorded in

Chapter 5 but the eldest girl, Charlotte, married Lieutenant Robert Joseph Debnam, an East Suffolk family, of the 65th (2nd Yorkshire, North Riding) Regiment of Foot, who arrived at Madras on *The General Stewart* in July 1803. Hot from the siege of Bhurtpore in February 1805, he left his regiment to go on leave to Calcutta where he married Charlotte on December 7th 1805. She was seventeen years old, a not uncommon age for brides in the predominantly male expatriate community in Bengal. Debnam's tombstone in Kensal Green Cemetery records his adventurous military career in the East.

> Robert Joseph Debnam born on 12th June 1781 at Chatham, died on 18th April 1876 at his residence 15 Kensington Gate. Major of 13th Light Infantry, entered the army in 1803 in H.M. 65th Regiment. He served in the Mahratta campaigns, in Burma and Afghanistan. An honoured life, 47 years spent in India, was closed in his native land, tenderly and devotedly loved, the stern simple faithful mind, strong and clear, with hallowed will he survived awhile the beloved wife of 67 years, living to see their childrens' children to the fourth generation. Wise and just and tender hearted, he lived and died in the love of Christ, a brave God-fearing man.
>
> Stand in awe, and sin not; commune with your own heart, and in your chamber, and be still. Offer the sacrifice of righteousness and put your trust in the Lord. (Psalm 4, verses 5 and 6).

It would seem that Charlotte shared some of his adventures for there is a story that on one occasion both of them with their eldest child were captured by a French frigate off Ceylon during the Revolutionary War, carried to the Isle de France (Mauritius) and remained there three months until, released by the French authorities, they took passage in an Arab ship to Muscat, eventually reaching Bombay. She was buried by her husband in Kensal Green Cemetery:

> Charlotte wife of Major R. J. Debnam late of H.M.'s 13th Light Infantry and eldest daughter of the late John Athanass, Esquire of Calcutta born 3rd January 1788 married 7th December 1805 died 2nd March 1873. The best of wives the best of mothers a true and faithful friend simple and unwavering in her faith dutiful in all the relations of her life, the beloved and devoted wife of 67 years. The rejoicing mother of 15 children - children to the third generation following her to the grave. She was called to her rest full of love in the true peace of Christ and his most holy assurance.
>
> Bless the Lord, O my soul, and forget not all his benefits. (Psalm 103).

At least three of her children had connections with India. George Athanass Debnam of Bilsee, Rohilkhand was born at Newport, Isle of Wight on 20th October 1821 and died on 30th July 1875 and was buried in Cawnpore. Her second daughter, Harriet Athanass Debnam married the Revd. James Justus Tucker, a chaplain to the East India Company. She was born on 25th September 1810 and died 31st July 1870. Another daughter, Helen, was born at Dinapore on 4th November 1827 and died in London on 21st April 1894. John and Sarah had

Charlotte Athanass

two other children whose tombstones in the South Park Street Cemetery give the following information: George b. 1790, d. 20th Sept 1809. Sophia b. 1791, d. 19th May 1797.

The year 1852 marks the end of an era. In that year Scott's Directory has a significant new entry in its list of Calcutta trading firms: "Ralli Brothers, 12 Lall Bazaar". The advent of this London-based firm with branches in several European and Levantine cities was to change the whole nature of Greek commercial activity in India. Against this colossus the old Greeks could not compete. One survivor who lasted for some years trading alongside the Rallis, was the firm of Peter John which began trading in 1840 at 2 Amratollah Street, and only ceased to do so in 1861. In 1859 Peter John was the Warden of the Greek Church and in that year the name of his son, A. C. John, appears as an assistant working for one of the new London-based Greek firms, Ralli and Mavrojani. Goliath had swallowed David.

As in the case of Calcutta, we have to wait until 1818 before Greek merchants are mentioned in Dacca in the Bengal Directories. In that year Alexander Panioty at last surfaces with five other Greek merchants - Demetrius Elias, Nicholas Kalonas, Lucas Theodoro, George Athanas Primo and Antony Foscholo - all based at Naraingunj. This river port, adjacent to Dacca, was a great mart for salt, oil-seeds, grain, sugar, ghee, tobacco, metals, timber and lime, and a depot for boats and boatmen engaged in the inland trade of Bengal.[15] From the beginning of the century to about 1839, the Greek presence in Dacca and Naraingunj expanded, but thereafter there was a rapid decline and it disappeared almost entirely after 1851 as the following table of Greek merchants operating there, taken from the Bengal Directories, indicates:

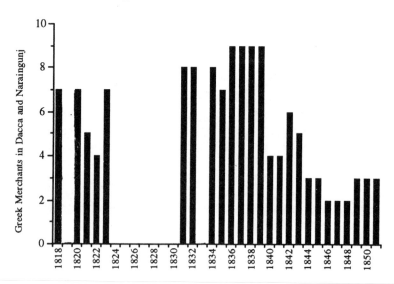

(The volumes of the Bengal Directories for the years 1819, 1825-1830, 1832/33 are unfortunately missing in the India Office Records.)

With historical hindsight, it is now possible to see that Alexios Argyree had played the role of a tragic pioneer. Like Moses, he led the Greeks to the promised land of Dacca but he was not to know that in the first thirty years of the 19th century the competition of Lancashire's cotton industry would destroy the prosperity of Dacca. In the very years when Greeks were crowding into the district, the economic ground was shifting under their feet. The reports of English visitors to Dacca made melancholy reading. In 1824 Bishop Heber noted that "factories of the Dutch, French and Portuguese nations are all sunk into ruin and overgrown with jungle". In 1840 James Taylor wrote "The place (Narayangunj) has declined considerably within the last thirty years....in the Armenian and Greek quarters of Dacca, there are several large brick built houses but most of them are falling into ruin".

Nevertheless, during this period a Greek community grew up around the church built by Alexander Panioty, creating a distinctive Greek way of life. Out of the thirty-seven names noted in the Dacca list of 1795 (Document E) only some eleven seem to be established as families of some consequence - Panioty, Ducas, Lucas, Athanas, Calogreedy, Calonas, Elias, Foscolo, Marrody, Esau and Jordan. In the case of the first, the reason for its pre-eminence is easy to understand since its members were the heirs of Alexios Argyree Panaghiotis. In the other cases we have unfortunately no means of knowing why they survived and other Greek names disappeared, only rarely emerging in some obscure record of birth, marriage or death.

Probably sometime in the last quarter of the 19th century, when Ralli Brothers had established a trading presence in Dacca, this firm, with a commendable sense of history, built a monument to the memory of its mercantile forbears. Originally it was situated on the Shahbagh Avenue and faced the Ramna Racecourse on a site which had been used as the Greek Cemetery in Dacca. Standing alone, it immediately attracted the eye, but today it stands in the University grounds in Mymensingh Road across from Suhrawardy Uddyan which is no longer a racecourse. It is a neoclassical structure built of brick and stucco and remains, at the time of writing, in fairly good condition. It has a central square core and from each of its sides projects a bay held up by two fluted pillars of the Doric Order on which rests the entablature and a triangular pediment, the whole forming a Greek Cross. Over the top of its eastern face is the following inscription in Greek: "Blessed are they whom you have chosen and taken to yourself".

Entrance into the interior is through the east door. Inside are ten memorial tablets of black stone, five in Greek and five in English, nine of which are affixed to the north, south and west walls and one lies broken on the floor and appears never to have been erected like the others. The oldest inscription is dated 1800 and the latest was carved in 1859. All of them seem to be headstones taken from the earlier Greek cemetery. The deciphering of the Greek inscriptions has proved irksome because time has eroded some of the characters and the stonemasons employed were clearly unfamiliar with the Greek language, so that some letters have been inscribed in a doubtful manner and the words are often jumbled together, making the task of the translator very difficult. Most of them are recorded in appropriate places in this narrative but two, which mention the wives of merchants, are as follows:

> A loving wife should not forget her husband therefore...
> because of her love and as a perpetual reminder of her
> marriage she has dedicated this memorial to her husband,
> Constantinos Georgiou Manrologlou whose homeland was
> Constantinople. After he had pursued a commercial life
> he died on July 24, 1806. Dacca.

> Here lies....Theodosia wife of Theodoro.....from Philippopolis
> .....who on April 10, 1807 was taken into eternity. Dacca.

Alexander Panioty probably had eight children - five sons and three daughters. One of his daughters, Sultana, married John Perroux, Head Assistant of the Salt Office in Calcutta. Another, Emiralda, married Celibi Constacki Mavrodoglio on April 28, 1799, in Naraingunj and a third, whose Christian name has not survived, married John D. Calogreedy in Dacca on Feb 1, 1813. Four of his sons, George, Anastasius, Alexander and John were born in Philippopolis and came out to India with their father in 1772 and their names are recorded on the the Hastings' Petition of 1788 (Document B) in the seventeenth to twentieth places. The youngest son, Constantine, from whose tombstone we can establish his date of birth as 1782, was born in Bengal. In the Sinai Petition of 1811 (Document F) the names of John and Constantine, alone amongst Alexander's sons, are found linked together "Joannes and Konstantinos Panagiotou", but it is something of a mystery why the names of their brothers do not appear on this document. Some years after the consecration of the Dacca Church, on November 3, 1812, the Dacca priest, Gregory of Syphnos, wrote to George and Anastasius Panioty, reproaching them for the neglect of their duties as wardens of the church, and this seems to be the last surviving mention of the name of Anastasius.[16]

The Bengal Directories list the names of G. Panioty, John Panioty and C. Panioty as Greek merchants of Dacca: George from 1834 to 1839, Constantine from 1834 to 1845 and John from 1834 to 1848. The last mentioned date was probably the date of death in each case but this assumption should be treated with caution since in the case of Constantine his tombstone shows that he died in 1844. Alone of the sons of Alexander his tombstone inscription has survived. He died in Barisal and was buried in the English cemetery (Grave no. 47): "Sacred to the memory of Constantine Panioty, Esq, who departed this life 16 Oct, 1844, aged 62 years".[17]

Greek Memorial, Dacca

John Panioty had two sons, Constantine and Emmanuel. It is significant that with the decline of Dacca as a commercial centre both these men looked for careers outside commerce. Emmanuel, born in 1800 in Dacca, qualified as a solicitor and about 1821 married a young girl who, within a year, died. All we know of her is on her tombstone in the Greek churchyard in Calcutta: "Sacred to the memory of Catherine, wife of Emmanuel Panioty, who departed this life on 21 Aug, 1821, aged 17 years and 17 days". [18]

Not long afterwards he married into another Greek family of Dacca, the Jordans. His bride was Erin and the marriage took place in Dacca on July 1, 1823. Her father was Joseph Jordanou who arrived in Bengal in 1788 just in time to sign the Hastings' Petition in the fifty-third place, and came from Caesarea in Asia Minor. His name also appears in the Dacca list of 1795 and the Sinai Petition of 1811. The English inscription of his tombstone is recorded in the Dacca Greek Memorial:

To the memory of Mrs Magdalene and Sophia Jordan
As also to that of their husband
Mr Joseph Jordan of Cesareah
Merchant at Naraingunge.
The latter departed this life the 10th of Feb 1819
aged about 60 years.
This monument is erected as a tribute of affection
to their memory by their afflicted orphan children.

His son, Jordan Joseph Jordan, like Emmanuel Panioty, chose a legal career and on May 7, 1821, married Anna Maria Gill in Dacca. In 1837 he was Sadr Ameen (an Uncovenanted Judge) of Backergunj and later of the Twenty Four Pargannahs. He was buried in the New Burial Ground, Circular Road, under the following inscription:

Sacred to the memory of J. J. Jordan,
late Sudeer Ameen of the 24 Purgannahs
who departed this life on 29/10/1841
Aged 42 years. [19]

He was almost the exact contemporary of Emmanuel Panioty and his brother-in-law.

In 1849 Emmanuel is noted in the Bengal Directory as a solicitor living at 18 Scott's Lane in Calcutta with his brother Constantine - the Lane was probably named after James Scott who owned extensive properties in Old Post Office Street, Camac Street and other places between 1780 and 1820. [20] It was here that Emmanuel died on January 29, 1852. In 'Bengal Administrations' of that year his name appears as 'intestate' and it is surprising that a lawyer should have neglected to prepare an adequate will. He died a fairly wealthy man and the administration of his will was granted to his elder brother, Constantine.

Constantine too moved from Dacca to Calcutta and found employment as a broker with the firm of Eglinton McClure. From 1839 to 1848 he lived at Hastings Street and from 1849 to 1852 with his brother at 18 Scott's Lane and probably died in 1856 as he is no longer mentioned as a resident in any of the Calcutta Directories.

The third son of Alexander Panioty was named after his father but little is known of this man except that he does not seem to have gone into trade but became a zamindar in Dacca. He married Catherine, daughter of Ignatius Barros of Portuguese descent, who died in 1846 in Calcutta some years after the death of her husband. She was buried in the Roman Catholic Church of Nostre Senhora de Dolores in Boitaconnah and her memorial still exists on the floor of one of the aisles of the Church:

> Sacred to the memory of Mrs Catherine Alexander Panioty,
> relict of Alexander Panioty, Esq, of Dacca and daughter
> of Ignatius Barros, Esq, also of Dacca, died 16 May, 1846,
> aged 66 years. Requiescat in Pace.[21]

Alexander and Catherine had at least one son, Ignatius Constantine, who inherited his father's zamindari and lived in Dacca till 1881 and married Dispinoo Lucas of another Greek Dacca Family.

There was another Panioty tomb to be found in the Greek Churchyard in Calcutta though its occupant cannot be identified with certainty but may have been the wife of Constantine Panioty of Eglinton McClure. Its inscription was as follows:

> Sacred to the memory of Mrs Greeny Panioty Jnr who departed this life on 10th February, 1833, aged 24 years.[22]

The only merchant who signed the Hastings Petition from the Island of Corfu was Angelo Ducas (Doucas). From the Dacca List of 1795 we learn that he arrived in Bengal in 1783 and that there was another Ducas, Constantine (perhaps Angelo's brother), in Dacca who came out a year later. A very early mention of this name in Indian Records is the case of John Ducas, a soldier, who died in Madras on Jan 4, 1715, but though this man was almost certainly a Greek it is impossible to know whether he was connected with the Corfu branch of the family. The origin of the name is fascinating for the Ducases were a dynasty of Byzantine Emperors in the Middle Ages and a branch of the family were Despots of Epiros.[23] The name 'Angelo' was the family name of yet another Byzantine Dynasty so that Angelo Ducas carried in his name the double memory of a gilded imperial lineage. Unlike the patronymics of most other Greeks in Bengal the name 'Ducas' was a true surname and in Corfu it appeared in the Golden List of Nobility under Venetian rule[24]. In the Bengal Directories of the first half of the 19th century, 'A. Ducas' is twice mentioned, seemingly referring to two brothers. One, Angelo, was a merchant at Dacca till 1852 and the other, Alexander, an indigo planter at Chinnispore near Dacca from 1824 to 1854. The daughter of the latter has her tombstone in St. Thomas' Churchyard, Dacca (grave No. 265):

Sacred to the memory of Miss Henrietta Eliza Ducas
who departed this life on the 13th Feb, 1837, aged
18 years 8 months 25 days.[25]

The son of one of these men, called 'Alexander Ducas', was noted as "the Keeper of the Register of Parwanas granted at other stations and fair copyest registers" in the Customs Service at Cawnpore in 1806.[26] After 1854 there is no further mention of the name in Dacca but it appears elsewhere. Angelo Ducas Jnr was working in 1865 for one of the new Greek firms in Calcutta, Argenti Schlizzi, and. C. Ducas became a civil engineer - in 1861 he was special assistant engineer on the Ooloobariah Canal; in 1862 Special Assistant Engineer of Public Works, Damooda Division, Morstaka, Burdwan; in 1863 the same post at Hidgelee; in 1865 an executive engineer, P.W.D. at Tumlook till 1870 when he retired and lived in Wellington Square, Calcutta. Another C. Ducas worked for the East Indian Railway from 1859 to 1862.

The twenty-seventh signatory of the Hastings Petition was Lucas Theodoro from Magnesia in Asia Minor, not far from the ancient city of Ephesus, and his name appears again in the Sinai Petition of 1812. He is tantalizingly described by a modern Greek writer (Spiros Loukatos) as "Loukas Theodorou, the Greek savant"[27] and one yearns to know in what branch of learning he excelled. However, this obscure description alerts us to the possibility that the standard of culture amongst the Dacca Greeks may have been of a reasonably high order. The Bengal Directory describes him as a merchant at Naraingunj from 1818 to 1820 and at Dacca until 1823. Two of his sons, Theodore and Andrew, were salt merchants in Dacca from 1831 to 1851 and in 1856 and 1857 are noted as 'zamindars'; they were also signatories to the Sinai Petition of 1811. Theodore Lucas' daughter Dispinoo (Despoina) married Ignatius Constantine Panioty on May 19, 1847, died in 1879 and was buried in the Golbadan Cemetery, Moulvi Bazaar, Dacca (Grave no. 7) with the following inscription:

In affectionate memory of Dispinoo, the beloved wife
of Ignatius C. Panioty, Esq, and daughter of T. Lucas, Esq:
Died 29 Dec, 1879, aged 50 years. This tablet is erected
by her sorrowing husband and comfortless children as the
last tribute of affection.
Weep not for me my children dear
Though I was once your sole delight,
For Christ has called me to appear,
And dwell with him in glory bright.[28]

Her brother, Lucas Theodoro Lucas, died in 1888 and was buried in the English Cemetery, Barisal (Grave no. 119):

> Sacred to the memory of Lucas Theodoro Lucas, Esq,
> Purganna Dukhim Shahozpoor, who departed this life
> on 7 Aug, 1888 in the hopes of a glorious resurrection
> and in the faith of his forefathers of the Eastern Greek
> Church. Aged 57 years, 7 months, 6 days.
> Calm on the bosom of my God
> Fair spirit rest thee now.
> Even while with ours thy footsteps trod
> His seal was on thy brow.
> Dust to his narrow house beneath
> Soul to the place on high:
> They that have seen thy look in death
> No more may fear to die.[29]

One of the most prolific of Greek families, whose members were to be found all over northern India, was that of Athanass.

We have already come across John Athanass, merchant of Calcutta, whose father returned from Calcutta to Philippopolis. On his return there he married a Greek girl and begot another son, Emmanuel or Manuel, born in 1778. Sometime after 1800, Manuel was sent out to Calcutta by his father and entrusted to the care of his half-brother John, under whose patronage he began a career in business. After some years' residence in Calcutta he launched out on his own as an up-country trader. He married a girl whose Christian name was Elizabeth and on December 4th 1813, the Bengal Directory records the birth of a son to his wife. Manuel is described as "a trader and merchant of Meerut," and subsequent records show that he continued his occupation at this place until his death on May 25th 1840. His son, Manuel Joshua Athanass is described as a portrait painter of Meerut in 1835 and "the owner of an estate near Dehra" which, with a fine Anglo-Hellenic flourish was called 'Byronopolis'. He died not long after his father and was buried in the cemetery at Dehra Dun under the following monumental inscription:

> Manuel Joshua Athanass who departed this life at Deyrah on the night of 27th
> January 1845 aged 31 years and one month. This tomb has been erected as the last
> tribute of affection by his beloved and affectionate mother Elizabeth Athanass. A
> pious Christian, sincere friend and lover in life.

In the records of Dehra Dun, the original purchaser of the estate in 1830 was recorded as J. Athanass. It is possible that this man was John Athanass of Calcutta who could have bought the estate for his half brother's son, but it might have been Joshua Athanass who is listed in the Bengal Directory as a resident of

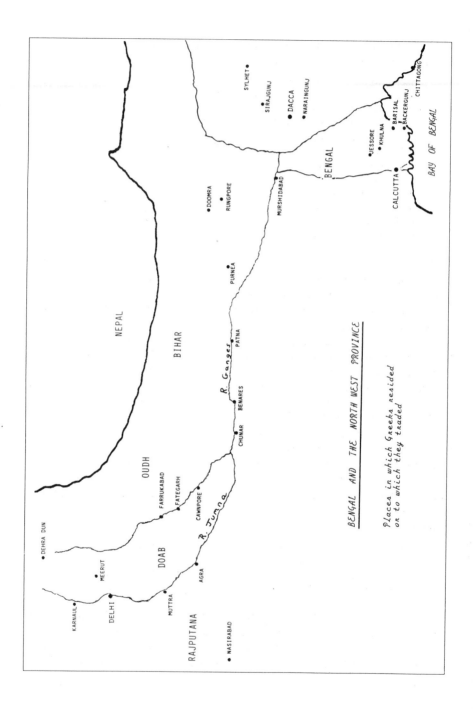

BENGAL AND THE NORTH WEST PROVINCE

Places in which Greeks resided
or to which they traded

Fategarh in 1837 and who may have been the brother of Manuel, the trader of Meerut. He may also have been the shopkeeper, Mr. Athanass of Nasirabad whom Bishop Heber met on his up-country travels in 1825 and who "had a brother also a shopkeeper at Meerut." Another member of the family, George Athanass, entered the Uncovenanted Civil Service and served in Delhi from 1840 to 1843 and then at Dera Ghazi Khan in the Deputy Commissioner's Office from 1855 to 1859, in Goojranwallah until 1861, and from 1863 was a copyist in the Military Secrets Office in Lahore.

A different branch of this family established itself in Dacca though it spelt the name with a single 's' while the Calcutta and up-country branches used a double 's'. The ancestor of the Dacca branch was George Athanasius of Philippopolis, thirtieth signatory of the Hastings Petition, who appears as 'George Primo' in the Dacca List of 1795. The Bengal Directory describes him as 'George Athanas Primo' a merchant of Naraingunj and Dacca from 1818 to 1835, who arrived in India in 1787. Almost certainly he belonged to the same family as the merchant from Philippopolis who fathered John Athanass of Calcutta and may have been his younger brother or his nephew. The 'Primo' in his name was probably used to distinguish him from other members of his family in Dacca. The sixty-second signatory of the Hastings Petition was Athanasius Demetrius from Philippopolis and there is a likelihood that he was the younger brother of George Primo. In the 1792 Petition for Firearms two of the conductors are named 'Dimitry Athanas' and 'Athanas Dimitry' and the Bengal Directory for 1827 lists a Greek merchant called 'D. Athanas'. George Primo's daughter, Miss B. Athanas married G. L. Esau from another Dacca Greek family in 1814 and one of his grandchildren, Celine (Selina) Athanas married Ignatius Constantine Panioty in Dacca in 1895, and another A. P. Athanas was a resident in the city in the mid 19th century and died there in 1882 and was buried in the Golbadan Cemetery (Grave no. 6) "under a plum tree": "Sacred to the memory of A. P. Athanas who died on 22 December 1882, aged 64 years."[30] In 1855 a M. T. Athanas was resident in Dacca and in 1857 was described in the Bengal Directory as "arriving in Calcutta from China by sea."

The thirty-fourth signatory of the Hastings Petition was Demetrius George Calograthy from the Aegean Island of Nio. It is likely that the man who signed the same document in the thirty-fifth place, also from Nio, as 'George Demetrius' was his son or brother. The latter was in Dacca in 1795 and he arrived in Bengal at the end of 1788 just in time to sign the Hastings Petition and also signed the Sinai Petition in 1811. The tombstone of Demetrius George Calograthy was in the Greek Churchyard in Calcutta:

> Here lies the body of Demetrius George. He was born in the Island of Nio in the Archipelago in Europe and departed his life in Calcutta on 17 October, 1790 aged 60 years.

His son John Demetrius Calogreedy (the anglicized form of Calograthy), married one of Alexander Panioty's daughters in 1813 but nothing more is known about him except the words added to the inscription on the tombstone of his father:

> Mr John Demetrius Calogreedy, son of the above. Died on 3 May, 1857, aged 69 years.[31]

Another inhabitant of Nio to sign the Petition of 1788 was Nicholas Marinus Calonas (also spelt Kalonas) in the thirty-sixth place, who arrived in Bengal in 1771, was present in Dacca in 1795 and 1811 and continued to operate there as a merchant until 1823, dying two years later. His son Marinus Nicholas Calonas was born in Bengal in 1787 and was a Dacca merchant from 1821 to 1835 and died on April 2, 1840. On August 3, 1812, he married Catherine Speridian (Spiridon) in Dacca who came from a Cretan family. Her father Nicholas Spiridon arrived in Bengal in 1781, signed the Petition of 1788 and was noted as a resident of Dacca in 1795. Catherine died after only five years of married life. Marinus Nicholas' brother, George Nicholas, is also mentioned as a Dacca merchant in 1835 and on December 23, 1825, he married Louisa Battye. Marinus Nicholas' daughters both married in 1847 - Margaret to J.A. Ricketts in Barisal and Erin Marin to C.J. Manook in Dacca. In the Burial Register at Barisal occurs the entry "Mrs. Desjines Kallonas died 3 May, 1877, widow of Mirium Miblas K."

One of the many citizens of Philippopolis to sign the 1788 Petition was Demetrius Elijah in the sixty-third place. In the 1792 Firearms Petition he was one of the conductors for whom a firearms licence was requested, and he was recorded as being an inhabitant of Dacca in 1795 and as having arrived in Bengal in 1787. He signed the Sinai Petition of 1811 as 'Demetrius Elias' - the change from 'Elijah to 'Elias' is the same as the name of the Hebrew prophet underwent at the hands of the Septuagint Translators. The Bengal Directory lists him as a merchant at Naraingunj and Dacca from 1818 to 1823 and he died in 1826. He had three sons, Nicholas, John and Constantine.

Nicholas Demetrius Elias was listed a Dacca merchant from 1831 to 1843 and married Theodosia Marrody, youngest daughter of Constantine Marrody on May 9, 1819 and is commemorated on the Dacca Memorial (west wall, third tablet from the left):

> Sacred to the memory of
> Nicholas Demetrius Elias
> Eldest son of Demetrius Elias, Esq
> Died 5th March 1845
> Aged 46 years.
> His desired verse:
> Duncaka Jomuza Hain
> Hurg Czca Cumnu Honoa

Churcha Aher Nhaga
Ufsose Hunnuhonga.
Erected by his sincere friend
Basil Demetrius in 1859.

Basil Demetrius was the clerk of the Anglican Church in Dacca and the 'desired verse' seems to be in the Persian language. If so, it is interesting that these two Greeks seemed to share a love of Persian poetry.

The youngest brother, Constantine, operated as a Dacca merchant from 1831 to 1838 and married Miss C. Lucas of Dacca on February 9, 1823. Born in 1803, he died on March 23, 1838. In the Old Baptist Cemetery of Wari, Dacca, a tombstone carried the following rather quaint inscription:

Three noble brothers lie mouldering here named Nicholas, John and Constantine, famed as brave hunters and to kindred dear, who erst to sport their merry lives continued. Erected by their cousin and godson, Manuel Elias Mitchoo.[32]

Perhaps their shikari techniques were too brave or too merry, for another tombstone in the same churchyard recorded the following:

Sacred to the memory of John Demetrius Elias, second son of Demetrius Elias, Esq, who was killed by a tiger whilst shooting at Mirzapore, 25 miles N.W. of Dacca on Sunday the 31st Jan, 1836. Aged 35 years.[33]

Another of the Dacca Greeks must originally have been of Venetian origin for his name 'Foscholo' was that of an ancient noble Venetian family, but this is not surprising as the Venetian maritime empire, before the Ottoman conquests, included many of the Aegean Islands. In Bengal the name (another rare example of a surname) underwent strange transformations as 'Phoskolos' and 'Pharsolees' before it finally settled into its original form. Anthony Foscholo came from the little volcanic Aegean island, variously called 'Irineus', 'Erini', 'Santorin' or 'Tino'; arrived in Bengal in 1786, signed the Hastings Petition in the sixty-fifth place, was recorded a resident of Dacca in 1795, and signed the Sinai Petition in 1811. On the last document is also the signature of his son, Joachim, who married a French lady, L'Aunette Benville, in Dacca in 1820. Anthony was recorded as being a merchant there from 1818 to 1833 and his tombstone is the one that lies broken on the floor of the Greek Memorial:

Sacred to the Memory of
A. Foscholo Esqr
Native of Tino
(Ar)chipelago in Greece
inhabitant of Dacca
?Decr 1833
82 years.
Interred also
the remains of his daughter

Catherine
who died 15th July 1813
Aged 20 years.

In 1855 a John Foscholo is mentioned in the Calcutta Directory as an assistant to George Grant, watch and clockmaker, and on February 5, 1889, a Walter Foscholo died in Lucknow.

One of the most puzzling variations in the spelling of Greek names in Bengal concerns the family which, in the end, came to be known as 'Marrody'. The second merchant signatory of the Hastings Petition was Marodes Thireacos of Philippopolis. In the Bengal Directories of 1790 and 1792 he is called 'Mavrody Kyriakos' and he signed the Firearms Petition of 1792 in the same way. He was one of the chief Greek merchants of Calcutta and his tombstone was to be found in the Greek Churchyard with a Greek inscription:

> Now this stone covers the body of Marodes Kyriakou, a native of the city of Phillippopolis, a merchant by profession and warden of this church who died on 10 Dec 1795 in Calcutta. [34]

A branch of this family established itself at Dacca. In the Hastings Petition occur the names: Christodulus Mavrody (fourteenth place) and Alexander Kyriakos (forty-second place) both from Philippopolis. There is clearly some familial connection between these men and between both of them and Mavrody Kyriakos. Alexander Kyriakos' name is on the Dacca List of 1795 from which we learn that he arrived in Bengal in 1771. His wife is commemorated in the Dacca Memorial (North Wall, third tablet from left) in both Greek and English:

Greek inscription:

> Here lies Sultanas wife of Alexander Kyriakou of Philippopolis who fulfilled the destiny common to all and died at Dacca 1800 Jan 25.

English inscription:

> Under this stone are deposited the Mortal remains of Mrs Sultana Alexander who departed this life on Tuesday the 6th of February 1800 Aged 34 years.

The difference between the recorded dates of death was probably due to the fact that the Greeks were still using the Julian Calendar which had been replaced by the Gregorian in most of Western Europe in 1582.

There was also in Dacca a Constantine Mavrody who arrived in Bengal in 1794. It is difficult to establish clearly the connections between these men. None of their names appear in the Sinai Petition of 1811 but in 1810 a D. C. Mavrody died in Dacca on December 26 and on May 19, 1819, Theodosia, youngest daughter of the late Constantine Marrody married N. D. Elias. Another branch of this family established itself at Fatehgarh. Here, on February 10, 1819, L. C. Marrody married Anne Busby at the house of Mr Rowland. In 1825 a Mrs

Marrody died on August 20 presumably the mother of L. C. Marrody who followed her on August 24, and on September 1 a posthumous son was born to his widow.

The last of the Dacca Greek families that established itself in Bengal was called Esau though the name was subject to the usual changes of Greek nomenclature in India. In the Hastings Petition the twenty-second signatory was Jacob Hauji Isaah from Caesaria and the twenty-sixth Johannes Hauji Isaah from the same place. Though neither man is mentioned in the 1795 Dacca List the name Jacob X Esaias occurs in the Sinai Petition of 1811 and clearly refers to 'Jacob Hauji Isaah' since the X is a symbol for 'Hauji' or 'Hadjee'. In the Bengal Directory Jacob is called 'Esau' and is listed as a merchant from 1818 to 1823. This is strange because he died in 1819 though it is not unusual for the Directory to go on listing a merchant for a few years after his death. His tomb inscription can be found in the Greek Memorial (West Wall, second from left):

Here lies....Jacob Essau Jacob....born in Caesaria died 1819, June 22.....I am informed that he lived about 48 years in this existence before his departure.

The inscription is very difficult to decipher so the above is only an approximate translation. A number of births and marriages are recorded in this name in Dacca during these years:

1813. Feb 28 a daughter to Mrs J. Esau.
1814. Sept 28 a son to Mrs G. Esau.
1814. Nov 6 Mr G. L. Esau married Miss B. Athanas.
1816 Ap 16 A daughter to Mrs J. Esau.

Much later, on September 22, 1847, George Athanas Esau married Jane Eliza Hamilton in Calcutta.

To complete the record of Greek merchants in this part of India we should note two other tombstones included in the Bengal Obituary:

At Dibrugarh: "Sacred to the memory of Athanas Mitchoo, Esq. A native of Philippopolis in Greece. Aetat 55 years". (No date given).

"Also in Memory of Ducas Athanas Mitchoo, Esq. Died at Dibrooghur, in Upper Assam, on the 21st Sept. 1840, aged 23 years and 3 months. Requiescat in pace".

Though the two main Greek communities were to be found in Calcutta and Dacca, some Greeks chose to seek their fortunes up-country between Bengal proper and Delhi, in the valleys of the Ganges and the Jumna, the power centre of the Mughal Empire. Communications between Calcutta and up-country were difficult in the late eighteenth and early nineteenth centuries for the roads were infested with robbers, particularly the sinister organisation of the Thugs before 1830. The main artery of communication was the mighty Ganges itself and boats were used for conveying grain, cotton, salt, textiles and human beings; some-times towed by men walking along the river-bank, sometimes rowed by boatmen they floated down stream at about four miles an hour, but going up-river they hoisted sail and were carried along by the prevailing southerly winds. These native boats, called budgerows, were lumbering keelless barges with large broad helms which was the only shape that would respond in the strong current. Two thirds of the length aft was occupied by cabins with Venetian windows[39] and a smaller boat was often towed behind, fitted up as a kitchen. Travelling by boat was fraught with boredom and occasionally dangerous so up-country traders had to be a tough, adventurous breed.

Before the arrival of the British, the area was dominated by the Marathas, and Agra was a nodal point of trade, but the power of the East India Company was catching up on the Marathas and in 1803 Agra was annexed to British rule. After the second Maratha War (1802-1806) the victorious Company controlled Delhi and the whole of the Gangetic valley came, either directly or indirectly, under its rule. Cawnpore and Fategarh were garrison towns and to a lesser extent Agra and Meerut, where British forces were maintained under the subsidiary system which bound Indian rulers to pay for a force of Company troops to be stationed on their territories for their protection. These cities "became home bases for a whole new generation of military contractors drawn from the commercial community who pushed forward the commercial penetration of the backward lands of the Banda to the south and the Himalayan foothills to the north. Firms at the base camp operated by sending agents with every detachment (of the Company's Armies) which was posted to a remote centre".[35] So Greek traders moved forward with the advance of British power.

"Compared with the Bengali entrepreneur in Calcutta inland wholesale purchasers had the great advantage of being closer to the source of supply. On the other hand, up-country market information was defective and the merchant was continually gambling on a large number of variables....European firms known as country produce brokers appeared in some numbers at Cawnpore and Delhi as agents of Calcutta and Bombay agency houses. In Cawnpore, for instance, Greek merchants were the largest dealers". [36] It was against this economic and historical background that the work of Greek up-country traders should be viewed.

Among the earliest Greek traders in this area was Anastas Treandaffelos who arrived in India in 1792 or 1793 and was given permission to proceed to the upper stations of the Army as far as Fatehgarh for nine months on 24 December 1801.[37] At Cawnpore in January 1792, Colonel Brisco, commanding the garrison, issued the following pass "This is to certify that John Manuel and Joseph Antonio Manuel who have been in the service of Sumer Raze Beegum have made their appearance at this station and applied for a passport to proceed through this District under my Command on their road to Calcutta. I have complied with their request and direct that these men be suffered to pass to Chunar. In witness whereof I have subscribed this passport at Cawnpore this 17th Day of January, 1792".[38] That these Greeks found employment with a minor Indian princess was a fact of some historical interest for "while merchants possessed an inner domestic culture, they had also developed the capacity to play the game of darbar and royalty, so that the old Indo-Persian culture provided, in North India, a neutral ground on which accommodation could be reached. Communities of Jewish, Armenian and Greek merchants sometimes acted as cultural brokers between European and Indian.[39] One of these men, or possibly a relation of theirs, Manuel, a shopkeeper of Cawnpore, in 1808 was present at the auction of the effects of a deceased British resident, Robert Baillie[40a], and the same name was noted as a trader in Cawnpore in 1835. George John, another Greek who arrived in India in 1795 was a trader in Agra between 1804 and 1812 and may have been related to Peter John, Merchant of Calcutta. It has already been related that Constantine Pantazes worked in Agra from 1795 to 1817. Another interesting arrival in this city was the family of Joannides who set themselves up in the jewelry business and remained to become owners and proprietors of the Agra Spinning and Weaving Mills in the 1880s. An early member of this family, Antonius Joannides (or Joanidies) came from the Levant, fought under Lord Combermere at Bharatpur and from 1801 to 1820 was a silversmith in Agra. He anglicised his name (circa 1820) to 'Antony John').[40b]

Amongst these up-country merchants we encounter once again the ubiquitous Paniotys. In the Kacheri Cemetery in Cawnpore there still exists a well-preserved tombstone with a Greek and English inscription:

Under this marble is laid the servant of God, Panyiotes Emmanuel. His wife Irene laid her dear husband to rest with due observance and mourned him; stricken with grief and inscribed these words to his everlasting memory. (Greek inscription).

Sacred to The Memory of Panioty Emmanuel Late Merchant who departed this life The 4th of June Anno Domini 1815 Aged 49 years 2 months 7 days. This tomb is erected by his affectionate wife As a tribute of love and esteem". (English inscription).[41]

These inscriptions are incised on a marble slab resting on a brick foundation, at the top of which is a carving of a cross flanked by the heads and wings of angels and at the foot of the slab are three cavities probably meant to contain votive lamps.

Who was this man? How was he connected with the Dacca Paniotys, if at all? It seems likely that he did belong to this family for the up-country Paniotys retained the same anglicized name when it was already clearly associated with the descendants of Alexios Argyree Panaghiotis, and one may hazard a guess that Emmanuel was a son of Alexios Argyree and brother of Alexander Panioty. He was born in 1766 and in that year Argyree had been in Philippopolis and then left the city to go back to Calcutta. If Emmanuel was indeed his son, he was born either in Philippopolis or in Bengal but probably in the latter place for had it been the former one would have expected the fact to be recorded on his tombstone as

Grave of Emanuel Panioty in the Kacheri Cemetery, Cawnpore

was the case with most other Greeks who were born in Greek-speaking lands. Furthermore, in the Bengal Directory of 1813 he is described as a 'British Subject' whereas all the Greek merchants in the Dacca List of 1795 are said to be subjects of the Ottoman Empire. In the record of 'Non Official Europeans in India, 1780-1820' he is described as a trader in Cawnpore in 1801 and the East India Directories from 1811 to 1814 use the same description.

In these years another Panioty, Constantine, is noted as a shopkeeper in Fategarh. The up-country proximity of the two names and the dates suggest that he was a brother of Emmanuel and, if so, another son of Alexios Argyree Panaghiotis. This Constantine Panioty is also listed in the Bengal Directory of 1821 as a merchant at Karnaul. In all probability it was a son of his, Emmanuel Panioty Jnr, who is mentioned in the Bengal Directory as an up-country merchant in 1818, 1820, 1822-24, 1831 and from 1834-39 a merchant in Muttra. That he was a son of Constantine rather than that of Emmanuel Snr is a deduction from the fact that it was very unusual for Greeks to christen sons with their own name; usually they were named after an uncle or grandfather. There was another Greek trader in Muttra, A. John, who appears in the Bengal Directory from 1834 to 1842.

Meerut, a British military station, claimed the attention of other Greeks. One of these, Gianacopulos, died there in 1810 but his tombstone in the Race Course Cemetery disappeared between 1889 and 1903. Another was Manuel Athanas who has already been mentioned as a Meerut trader; and the Bengal Directory of 1821 also mentions a George Paul. A friend of Manuel Athanas, Michael Keryack, was a shopkeeper of Delhi and died there in 1828:

Sacred to the Memory of Michael Keryack Shopkeeper at Delhi who departed this life on the 16th Day of August 1828. Born in Vienna of Greek Parentage Aged about 46 Years.
Erected by his Friend Manuel Athanas.

The lettering on his tombstone was carved by a trooper of the 16th Lancers who added his signature at the bottom: 'M. Fennerty 16th L'.[42] He seems to be the only instance of a Greek from the Habsburg diaspora whose place of origin is recorded in India. Another 'Delhi' Greek whose name is recorded in 1835 was A. Banass.

Not all the up-country Greeks were traders. Some of them were engaged in other occupations and some began as traders but transferred their attentions to other activities and this, of course, was also true of their compatriots in Calcutta and Dacca. John Verdony, who arrived in India in 1794 was a teacher who began as an assistant master at the Free School, Thoolutallah, Calcutta, and eventually became its Superintendent. A number of Greeks became indigo planters. The Company held a monopoly of all opium grown in India and vast quantities were exported through Calcutta to China in exchange for tea and silks. The life of a planter was one in which an affluent domestic style was mixed with hard unrelenting toil for the greater part of the year. One Greek family that settled into this life was called Nicholls. Despite the English name, it was officially listed as Greek and had undoubtedly anglicized its name from a probable original of 'Nikolas'. George Nicholls arrived in India in 1790 or 1791 and began as a trader in Rungpore but in 1811 he switched to indigo planting, first at Rungpore and later at Doomra. Another member of the family (probably a younger brother) M. G. Nicholls came out in 1806 and was listed as an indigo planter at Doomra, Gungtee and Tirhoot. Two other Greeks are mentioned as indigo planters in 1835 - A. Nicholls at Jessore and F. Boutros at Purneah.

An interesting example of a Greek merchant family which began as traders and then found employment outside commerce was Paliologus. It bore the name of the last Imperial dynasty of Byzantium and a Phanariot Greek family of the same name in Wallachia (part of modern Rumania) confidently claimed descent from the last Emperor of Constantinople, Constantine Palaeologus. Nicholas Palaiologou was a signatory of the Sinai Petition of 1811 and his son Nicholas (rare example of a Greek bearing the same Christian name as his father) was an attorney and notary of Calcutta. He was buried in the South Park Street Cemetery under a headstone which recorded nothing more than his name. His infant daughter was interred in the same place:

Sacred to the memory of Jane Ann, daughter of N. and J. Paliologus, who died 30 Nov, 1833, aged 4 years, 3 months, 7 days.[43]

In the Protestant Cemetery at Agra three inscriptions from Greek graves were recorded in 1911. They were as follows:

Sacred to the memory of Andrew Pythagoras Constantine who died on 12 August, 1855, aged 22 years. R.I.P.

Sacred to the memory of Andrew Constantine born at Corinth, a Greek who died on 29 July, 1855, aged 77 years. R.I.P.[44]

Sacred to the memory of Georgiana, the beloved wife of Archimedes Constantine born 5 Oct 1832, died 6 August 1865 aged 32 years 10 months 1 day.
Ah, only to the ardent heart,
Where love and friendship dwell,
Is known how dreadful is to part,
How sad the last farewell.
Oh! Jesus kind, Thy mercy show,
Unto her soul who lies below.[45]

Who these people were, what work they did remains a secret buried in the grave of time. Their funerary epitaphs serve to remind us that, in all probability, in the first half of the 19th century there was a large number of Greeks whose occupations were relatively humble and who made little mark on the society in which they found themselves. They toiled in a foreign and exotic clime and then oblivion claimed them for her own.

References: Chapter Seven

1. Loukatos, op. cit. Chapter 3
2. Imperial Records XII, 465 pp No. 21 I.O.R. See Appendix A
3. Press Lists Public Records Vol. XIV, 27 I.O.R.
4. Bengal European Inhabitants. 1783-1807. I.O.R. See Appendix B
5. Loukatos, op. cit. Chapter 3. See Appendix C
6. Asiaticus, op. cit. Recorded Inscriptions Nos. 2 & 3
7. Loukatos, op. cit. Chapter 3
8. Bengal Obituary
9. Loukatos, op. cit. Chapter 3
10. *The Greek Merchant Marine* Ed. Stelios (A. Papadopoulos, National Bank of Greece, 1927) p97
11. Loukatos, op. cit. Chapter 3
12. *Travels in the Ionian Islands, Albania, Thessally, Macedonia etc. during the years 1812 and 1813*, Henry Holland (London, 1815)
13. *Travels in Northern Greece*, William Martin Leake (London, 1835)
14. Bengal Obituary
15. A H Dani, op. cit. p43
16. Loukatos, op. cit. p26 note 2
17. Bengal Obituary
18. *Ibid.*
19. *Ibid.*
20. *A History of Calcutta Streets*, PT Nair, p737
21. Bengal Obituary
22. *Ibid.*
23. *Roumeli*, P Leigh Fermor (John Murray 1966) pp83-84
24. List of the nobility of Corfu, 1803 P.R.O. Kew
25. Society of Genealogists, London. Buff files unclassified
26. *Traders and Nabobs*, Zoë Yalland (Michael Russell, 1987) Appendix 10
27. Loukatos, op. cit. Chapter 3
28. Society of Genealogists, London. Buff files unclassified
29. *Ibid.*
30. *Ibid.*
31. Bengal Transcriptions of Tombs, Vol. 1 I.O.R.
32. Society of Genealogists, London. Buff files unclassified. Also on the Dacca Greek Memorial
33. *Ibid.* Also on the Dacca Greek Memorial
34. Asiaticus, op. cit.
35. Bayly, op. cit. p215
36. *Ibid.* pp247,434
37. Bengal European Inhabitants. 1804. I.O.R.

38. I.O.R. P/4/14 No.45
39. Bayly, op. cit. p239
40a. I.O.R. L/AG Bengal Inventories, 1808
40b. *The Makers of Indian Colonial Silver*, Wynyard RT Wilkinson (London, 1987) p106
41. *A Guide to the Kacheri Cemetery and the early history of Kanpur*, Zoë Yalland (BACSA, 1983) p443
42. *Two Monsoons*, Theon Wilkinson (Duckworth, 2nd edn. 1987) p145
43. Bengal Obituary, op. cit.
44. *Inscriptions on Christian Monuments in the U.P.*, E A M Blunt (Allahabad, 1911) It is possible that this man was a signatory of the Sinai Petition, 1811: 'Andreas Constantinou'.
45. *Ibid.*

8

The Chiots

Over the seas our galley went.

(Browning)

An 18th century traveller approaching the island of Chios from the sea could smell, if the wind was right and the day was young and there had been a fall of dew overnight, the tantalizing scent of its citrus groves and, as his ship entered harbour, he could detect the pervading odour of dust, lemons and rock honey. The island has always claimed to be the birthplace of Homer - "the blind old man from rocky Chios" - and from ancient times has been famous for the production of mastic, a white chewy substance with a delicious flavour, derived from a plant grown on the island, which found its chief market in the seraglios of Turkey, whose inmates valued it as a breath sweetener and an aid to digestion. Over the chief town in the island loomed the brooding presence of the promontory of Karaburna on the Asiatic mainland, an apt symbol of the proximity to the Chiots of the malign, imperial Ottoman power.

The history of Chios, like many other Greek islands, is mainly one of foreign occupation. The Macedonians, then the Romans and the Genoese and lastly the Turks brought it within the orbit of their empires. In one respect, however, Chios was different from most of the other Greek Aegean islands. The Chiots escaped the degredation, both physical and moral, that afflicted many other Greek communities under Ottoman rule. The English traveller, Finlay, observes "they were alike destitute of the insolence and rapacity of the Phanariots, and of the meanness of the trading Greeks of the continent. The marked difference which existed between them and the rest of their countrymen was observed by early travellers and foreign merchants".[1] The causes of this superiority are described by Finlay and by the Greek scholar, Coray, in 1803, who both noted how the island managed to be a haven of Greek prosperity in the desolation of Greek life in many parts of the Ottoman Empire.

Chios possessed remarkable physical advantages. It was fruitful and almost every article the Chiots produced was of an immensely superior quality which readily found a market abroad. But this advantage in itself would have been useless had it not been accompanied by the human attributes of the islanders. "The superior moral qualities of the Chiots was recognized throughout the Levant".[2] They valued education and every Chiot family sought to instil in its children pride in Hellenic culture. They set up academies which imported modern western ideas and which became so famous that they were attended by Greek pupils from other parts of Greece. The uncle of Adamantios Korais, one of the foremost modern Greek intellectuals and propagandist of the movement of Greek independence, taught at this school. In 1819 it had 476 pupils of which 400 were Chiots, 74 from other parts of Greece (largely Cephalonians and Peloponnesians), and most remarkable of all, two Americans called Parsons and Frisk. They were an industrious people who scorned to solicit from their Turkish rulers the posts of tax collectors and other degrading sinecures. Every family was actively engaged in agriculture, industry or trade and there was in particular a thriving silk manufactory on the island. Nearly all the silk was used in the manufacture of velvets, damasks and other stuffs for export to Asia, Egypt and the Barbary states. Sometimes gold and silver were woven into these materials, according to the taste of the workmen or the demands of the market. Work, education and prosperity had their effects on character so that Finlay can say "The superior morality of the Chiots in all the relations of life, their truth and honesty, rendered the island for several centuries the most happy and flourishing portion of Greece". Coray calls Chios "the garden of the Archipelago", and the Chiots "the French of the Levant", and even says that their natural joviality and panache should deserve the appellation of "the Gascons of the Levant".[3]

But none of these institutions, activities and traits of character could have developed under Turkish rule had it not been for the political sagacity of the islanders. The Chiots elected their own municipality. Aware of their political weakness, they eschewed rivalries and bitterness amongst themselves and presented a united front to the Turks. The Municipality took pains to despatch able Chiots to Constantinople where they acted as 'resident ambassadors' and agents for Chiot interests. They obtained the protectorship of some eminent Turk and, backed by his influence and the concerted will of the entire island, they managed to secure the appointment of Turkish administrators who were known to be willing to acquiesce in the liberties they enjoyed and to veto immediately the appointment of those who were not. The Turks found they could do nothing on the island without the co-operation of the Greek Municipality, annually elected and wielding almost unlimited power. Such was its influence that any Turkish officer who fell foul of the inhabitants was immediately removed once he had been reported by the Chiots to Constantinople. Fermin Didcot, a French visitor to Chios in 1816, noted that "the Turks seem to be much softer in this island than elsewhere and while in almost the whole of Turkey, where the Greeks alone speak two languages, the Turks believe it dishonourable to speak another language other than their own, here they all know how to speak Greek, and sometimes are even ignorant of their own tongue". It was this state of affairs that produced the judgement of the great French historian, Fustel de Coulanges, that Chios was a Greek state and that Turkish power was practically non-existent on the island. In addition to all these advantages of independence and prosperity, yet another traveller, a Scotsman, William Lithgow declared that "the women of Scio are the most beautiful dames or rather Angelical creatures of all Greeks upon the face of the earth".

Chios possessed a nobility of forty families whose origins went back to the city of Genoa who had ruled the island before the Turks. These families were divided into two groups, the Pentada and the Dodecha and their landholdings and their pleasant, shuttered country mansions, surrounded by high walls and deep gardens, were situated in a beautiful green plain in the island called the Campos. In one of these lived the family of Rallis and it is here, in the Campos that we must seek the origin of the trading company, Ralli Brothers, which established a great commercial empire on the banks of the Hugli. And not only the Rallis but the Petrocochinos, the Schlizzis, the Argentis, the Sechiaris, the Sagrandis and the Vlastos, all of whose names graced the late 19th century commercial world of Calcutta. It is without exaggeration that we can say that Greek commercial activity in mid and late Victorian Bengal can be traced back to its origin in the emerald haven of the Campos in the tiny Aegean island of Chios.

The name 'Ralli' harks back to the 11th century but the earliest mention of a Ralli in Chios is that of Michael Rallis who acted on behalf of the islanders in 1511, and a little later John Rallis, nicknamed 'Kalogiannis', who put his signature to a document as an Archontas of the island. In 1784 Stefanos Zanni Rallis, aged 29, and his young wife Julia Avgousti Sechiari, aged 16, began their married life on one of the Ralli estates in the Campos. Of their ten children, their third son Pandias Stephanos Ralli was destined to become the real founder of Ralli Brothers.[4] Born in 1793 his early years were spent on Chios where his father was a wealthy merchant belonging to the Dodecha who expanded his commercial business to Livorno. Seeing that the greatest number of his customers were English, he decided that it would be in his interest to open a branch of his business in London. In 1818 his eldest son Zannis, and his youngest Eustratios, arrived in London and opened a branch of their firm under the name of 'Ralli and Petrocochino' at 5 Union Court, Old Broad Street. In contrast to the landed class of contemporary England and especially in contrast with the nobility of most European countries, the Chiot nobility saw no disparagement to their blood in the pursuit of trade. The Rallis, especially, were equally proud of their ancestry and their commercial success. On the Ralli memorial in Marseilles, erected to the memory of Stephanos Ralli, are carved the arms of the family: azure a lion rampant or covered with lozenges, in chief a crescent between two crosses argent and underneath the splendid motto so expressive of Ralli achievement: 'Badize ten eutheian' (Advance in a straight line).

The even tenor of life in Chios was disrupted by the Greek War of Independence. In 1821 a Greek nobleman and officer in the Russian Imperial Army, Prince Alexander Ypsilanti, began in Moldavia a revolt against the Turks, issuing a proclamation to all Greeks urging them to rise against Ottoman rule. He

111

was encouraged by the belief that Czar Alexander I of Russia would intervene on their behalf and that the network of Philiki Etairia, the Greek Secret Society with branches in most of the large cities of the Ottoman Empire, would be able to activate an armed revolt against the Turks. Neither of these hopes materialized and Ypsilanti's revolt was easily crushed. But this initial uprising sparked off a rising amongst the Greek mountaineers of the Morea on the Greek mainland which successfully beat off all the attempts of the Ottoman Army to suppress it. The Patriarch of Constantinople, Gregorius V, condemned the revolt in the strongest terms and urged Greek loyalty to the Turkish overlord. It did him little good for the Ottoman authorities hanged him, exposed his corpse at the gate of the Ecumenical Patriarchate in Constantinople and proceeded to liquidate many other Greek notables in circumstances of barbaric ferocity. These massacres simply heightened the resolve of the Moreates to continue the struggle. In a last desperate measure to crush them, the Sultan called in the help of Mehmet Ali, the powerful Pasha of Egypt, who sent his son Ibrahim to the Morea with an army trained by ex-Napoleonic officers and conveyed there by a formidable fleet. Foreign volunteers flocked to the Morea to fight for the Greeks, among them Lord Byron who succumbed in the fever-ridden atmosphere of Missolonghi. The pressure of liberal opinion and, more importantly, the political and commercial interests of Britain, France and Russia brought about their intervention on the side of the Greeks. In 1827 Admiral Codrington, commanding the combined navy of British, French and Russian ships, battered the Egyptian and Turkish navy into submission in Navarino Bay and so virtually obtained for the Greeks the freedom they were fighting for, though it was not until 1833 that a sovereign Greek Kingdom emerged, fully independent of Turkey.

These stirring events in the Morea and on the western side of Greece found their counterpart in Chios. Here, the proximity of the island to the Asiatic mainland made revolution a perilous matter but the Chiots were so independent and freedom-loving that the dangers of insurrection were overlooked. They were encouraged to raise the banner of revolt by the fact that Greek fleets in the Aegean soon began to dominate the sea and make maritime movement perilous for the Turks. On April 26, 1822 a small Greek fleet anchored near Chios and the news stirred the patriotic feelings of the islanders. Unlike the Metropolitan See of Constantinople, the See of Chios was occupied by a patriotic bishop, Platon Emmanuel Franghiadis, who urgently summoned a meeting of the notables of the island. What followed is related by the Greek historian, N. S. Kroussouloudis: "At this meeting thirty of the Archontes were present but only three names are recorded - Alexander Rallis, Andreas Manoukas and Nicolaos Petrocochinos. Alexander Rallis, who was boiling with the enthusiasm of his youth, advised an immediate insurrection. Manoukas and Petrocochinos, however, had different views. They deployed arguments and disagreed with him". But how was cold and cautious realism to control the hot blood of youth, inflamed by stories of Turkish atrocities and of Greek bravery elsewhere? Alexander Rallis had his way and Manoukas and Petrocochinos saw their forebodings fulfilled. The Chiots revolted but the Turks crushed the revolt and rounded up seventy prisoners whom they incarcerated in the citadel of Chios. Their execution was begun on May 6 1822. "While many of the hostages were already hung, the Moulas (Islamic clergymen) approached the Bishop and said to him 'look how the great Prophet punishes the infidel slaves'. And saying so they spat on the Bishop's face, while many of the other Turks followed their example. Alexander Rallis, who stood by seeing all this, fumed with anger and blasted them with an angry curse. 'Bloody murderers! Is not your bloodthirstiness quenched with the blood of so many innocent people? But God will not overlook your crimes. He is looking at your dishonest bloodstained hands! He listens to the sigh of these innocent people and will not fail to give you the right punishment'. Before he was able to finish his words, he was stormed by the soldiers who stood by who drew their swords and butchered him"[5]. Bishop Franghiardis' execution followed hard upon, as did that of the other hostages including Theodore Rallis, Alexander's elder brother, and Peter Scaramanga. The massacre moved Victor Hugo to its commemoration in a moving passage of literature and Delacroix to depict it in a graphic painting. The names of Ralli, Petrocochino, Franghiadis and Scaramanga all appear later in the commercial annals of late 19th century Calcutta.

The bloody reprisals of the Turks in Chios caused an exodus of refugee families who found homes in the West and brought with them their commercial expertise, not least amongst them Pandias Stephen Rallis who found his way to Regency London. His actual date of arrival cannot be established with certainty but it was sometime between 1822 and 1825. He joined the firm his brothers had founded and it was probably due to his drive and inspiration that in 1825 it expanded its operations, changed its name to 'Ralli Brothers' and moved its offices to 25 Finsbury Circus where it remained for almost a century and a half until its sudden collapse in 1961. Pandias Ralli and his brothers had, by shrewd thinking and good fortune, chosen the right time to move to London for the arrow of history was pointing inexorably in the direction of a vast British commercial expansion and Ralli Brothers was to benefit immeasurably from its ability to exploit these circumstances.

In the last twenty years of the 18th century there was a rapid economic growth in Britain which, among a host of other minor factors, was largely due to a rapid improvement in methods of transport, a phenomenal growth in industrial production and an increase in Anglo-American trade. Britain was about to pioneer that massive change in the history of the human race called 'The Industrial Revolution'. The writer and naturalist W. H. Hudson noted that the shepherds he met in early 19th century Wiltshire were men whose lives were not greatly different from the Biblical Patriarchs but between them and the modern city dweller lay an abyss of thought and feeling which was as great as the difference between our ape-like ancestors dwelling in trees and the peasant who had mastered the technique of tilling the soil and making the earth serve his needs. Such was the scope of the Industrial Revolution.

The quick commercial growth of the last years of the 18th century was followed by the Revolutionary and Napoleonic Wars which damaged Britain's trade with Europe but greatly expanded her commercial operations with America and Asia where her navy eliminated French and Dutch competitors. Between 1800 and 1850 Britain was in an unique economic position. As her economy became industrialized she exported the products of her factories, workshops and mines in exchange for food and raw materials while the rest of Europe lagged behind, clinging to self-sufficient rural economies. Britain became the workshop of the world and this led to a massive increase of her commercial activities. Until the middle decade of this century this was hindered to some extent by the protectionist policies which her government adopted to protect her agriculture and the measures foreign governments took to defend their infant industries against British competition. The real expansion of British trade was in the direction of America and Asia, not least of all to the sub-continent of India.

This spiralling movement was not without its difficulties for the economy. It was subject to considerable fluctuations in which trade cycles alternated between boom and slump. These made fortunes and unmade them just as rapidly and this fact has to be taken into consideration to appreciate Pandias Ralli's skill to keep Ralli Brothers buoyant and expansive while so many other firms plunged to financial ruin. The years following the Napoleonic Wars until about 1822 was a period of great difficulty caused by the slow recovery of Europe and the unimaginative economic and social policies followed by Begum Johnson's grandson Lord Liverpool and his government, particularly the retention of protectionist tariffs. In 1820, a few years before the arrival of Pandias Ralli in London, the City merchants presented a petition to Parliament in favour of Free Trade. From then until the fifties, Britain moved steadily towards Free Trade which made economic sense as long as Britain remained the dominant industrial producer of the world and could exchange her industrial products for the food and raw materials of other countries on reciprocal terms. It was in this economic soil of expanding commerce and the advance of Free Trade principles that Ralli Brothers took root in London.

After the Napoleonic Wars the carrying trade of the world was largely in British hands. Her merchant tonnage had risen from a million to two and a half millions. Her commerce with South America had increased fourteen fold. Her conquests in India, the Cape, Ceylon and Malta and her possession of Australia, Canada and eventually New Zealand had extended her tentacles to every part of the globe and the population of her Empire had leapt from twenty to seventy millions. Perhaps no other country in the history of the world had attained such astonishing prosperity and glory. "Everything" says Arthur Bryant "testified to her wealth, power and empire: The interminable masts on the Thames, Tyne and Mersey, the Chinese, Persian, Parsee and Armenian traders in the Customs Houses... even the humblest artisans seem to share in that flood of prosperity".[6] British imagination was fired with the romance of its Indian conquests. Even a country boy, listening to the tales of some humble traveller, could be affected: "He used to tell us the most delectable tales about elephants and tigers.... of guavas, bananas, figs, jacks and cashew apples, and your hat full for the value of a farthing.... Miller and I often vowed we would go to that grand fruitful country when we became men".[7] Sixty million Indians were the subjects of a Commercial Company whose headquarters was not in some marble and gilt palace but in a rather dingy building in Leadenhall Street, London, where Charles Lamb, one of the foremost prose writers of the age "sat at his desk totting up the price of tea, drugs and indigo".

The London in which Pandias Ralli settled contained bizarre contrasts. In the West End, where Ralli Brothers had established itself, there was mile after mile of splendid mansions, inhabited by wealthy people with their smart barouches and landaus. But in the nightmare extensions of London to the east and beyond the river and in the rookeries and foetid courtyards that huddled behind the haunts of fashion and commerce, pallid, diminutive-looking men, women and children dragged out their existence amid heaps of garbage. 'Punch' was to castigate these sordid conditions with its grim humour: "The names of our London streets exhibit a disgraceful tautology. We are afraid to say how many Peter Streets, John Streets, and above all Wellington Streets there are in the metropolis. Let this fault be amended. Let the streets be called by their proper names.... by the various nuisances or diseases which infest or pollute them, respectively, as Open Sewer Street; Gully Hole Court, Slaughter House Buildings, Shambles Place; Knacker's Yard; Grave Yard Crescent; Charnel Square; Typhus Terrace; Scarlatina's Rents; Intermittent Row; Consumption Alley; Scrofula Lane. Let such, at least, be the provisional nomenclature of the streets of London, till this filthy capital shall have been properly drained and watered; shall have its churchyards closed, its atmosphere disinfected and plague and pestilence expelled from its inhabitants".[8] It would seem that in some respects, at least in the contrast between the living quarters of the rich and poor, there was not a great deal to choose between London and Calcutta.

Pandias Ralli threw himself with fervour into the business of his firm, fired with the ambition to create a Greek firm of commerce in London which would compare with the leading giants of commerce in the City. With his strong will and keen intellect, he laid the foundations on solid principles of business which saw Ralli Brothers through the financial crises of the 1820s, 30s and 40s which destroyed many other city firms. Business expanded rapidly in many directions. Pandias' four brothers wholeheartedly accepted his overall management of the firm from Finsbury Circus but each of them provided a key element to the success

115

of the Company. The eldest brother, Zannis Stefanou Rallis, went to Odessa to organise the grain exports from Russia. The second brother, Avgoustis, became head of the Marseilles branch. In later years his son, Stephen Avgousti, took over the direction of Ralli Brothers after the death of Pandias in 1865. His reputation as a shrewd businessman led to an offer from the Bank of England to become one of its Directors. This he refused, though he was often consulted by the Bank on financial matters. He mediated successfully in a dispute between British ship-owners and the Suez Canal Company and advised a Royal Commission on the question of Indian currency. His son Anthony, a major in the 12th Lancers, was killed in the Boer War. Toumazis, the third brother of Pandias, took over the branch at Constantinople and was responsible for operations in South East Asia. His son, Pandelis T. Rallis, became a Liberal M.P. for Wallingford and an intimate friend of Field Marshal Kitchener. His house at 17 Belgrave Square was used by Kitchener as his London home for many years. He even tried, unsuccessfully, to arrange a marriage between the Field Marshal and a wealthy heiress of the Anglo-Greek community. His sister Jenny married Richard Moreton, Queen Victoria's Master of Ceremonies. Pandias' youngest brother Eustratios settled in Manchester as head of the branch dealing mainly in textile export.

The expansion of the firm was so dramatic that already by 1830 it was larger than any other Greek business house in London and Pandias was rapidly being accepted as the foremost businessman of the London-Greek Community so that he had attracted the nickname of 'Zeus'. He was the first to organise the system of trading in cargoes of grain while still in passage from the Black Sea, "a system which for more than two generations was the recognized rule and custom of the corn trade in England".[9] In 1846 Sir Robert Peel, pressured by the Anti-Corn Law League of Cobden and Bright and by a tragic failure of the potato crop in Ireland, repealed the Corn Laws, the bastion of Protectionist Policy. As a result, Ralli Brothers was able to make good profits through the import of grain to Britain. Apart from this commodity the firm traded mainly in silk, cotton piece goods, metals, natural indigo and tallow. Already in 1837 a trading firm in Tabriz, Persia was opened as a branch of Ralli Bros, London and Ralli, Schlizzi and Argenti, Marseilles under the name of Ralli and Agelasto.

In 1831 Pandias married Marietta Scaramanga (another name to appear later in Calcutta) of a noble Chiot mercantile family, established there since the 16th century. Its name was derived from 'scaramanghion', a fine silk material from which clothes had been made for the Byzantine nobility, and were therefore presumably in origin silk traders. In 1835 he was appointed Consul for Greece in London by the new Greek Government of King Otho and he used his house as the premises of the Greek Consulate. When, in 1834, Greece was to be repre-sented in European capitals by Chargés d'Affaires, the Greek Ambassador in London, Spyridon Tricoupis, wanted his friend Pandias to fill this honourable post in London but his appointment was blocked by the unrelenting hostility of the British Ambassador to Athens, Sir Edmund Lyons, on grounds of blatant snobbery. In a letter to the Foreign Secretary, Lord Palmerston, he expressed his Olympian disdain for men of trade: "It would scarcely be fitting that a person who has long pursued a secondary mercantile career in London should, even though he were now to join it, appear at Her Majesty's Court as a Diplomatic Agent holding the rank of Chargé d'Affaires".[10]

As his wealth and status as a businessman increased, Pandias became more and more involved in the affairs of the Greek Community. It was largely his initiative that moved it to abandon its small chapel in Finsbury Circus and build a new 'Church of the Saviour' at London Wall. In 1851 he rented a fashionable house, No. 5 Connaught Place, and here he lived till his death in 1865. It was in the last years of his life, 1850 to 1865, that he reached the peak of his career, commercially and socially. His son Peter went to Eton and his only daughter Julia married Charles Monk, son of James Henry Monk, Bishop of Gloucester and Bristol, who, as a Liberal M.P., frequently championed the cause of Greece in international affairs. At the time of Pandias' death Ralli Brothers, London, and its partners had established branches in Calcutta, Bombay, Karachi, Manchester, Liverpool, Marseilles, Constantinople,Trebizond and Tabriz, and were associated with the firms of John Eustratio Ralli & Co. in Odessa, Ralli & Scaramanga in St. Petersburg and Taganrog & Stamati E. Scaramanga in Rostov. Soon after his death in December 1865 the old firm of Ralli Brothers was dissolved and reconstructed in a new form on January 1 1866, with Stephen Augustus Ralli and John Eustratio Ralli as partners.

In the eighteen fifties, Ralli Brothers continued to surge ahead in the world of business. It employed 4,000 office clerks and 15,000 workmen in the manual task of loading and unloading goods. It owned ships of its own to carry cargoes, vast areas of farmland in France and other countries and transported thousands of tons of cereals, foodstuffs, spices and other commodities of the Near and Far East across the Black Sea and from the Levant ports to Europe. In 1851 Pandias began to make plans to extend his firm to India. By the mid-nineteenth century Britain's Indian trade was assuming a vital importance. Already between 1814 and 1832 "the export of Lancashire cotton goods to India had risen by a fabulous 7,500%, while the muslin industry of Dacca was destroyed because its hand-loom weavers simply could not compete with their power-driven rivals seven thousand miles away, who could produce cloth more cheaply and in much greater quantity".[11]

This inability to compete was not simply due to the introduction of steam-powered machinery in Britain but more to a deliberate policy of the British Government to place heavy duties on Indian imports to Britain. These were raised in 1799 and reached a maximum before the end of the Napoleonic Wars. In his continuation of James Mills' 'History of India' Vol I (1845), Professor H. H. Wilson noted "It was stated in evidence (in 1813) that the cotton and silk goods of India up to this period, could be sold for a profit in the British market at a price from 50 to 60 percent lower than those fabricated in England. It consequently became necessary to protect the latter by duties of 70 or 80 percent on their value, or by positive prohibition. Had this not been the case... the mills of Paisley and of Manchester would have been stopped in their outset, and could hardly have been again set in motion, even by the powers of steam".

What was financial disaster for the descendants of Argyree in Dacca was a great commercial opportunity for Ralli Brothers, particularly for that branch of the firm established in Manchester under the aegis of Eustratios Rallis. Moreover, India was becoming a supplier of raw cotton to Lancashire. Until 1846 the British cotton textile industry relied on the USA for 75% of its supplies but in that year a disastrous harvest in America began to turn the attention of Lancashire mill owners to India as a source of supply which had hitherto only provided 13% of their raw cotton. Imports of Indian cotton began to grow and from 1863 to 1865, as a result of the American Civil War, £36.5 million was exported from India to Britain.

The Irish potato famine of 1846 led to a vastly increased production of rice in Bengal and Burma for export to Britain and Europe and this too was good news for Ralli Brothers. Between 1854 and 1856 during the Crimean War the Black Sea trade of Ralli Brothers, under the direction of Zannis Rallis at Odessa, suffered losses. The war prevented the export of Russian hemp to Britain and other European countries who were dependent on it for the manufacture of rope, cordage and bags. So jute came into its own. It was a native product of Bengal and large quantities of its raw fibre were shipped to Britain. In 1833 a new industry, centred in the Douglas Foundry in Dundee which possessed a spinning machine to handle jute, grew and prospered. The Repeal of the Corn Laws greatly expanded the amount of grain imported into Britain and created an enormous demand for jute sacks. Jute therefore was at hand to replace the lost supplies of Russian hemp during the Crimean War and another outlet of expansion was opened for Ralli Brothers.

The British had established indigo plantations in Bengal by the end of the 18th century and this product continued to be in demand on world markets until German chemists developed an aniline substitute dye in 1897 which gradually destroyed the market for indigo. Another sort of plantation which began to make commercial profits for Britain in the 19th century was tea, with plantations springing up in Assam, Darjeeling and elsewhere along the lower Himalayas. By 1874 nearly four million pounds of Indian tea were being produced from 113 gardens, displacing in popularity the original Chinese brew which had been a staple of British trade in the 18th century, and in the Boston Tea Party added an event to history to be remembered with patriotic pride by generations of Americans.

Camels carrying seed cotton for Ralli Brothers Ltd. (1951 Report)

The logic of Britain's vast commercial expansion led to a huge increase of her mercantile marine. The biggest London trading firms, including Greek ones like Ralli, Papayanni and Lascaridi, owned their own ships. There is even a mention of the sale in India of an iron screw steamer, 'Prince Arthur', to the Greek firm of Schlizzi & Co. in 1857.[12] Other smaller Greek companies had to charter ships from British Shipping Companies. This led to an enterprising but ill-fated attempt by a Greek entrepreneur, Stefanos Xenos (yet another name to be met with later in Calcutta), to form a Greek shipping firm in London specialising in carrying cargoes to the Levant and Asia, 'The Greek and Eastern Shipping Company'. It owned a fleet of twenty two vessels carrying romantic names like 'Nea Hellas', 'Valiant', 'Lord Byron', 'Olympios' and 'Asia'. Its initial success was considerable but it foundered on the rash journalistic aspirations of its promoter who funded his ill-starred publications with the profits of his shipping company.[13] It was these economic facts and the involvement of Ralli Brothers since the 1820s in Levantine trade that, no doubt, influenced Pandias' inauguration of a branch of his business in Calcutta in 1851, under the management of John Eustratio Ralli (son of Eustratius Stephanou Ralli) and Nicholas George Paspati.

The easy-going ways of commerce in the days of Clive and Hastings were in the new century disappearing to be replaced by the stricter, stingier, more ascetic and moral attitudes of the Victorians. Charles Lamb, at the beginning of the century, castigates his employers, the East India Company, for cutting the old saints' days holidays almost to nothing and for discontinuing the practice of allowing their employees' correspondence to travel free in the Company's bag. In the 1760s young William Hickey, working in his father's legal business in London, managed to combine the life of a clerk with gargantuan dissipation. He purloined the receipts of the firm to squander them in gaming houses and on prostitutes. "My error commenced in not keeping my pocket money distinct and separate from that belonging to the office..... not a night but I passed a considerable portion of in every degree of dissipation and debauchery, mixing with the most abandoned of both sexes... returning home from these intemperate scenes, if my father was out of town, as he generally was, I went to bed for four or five hours but, if in town, I went directly to my desk where, laying my head down upon it, I soon fell asleep, in which state Mr Bayley (the senior clerk) would often find me, when, awakening me, he with a solemn face would say 'Indeed William, these are sad doings, and God only knows to what a life of such excess will lead you'."[14] It led, through the tolerance of his employers, to a highly successful law business in Calcutta. In the early years of the 19th century, however, attitudes had certainly changed. Lamb's fellow clerk, Tommy Bye, coming into the East India Office a little hazy one morning after an evening's conviviality was instantly dismissed by the Directors, notwithstanding his twenty seven years' faithful service.

It was this new, if extreme, probity of work and conduct in the emerging ethos of commerce which Pandias had to take into account in his organisation of Ralli Brothers. The principles upon which he based the ethics of his firm are described by John Gennadius as, firstly an absolute honesty and straightforwardness in all his business dealings, qualities particularly necessary in London because of the common belief, not always unjustified, that Levantines could not be trusted in commerce. Profit, of course, was a paramount objective but Pandias was insistent that Ralli Brothers should always aim at a reasonable profit acquired fairly. His business transactions were always above-board, absolutely eschewing any sort of secretive or shady dealing. Everything was to be conducted on sound economic principles, avoiding paper transactions and trading only to the extent of the firm's own cash resources. In this way, it came to enjoy a reputation for stability unperturbed by financial crises in the City. With regard to his employees, he demanded an iron discipline which regulated relations between superiors and inferiors in a strict hierarchical manner - deference to seniors by juniors and consideration of the latter's interest by senior partners. The relationship was governed by the kind of patriarchal tradition that subsisted between noblemen and their dependents. Despite the apparent rigidity of the system, it was tempered by Greek humanity. When financial or personal tragedy affected members of the Greek community, those who suffered often found a refuge in the firm which was described as "the friary of Hellenism".

Entrance into Ralli Brothers was phenomenally strict. Vacant posts were filled as a result of an intense and difficult competitive examination. Promotion was only by merit - rich young men with connections found that these apparent advantages did not avail much in the absence of more sterling qualities. Zeal, hard work and a natural aptitude for commerce were the only keys to success. A life of luxury and extravagance was disapproved of and a rigid adherence to punctual attendance at work was demanded. Young Hellenic Hickeys would not have lasted long. Learning from the earlier experience of the East India Company, Pandias insisted that none of his employees should engage in trade and business on his own account. Loyalty was required not only to superiors but to the firm itself - one had to be 'a Rallis man', proud of the Company and anxious to promote its interests. It was one thing to insist on rules and regulations but quite another to achieve adherence to them. Pandias was, in fact, not only the architect of Ralli Brothers but also its builder - the firm worked in the way he wanted it to because of his own hard work, skill and dedication. He benefited from the ancestral respect of Chiots for a conservative and moral business tradition. Because the Directors of the business kept the rules and set the tone they inspired emulation in their employees.[15]

According to Scott's Directory of 1852, Ralli Brothers was trading in Calcutta in that year at 15 Lal Bazaar. From the middle of the century to 1919, economic conditions in India provided immense opportunities for London-based firms. Ralli Brothers, for instance, opened a branch at Bombay in 1861 under the management of Pandia Theodore Ralli and Ambrose Theodore Ralli and also, briefly, one at Karachi under the control of John Negroponte - this branch was closed in 1866 but was reopened in 1882. The building in India of a vast internal railway network, huge irrigation projects, construction of new harbours and improvement of old ones created an infra-structure which could take advantage of external economic forces. The railways alone had immeasurable consequences, economic, social and political. An English journalist, Edwin Arnold, during the Governor-Generalship of Dalhousie, predicted that "Railways may do for India what dynasties have never done - what the genius of Akbar the Magnificent could not effect by government nor the cruelty of Tipoo Sahib by violence. They may make India a nation". "The total value of imports and exports rose from £39.75 million in 1856 to £155 million in 1887".[16]

The tragedy of the Mutiny and the subsequent transfer of authority to the Crown helped in the long run to change the economic climate of India to its advantage. The opening of the Suez Canal in 1869 drastically changed the economic geography of India's communications with Britain. Eventually it was to benefit Bombay rather than Calcutta but it did not check the rising scale of commercial activity in the latter place. Steam vessels began to tie up in the Hugli but as late as 1880 much of the export trade to Calcutta was still arriving in three-masters and by that date the city was probably at the zenith of its commercial prosperity. Pandias had timed the arrival of Ralli Brothers in Calcutta well.

Soon after their establishment, a whole number of new London-based Greek firms began their operations in Calcutta as well - Ralli and Mavrojani from 1852 to 1886, Argenti Sechiari from 1859 to 1876, Agelasto Sagrandi from 1870, P. T. Ralli & Co. from 1857 to 1862, Schlizzi & Co. from 1852 to 1873, Petrocochino Brothers from 1866, Tamvaco & Co. from 1872, Paul Tambaci & Co. from 1873 to 1882, Georgiardi & Co. from 1883, N. Valetta & Co. from 1875, Ziffo & Co. from 1899, F.C. Pallachi & Co. from 1881 and J.S. Vlasto & Co. from 1898. Some of these businesses did not last long and were replaced by others but the one inexorable fact was that Ralli Brothers outpaced them all and like the Coldstream Guards could say "Nulli Secundus".

A close look at the names of some of these companies and a scrutiny of the marriages that the Rallis made with other Greek families reveals an interesting fact - Greek commercial activity in Calcutta in the late 19th and first decade of the 20th century was dominated by a close-knit clan of Chiot noble families related by marriage. In Bishop Catsiyanni's book on the founder of Ralli Brothers records of the following marriage alliances in the 19th century show that the Rallis were connected in this way to the founders of other Greek firms in Calcutta like Argenti Sechiari, Schlizzi & Co., Petrocochino Brothers, J. S. Vlasto & Co., Tamvaco & Co. and Agelasto Sagrandi:

Helene Rallis married Pandelis Argenti
Zorgis Rallis married Marietta Schlizzi
Stefanos Rallis married Julia Sechiari
Ambrouzis Rallis married Penelope Petrocochino
Iacovos D. Z. Rallis married Zenou Vlastou
Toumazis Rallis married Marouko Argentis
Marouko Rallis married Leonis Argentis
Antonios Alexander Rallis married Minousca Tamvaco
Julia A. Rallis married Leoni Argentis
Calliopi Rallis married Alexandros Vlasto
Vierou Stefanou Rallis married Cozi Agelasto
Marigo Stefanou Rallis married Peter Schlizzi
Pandias P. P. Rallis married Argyro Sechiari.

Apart from the fact that Calcutta Greek firms employed members of their own families in their branches in Bengal, they also regularly employed members of other Chiot families with whom they had intermarried. This is revealed by a comparison of a second list of Ralli marriage alliances with entries in Thacker's Directories of employees in the firms noted above: Ralli marriage alliances in 18th and 19th centuries listed by families:-

Stephanos Rallis	m.	Marietta Mavrocordatou
Stratis Rallis	m.	Zambeloy Mavrocordatou
Ambrouzis S. Rallis	m.	Anastasi Mavrocordatou
Eustratios Rallis	m.	Marigo Mavrocordatou
Marietta Rallis	m.	Matthew Mavrocordatos
Despina Rallis	m.	Emmanuel Mavrocordatos
Zannis Rallis	m.	Ploumou Scaramanga
Mina Rallis	m.	Marietta Scaramanga
Pandias Rallis	m.	Marietta Scaramanga
Marietta P. P. Rallis	m.	John Pandia Scaramanga
Loucas D. Z. Rallis	m.	Despina Rodocanaki
Marigo A. Rallis	m.	Peter Rodocanaki
Mary P. P. Rallis	m.	Emmanuel Rodocanaki
Stefanos Ambrosius Rallis	m.	Despina Omiro (Amiro)
Iacovos D. Z. Rallis	m.	Zenou Vlastou
Argyro Stefanou Rallis	m.	Emmanuel Psycha
Demetrios Rallis	m.	Aikaterini Negroponte

The previous lists of Ralli marriages taken together should be compared with the list below of employees in Calcutta Greek firms taken from Thacker's Directories between 1857 and 1896:-

1857	Ralli Brothers:	E.C. Petrocochino
	Schlizzi & Co:	J.C. Negroponte
1859	Ralli Brothers:	N. Argenti
1860	Petrocochino Bros:	N. Argenti
1862	Argenti Sechiari:	Michael Geo. Schlizzi
		John Theo Rodocanaki
1864	Argenti Sechiari:	T.E. Schlizzi
	Petrocochino Bros:	A.K. Agelasto
	Ralli Brothers:	J.E. Scaramanga
1865	Schlizzi & Co:	P.Z. Amiro
1869	Argenti Sechiari:	J.A. Negroponte
	Petrocochino Bros:	T.P. Vlasto
1872	Petrocochino Bros:	P.J. Ralli
1873	Agelasto Sagrandi:	J.A. Ralli
1874	Ralli Bros:	T.A. Vlasto
	Petrocochino Bros:	S. Mavrocordatos
1875	Argenti Sechiari:	G. Negroponte
1876	Agelasto Sagrandi:	S.J. Psycha
	Petrocochino Bros:	J.P. Ralli
1879	Tamvaco & Co:	C.J. Scaramanga
		A. Mavrocordato
1881	Ralli Brothers:	C.C. Scaremanga
1885	Ralli Brothers:	D.P. Petrocochino
1886	Ralli Brothers:	J.E. Schlizzi
1887	Ralli Brothers:	J.S. Vlasto
		J.J. Mavrocordatos
1892	Ralli Brothers:	A.A. Vlasto
		E.A. Vlasto
1893	Ralli Brothers:	A.P. Negroponte
1895	Petrocochino Bros:	S. Psycha
	Ralli Brothers:	A.P. Sechiari
1896	Ralli Brothers:	A.P. Rodacanaki

The Thacker's entry for Petrocochino Bros. in 1865 and subsequent years describes the firm as agents for Agelasto, Petrocochino & Co., London; J. Sagrandi, Manchester; Petrocochino, Sagrandi & Co., Marseilles; Agelasto Vouro & Co., Constantinople. This reveals the far-reaching tentacles which the Chiot nobility clamped on to the Greek network of trade between India and Europe. An examination of the names of the Church Wardens who served the Greek Chapel in Finsbury Circus reveals the same pattern of names which occurs in Calcutta:

124

1839 N. Tamvacos
1840 P. Rallis and A. Mavrojannis
1841 A.T. Rallis
1842 A. Argentis
1843 A.A. Rallis
1844 C.T. Rallis
1845 P.T. Rallis
1846 I.S. Schlizzi and D. Georgiardis
1848/9 A.P. Petrocochino.

In West Norwood the Greek community of London established a magnificent cemetery of about half an acre in 1842. Here the great 19th century London Greek families buried their deceased members under memorials of classic magnificence that make the cemetery one of the most beautiful in Britain. Here, too, the same names which dominated Greek commerce in Calcutta reappear: Rallis, Scaramanga, Schlizzi, Argenti, Sechiari, Mavrocordatos, Agelasto, Petrocochino, Calvocoressi, Rodocanaki and Mavrojanni. As an example of the anglicization that many of these families underwent (whilst preserving their Hellenic heritage), is an interesting memorial tablet in the Parish Church of Clyro, the Radnorshire village nestling under the green-dark mountains of Wales, forever, to English minds, associated with the gentle, clerical diarist, the Revd. Francis Kilvert, who served as a curate in the village. In his day the Great House in the parish was Clyro Court, home of the Baskerville family after whom 'The Baskerville Arms' in the village is named. In the early 20th century, however, the squire was an Anglo-Greek of the Phanariot Mavrojani family who with the Rallis established the firm of Ralli and Mavrojani in Calcutta. The memorial on the north wall of St. Michael's Church reads:

To the Glory of God and in loving memory of Spiridion Mavrojani, late of Clyro Court, Radnorshire. Captain 5 Battalion, Royal Fusiliers who died at Jerusalem, March 1, 1930, aged 63. Also Dorothy, his wife, who died at Clyro Court, Jan 2, 1931, aged 54. Rest in Peace.

Another of these London Greek families was that of the Phanariot noble, Mavrocordato. Prince Alexander Mavrocordato was the friend of Byron and Shelley and one of independent Greece's first premiers.

Employment in Calcutta Greek firms was not the exclusive preserve of certain families. These firms gave employment to a very large number of Greeks and also, to a more limited extent, to British people. These Greeks were not, in the main, like the old Greek families who settled in India, for most of them returned to Greece when their working days were over. The total number of these men would be difficult to determine but Thacker's Directories from 1852 to 1902 contain the following Greek names in the service of Calcutta Greek Houses. Though the following list is not exhaustive it gives some idea of the Greek presence in Calcutta:

Acatos, Andreades, Anninos, Apostolides, Assilanopoulos.
Beinoglou, Brouzis.
Calomiris, Calvocoressi, Camillatos, Candia, Caridia, Carras, Carrimatis, Casanova, Cocolas, Condoleon, Consolo, Constanidi, Contarini, Convelos, Coroneos, Couvela, Coveos.
Dalbusset, Damala, Damiano, Demetriadi, Desylla, Dimoca.
Elefteriades, Eliopolos.
Falle, Fardulides, Flamburiari, Fotiades, Fraghiadis, Frangopoulos.
Georgacopulos, Giannacopulos, Gino, Grimaldi.
Handris, Hilduvachi.
Kalageros, Kalomiris, Kazakos, Klemis, Konios, Kyprianados, Kyriazi.
Lambrinudi, Lambropoulos, Logothetis, Lutrari, Lyrioti.
Macrinos, Magariti, Mamachi, Mangakis, Mangana, Mangos, Maniachi, Marchetti, Massaouti, Masson, Mavrogortlah, Mayorachis, Melanos, Menelas, Michellatos, Micrulachi, Mikas, Millacludes, Minghis, Minettos.
Nicholas, Nicolaides, Nicolini, Nomicos.
Orimaldi, Orvanitelis.
Pallachi, Panas, Papachistopulo, Parodi, Paspatti, Pendelides, Phardonlida, Phocas, Pitta, Proios, Proveleggios.
Ralli, Raphael, Rizo.
Sackerlaropolos, Salamora, Samiotakis, Scouloudi, Scoursos, Scrini, Sergiades, Sevastopulo, Skyridos, Sophianopoulos, Spanos, Stavrides, Stephanides, Sypsomo, Syrioti.
Takidelos, Triandos.
Vafiadis, Valetta, Vassilopoulo, Velisariados, Verdeau, Vermadachi, Vertannes, Vlasto.
Xenos.
Yakinthes.
Zalichi, Zanapulo, Zenos, Zevelachi, Ziffo.

In addition to Greek Trading Houses there were also three Greek tobacconist firms in Calcutta: S. Z. Andricopoulos at 10 Dalhousie Square and Theo. Vafiadis & Co., 4 Dalhousie Square, cigarette manufacturers and tobacconists. Vafiadis was a Greek from Cairo and branches of his firm were to be found in London and Rangoon with agencies in Colombo, Penang and Melbourne. The third firm was Pisti and Pelakanos (L. M. Pisti and M. C. Pelakanos) at 104 Clive Street.

Many of the Greek employees lived in boarding houses some of whose names have survived: Mme Courets Boarding Establishment at 1 Theatre Road; Miss Bobonau's Boarding Establishment, 49 Park Street; Mrs Bett's Boarding Establishment, 2 Russell Street. As they advanced in their careers some took up residence in the Grand and Continental Hotels. Just as Pandias Ralli in London was to encounter British official disdain for men engaged in trade, so in Calcutta officialdom spoke contemptuously of Box Wallahs or Counter Jumpers. Commercial gentlemen found it very difficult to gain admission to the grandest clubs in Calcutta. Official contempt for trade was incomprehensible since commerce was the very life-blood of the Empire, the keystone of an arch which held the whole edifice together. One has the impression that the Calcutta Greeks mixed easily with their British counterparts while retaining a vigorous Greek social life.

By the end of the 19th century Calcutta was the second largest city of the British Empire and the capital of the British Administration in India. As Jan Morris says "Its pattern was deliberately grand. It was laid out as a great capital must be, with authority. It occupied two sides of a square, on the north and the east. The western side was formed by the Hugli River, the southern was left open to suburban development. Around the whole, a defensive ditch was dug, later to delineate the city's inner road, and the centre of the square was occupied by the grand expanse of the maidan, with the protective stronghold of Fort William at its south-west corner".[17] The northern side of this square was formed by the Esplanade where most of the great public buildings were grouped, particularly Government House, modelled on Kedlestone Hall in Derbyshire, the grand sanctum of political power.

To the north of the Esplanade lay the old commercial heart of Calcutta, bounded by Canning Street to the north, the Hugli to the west, Cositollah Street to the east and the Esplanade to the south. It was here that the Greek business firms found their homes and the locus of their commercial operations. Running west from Cositollah Street and in line with Bowbazaar Street and the Writers' Building was Lal Bazaar where in 1852 Ralli Brothers began its life at No. 12, shifting in 1855 to No. 15. Its partners were N. G. Paspati, E. C. Petrocochino and J. E. Ralli. It was one of the oldest streets in Calcutta whose existence was recorded in a French map of the city in 1742 as "Battarie de Lal Buzar". In the early days of the 19th century it was known to soldiers and sailors as 'Flag Street' because across it was festooned a string of flags advertising the existence of a multitude of poor restaurants, grog shops and brothels. It was not a bazaar in the normal sense of that word and its name was probably a corruption of 'Loll Bazaar' (or Red Bazaar). 'Loll Shrub' was the vernacular term for claret. Two early taverns in the street were the London Tavern and the Harmonic House where customers could drink coffee and peruse the newspapers for a rupee. John Palmer 'the prince of merchants' resided in a palatial house here in the early years of the 19th century.[18]

Moving westwards along Lal Bazaar towards the Writers' Building two roads branched off it towards the Esplanade - Mission Row and Old Court House Street. The early name for the former was 'Rope Walk' because the Company's Rope Works were situated there. It derived its 'new' name from the Old Mission Church, built in 1770, by a Swedish missionary the Revd John Zachariah Kiernander. No. 1 was the home of Colonel the Hon. George Monson, a friend of Hastings' arch-enemy Philip Francis, and No. 8 of General Sir John Clavering, another of the Calcutta Councillors. In 1879 Agelasto Sagrandi set up its offices

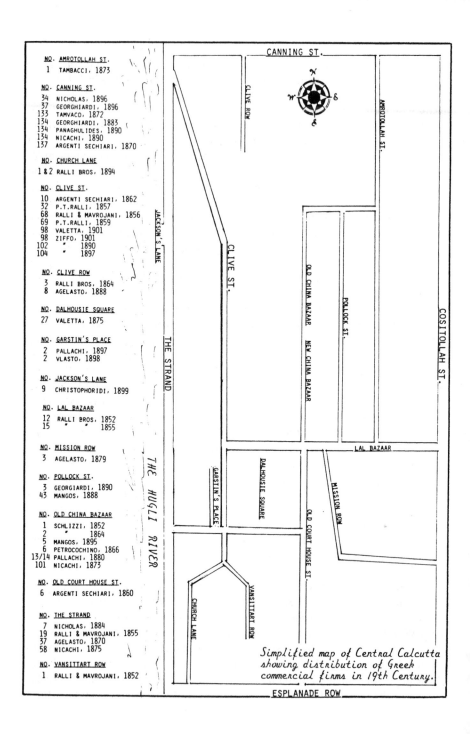

NO. AMROTOLLAH ST.
1 TAMBACCI, 1873

NO. CANNING ST.
34 NICHOLAS, 1896
37 GEORGHIARDI, 1896
133 TAMVACO, 1872
134 GEORGHIARDI, 1883
134 PANAGHULIDES, 1890
134 NICACHI, 1890
137 ARGENTI SECHIARI, 1870

NO. CHURCH LANE
1 & 2 RALLI BROS, 1894

NO. CLIVE ST.
10 ARGENTI SECHIARI, 1862
32 P.T.RALLI, 1857
68 RALLI & MAVROJANI, 1856
69 P.T.RALLI, 1859
98 VALETTA, 1901
98 ZIFFO, 1901
102 " 1890
104 " 1897

NO. CLIVE ROW
3 RALLI BROS, 1864
8 AGELASTO, 1888

NO. DALHOUSIE SQUARE
27 VALETTA, 1875

NO. GARSTIN'S PLACE
2 PALLACHI, 1897
2 VLASTO, 1898

NO. JACKSON'S LANE
9 CHRISTOPHORIDI, 1899

NO. LAL BAZAAR
12 RALLI BROS, 1852
15 " " 1855

NO. MISSION ROW
3 AGELASTO, 1879

NO. POLLOCK ST.
3 GEORGIARDI, 1890
43 MANGOS, 1888

NO. OLD CHINA BAZAAR
1 SCHLIZZI, 1852
2 " 1864
5 MANGOS, 1895
6 PETROCOCHINO, 1866
13/14 PALLACHI, 1880
101 NICACHI, 1873

NO. OLD COURT HOUSE ST.
6 ARGENTI SECHIARI, 1860

NO. THE STRAND
7 NICHOLAS, 1884
19 RALLI & MAVROJANI, 1855
37 AGELASTO, 1870
58 NICACHI, 1875

NO. VANSITTART ROW
1 RALLI & MAVROJANI, 1852

CANNING ST.

CLIVE ROW

AMROTOLLAH ST.

CLIVE ST.

OLD CHINA BAZAAR

NEW CHINA BAZAAR

POLLOCK ST.

COSITOLLAH ST.

JACKSON'S LANE

THE STRAND

THE HUGLI RIVER

LAL BAZAAR

GARSTIN'S PLACE

DALHOUSIE SQUARE

MISSION ROW

OLD COURT HOUSE ST.

CHURCH LANE

VANSITTART ROW

Simplified map of Central Calcutta showing distribution of Greek commercial firms in 19th Century.

ESPLANADE ROW

128

at 3 Mission Row, having previously traded from 37 Strand Road North. Old Court House Street stood where St. Andrew's Church now stands. It was named after the old Court House building in which the Mayor's Court held its sessions and also served for a time as the Town Hall of the city before it was demolished in 1792. From 1860 to 1862 Argenti Sechiari traded from 6 Old Court House Street.

Continuing westward past Writers' Building lay Dalhousie Square once known as Tank Square. The Tank dug in 1700 was known to Bengalis as 'Lal Dighi'. N. Valetta and Co. had their offices at No. 27 from 1875 to 1897. Issuing from Dalhousie Square was a short cul-de-sac called Vansittart Row, named after Henry Vansittart, Governor of Calcutta between 1760 and 1764 who owned property here. Ralli and Mavrojani (trading in London, Liverpool, Manchester, Corfu and Alexandria) occupied No. 1 Vansittart Row from 1852 to 1855. Southwest of the Square, Church Lane ran south to the Esplanade. It got its name from St. Anne's Church, built in 1709 but destroyed by Siraj-ud-Daulah in 1756. As late as 1870 No. 3 housed the well-known firm Moran and Co. where indigo sales were held. In 1894 Ralli Brothers, who had in 1864 moved out of Lal Bazaar to Clive Row, established their headquarters at 1 and 2 Church Lane.

Along the north side of St. John's Church compound lies a blind alley known to Bengalis as 'Garstin Sahib Ka barrack'. It was named after John Garstin who rose in the Company's service to become a Major General in the Engineers and Surveyor General of Bengal. The Old Court House was demolished under his supervision and he used the materials and fittings to build Garstin's Place. He is also famous as the architect of the Old Town Hall and the architectural masterpiece of the Gola, a storehouse for grain in Patna. Garstin's Place was the original home of the Company's Hospital where, as Alexander Hamilton said, "many go in to undergo the penance of physic but few come out to give an account of its operation". No. 2 Garstin's Place was the home of both F. C. Pallachi and Co., General Produce Brokers, and the Greek Merchant firm of J. P. Vlasto.

Running northwards from the northwestern corner of Dalhousie Square was the famous Clive Street. Robert Clive lived in a house here in which Begum Johnson later held her famous whist parties and which later still became the site of the Royal Exchange Building. One of the oldest and most famous streets of Calcutta, it teemed with the affairs of commerce. A modern Bengali poet, Dinesh Das, so describes it in one of his poems:

Here in a hundred snake-like veins,
Streams of people come and go:
Through these shrunken veins the blood
of the country must flow...
O mighty city's burning heart,
O Clive Street of Bengal,
A thousand dumb veins freeze to make
The cornerstone of your high hall.

It was a favourite location of Greek commercial houses. From 1856 until its demise in 1886 Ralli and Mavrojani were at No. 68 and here a member of the family of the martyred Bishop of Chios, E. G. Franghiadis, worked for the firm. Argenti Sechiari were at No. 10 (at the corner of Jackson's Ghat Street) from 1859 to 1860, and again from 1862 to 1870; P.T. Ralli and Co. at No. 32 from 1857 to 1859, moving to No. 69 until it ceased trading in 1862; Ziffo and Co. (freight brokers) at No. 102 in 1890, at No. 104 in 1897 and at number 98 in 1901; N. Valetta and Co. moved from Dalhousie Square to number 104 in 1897 and transferred to No. 98 in 1901.

West of Clive Street and running almost parallel to it was the Strand. In 1820 the Lottery Committee proposed the construction, on what was a low sedgy bank of land, of a road and wharf along the western boundary of Calcutta, to the north of Old Fort Ghat. Construction began in 1828 and the road became the Strand. There, in 1831, the Company built its Mint where its supplies of specie were stored or converted into currency. Designed by the Mint Master, W. N. Forbes, it had a Doric portico and was build around a central courtyard. Ralli and Mavrojani had its offices here from 1855 to 1856 at No. 19, Agelasto Sagrandi at No. 37, Nicholas & Co. at No. 7. At the northern end of the Strand was a thoroughfare leading down to the river known as Jackson's Lane, named after William Jackson, the Company's Attorney General in 1787 who died in Calcutta in 1807. No. 9 Jackson's Lane was the office of Christophoridi & Co., Jute Brokers, from 1895 to 1899.

East of Clive Street was one of the most fascinating areas of Calcutta, Old China Bazaar. Its name was derived from the sale of Chinese goods there brought by ships that plied between Calcutta and Canton. A highly diverting description of the area is given in an editorial note in The 'Statesman' of November 14, 1876: "Leaving St. Andrew's Church on the left and driving due north, we find ourselves approaching a very unfashionable quarter. We are in a very narrow street, on either side of which are little dens of native shops of all shapes and sizes.... in the windows, Eau de Cologne, Burmese Cigars, and tenpenny nails lie fraternally side by side in repose, whilst spiders, flies and mosquitoes, disport amongst them, fearless of the avenging chowrie (fly whisk). Turning a sharp corner, we find ourselves at once in an Indian Babel. A roar of many voices, increasing every moment as we advance, is sufficiently suggestive to the hardy explorer, of the vultures that are awaiting him at no great distance. Suddenly we come to a dead stop.... we find a line of heavily laden wagons blocked across the road. One of the leading bullocks is half inside a barber's shop... there seems to be no likelihood of moving for a couple of hours. We are deafened by the excited jabbering of the touts, who in pithy but unparliamentary language contradict each other's vigorous recommendations of their respective employers. Above the din, a highly pitched insinuating voice shrieks on our right, 'Mine very good shop, Sir! Hats, bonnet and stationery got! Not want? Then Sahib say 'What will have my shop all got?' A fortissimo bass on the left drowns every other sound by his denial of number one's statement. 'You do not believe him, Sar, I know him long time; him very big scoundrel; my shop here close got all things very cheap'." Only Nicachi and Co. occupied 6 Old China Bazaar in 1902 but in 1908 a New China Bazaar came into existence as a large block of shops erected near the Writers' Building. A large number of Greek firms occupied this site - Schlizzi & Co. at No. 1 from 1852 to 1864 and at No. 2 from 1864 to 1873; Petrocochino Bros. at No. 5 from 1866 to 1882; C. D. Mangos & Co., Jute and Produce Brokers, at No. 5 from 1895; F. C. Pallachi & Co. at Nos. 13 and 14 from 1881 to 1897. At the northeast corner of New China Bazaar lay Swallow Lane, named after Captain William Swallow who owned property there. At No. 7 Christophoridi and Co. had its offices from 1895 to 1897. To the east of Old China Bazaar appeared Pollock Street, named after a property owner, Hugh Pollock. At No. 3, Georgiardi & Co. operated from 1890 to 1896 and C. D. Mangos & Co. at No. 43 from 1885 to 1895.

Running eastwards from the Strand to Chitpore Road and at right angles to Clive Street was Canning Street, named after the first Viceroy of India. Its old name was Moorghihatta (Fowl Market) and was the place where the first Portuguese inhabitants of Calcutta had once lived. In the early 19th century it was divided into two sections by an ancient building with a flagged courtyard in front surrounded by a high brick wall called Aloo Godown, occupied by George Henderson & Co., Agents for the Borneo Jute Company. This was knocked down to afford continuous communication along the street. Before it ceased trading in 1876, Argenti Sechiari had its office at No. 137; Tamvaco & Co. operated at No. 133 from 1872 and next door at No. 134, Georgiardi & Co., Jute and Jute Fabric Merchants, from 1883 to 1890 and at 37 from 1896, while, finally, Panaghulides & Co. occupied 134 from 1887. At the eastern end of Canning Street was the old home of Greek commerce containing the Greek Church of The Transfiguration, Amratollah Street. The Church was still there but it was no longer as it had once been, the main centre of Greek commerce. However, from 1873 to 1882 Paul Tamvaci & Co. traded from No. 1. Running south from Canning Street to the western side of Old China Bazaar was Clive Row. Before its establishment at Church Lane, Ralli Brothers had its offices here from 1864 to 1894 at No. 3 and Agelasto and Sagrandi at No. 8 from 1888.

To obtain some idea of the kind of commercial operations that Ralli Brothers was engaged in during these years we can examine one of the handbooks issued by the firm annually in Calcutta. To leaf through the faded pages of Ralli Brothers Calcutta Handbook for 1888 is to enter at once into a world of mercantile romance in which exotic names like teelseed, mowaseed, turmeric, borax and tincal jostle with sober commodities like saltpetre, rice, jute and ginger. Pride of place, however, was reserved for jute, the prince of products which made the fortunes of the firm in Bengal and is dealt with in the first chapter of the

Handbook. The word and the product was Bengali in origin and was also used to describe the plant (Corchorus Capsularis) and the fibre derived from it which was used for a variety of purposes but chiefly for the manufacture of sacks. The first extant English use of the word goes back to 1746 and in 1795 Dr. Roxburgh drew the attention of the Court of Directors of the Company to "the value of the fibre called jute by the natives".[19] The popular trading name for the coarse sacking made from jute fibre was 'gunny'. In the early days of the Company, a limited amount of jute fibre was produced on village looms but from 1833 raw jute began to be shipped to Dundee where jute sacks were manufactured. In 1854 Dundee machinery was installed at a mill at Serampore and the close connection between this Scottish city and jute manufacture in Bengal, making the fortunes of innumerable Lowland Scots, was born. Profits from it were enormous. Unlike those from other commodities they increased steadily and were not subject to fluctuations. The first World War was not a tragedy for jute manufacturers and merchants for it expanded the sales of gunnies which were urgently required as sandbags for trenches in the various theatres of war. When the Armistice was proclaimed on Friday November 11, 1918, the date was dubbed, with grim humour, by jute manufacturers 'Black Friday'. A prestigious Scottish firm, Andrew Yule & Co., had its own jute factory 'Cheviot Mills' on the banks of the Hugli as did many other firms.

Ralli Brothers had its own jute mill at Naraingunj and two steam launches, 'Alexandros' and 'Georgios' moored at its wharves. A number of Greeks worked at this station for the firm and among them we encounter the name of C.D. Giannacopulos who was an Honorary Magistrate in Dacca. It is very likely that he belonged to the Greek family of this name who provided the first verger of the London Greek Church, Dimitrios Giannacopulos and the Greek Consul at Liverpool in 1863 D. K. Giannacopulos. He may even have been connected with the merchant of Meerut of that name who died there in 1810. Even at a later date signs of old Greek commercial activity continued at Naraingunj. In 1897 and subsequent years there was a jute pressing concern, Lucas Brothers, there with Andrew and Abraham Lucas as partners. The Handbook informs us that between 1829 and 1863 exports of jute had increased sixteenfold. About 1864/65 this caused cultivation to spread to districts other than Cuttack and Balasore, the traditional areas of jute production. The European countries to which it was exported by Ralli Brothers were, in order of quantity, the U.K., France, Germany, Austria, Belgium, Holland, Spain, Italy and Russia - the USA importing slightly less than Austria. The Handbook says that the firm shipped gunnies to the Levant through the agency of E. Decipri and T. Fachiri at Smyrna under the guarantee of M. L. Calvocoressi.

Chapters II, III and IV of the Handbook deal with the export of wheat, pulse and various seeds from which oil and other products like cattle food could be extracted: linseed, rapeseed, poppyseed, teelseed (Indian sesame) and

Boats and towing launches of Ralli Brothers Ltd. at Naraingunj (1951 Report)

mowaseed. Chapter V is concerned with rice and lists the various countries to which it was exported by the firm: U.K. (London, Liverpool), France (Marseilles, Bordeaux, Havre, Rouen), USA, West Indies, Mauritius, Isle of Bourbon and Bombay. Chapter VI deals with saltpetre from which gunpowder was manufactured and was also used in the dyeing and metallurgy industries. Shellac is the subject of the next chapter and the Handbook informs us that it was "used for hat stiffening, varnish, sealing wax, coating the inside of barrels, painting the bottom of boats and as undercoat". Next, in Chapter VIII, comes 'Jaggery, the coarse brown, almost black, sugar which is made from the sap of various palms, particularly the date palm in Bengal. It was produced in the form of small round cakes'. The four following chapters deal respectively with castor oil, turmeric and ginger (produced in East Bengal) and India rubber. Chapter XIII is about cutch, imported from Burma, also known as catechu. The Handbook says it is used for dyeing and tanning nets and sails of fishing boats and in India it is eaten by the natives mixed with areca and betel. The last chapter concerns borax, a salt formed by the combination of boracic acid with soda which occurs in a crude state in Eastern India known as tincal and used for glazing china and pottery.

As the 19th century moved to its close, the operations of Ralli Brothers were expanded from Calcutta to the Mofussil. There were branches of the firm in Patna, Cawnpore, Seragunj, Saidpore, Buxar, Delhi, Revilgunj and Naraingunj. Strangest of all, in Calcutta itself there appears in Thacker's Directory of 1892 the mention of a business "S. S. Ralli & Co., 1 Bhowanipore Road, Tatersall's Horse Repository, horse importers, commission agents, veterinary surgeons, hack and race stables, crush food mills". It does not seem to have lasted long but it is a tribute to the thrusting commercial enterprise of the remarkable Chiot family who replaced the trading activity of the old Greeks from Philippopolis and brought a new more sophisticated dimension to Greek enterprise in Bengal.

It is interesting to compare and contrast the fortunes of the two Levantine communities of Greeks and Armenians in Calcutta. The latter were there first and their commercial prosperity exceeded that of the early Greek community of merchants but was easily overtaken by Ralli Brothers and the new Greek firms. But the Armenians are still in Calcutta whereas the great Ralli Brothers, as such, suddenly ceased trading in 1961. These facts may perhaps be explained by the observations in 1836 of an English traveller in Turkey, J. Pardoe: "All the steady commerce on a great scale in Constantinople may be said to be, with very slight exceptions, in the hands of the Armenians, who have the true, patient, calculating spirit of trade; while the wilder speculations of hazardous and ambitious enterprise are grasped with avidity by the more daring and adventurous Greeks; and hence arises the fact, for which at first it is difficult to account, that the most wealthy and the most needy of the merchants of Stamboul are alike of that race while you rarely see an Armenian either limited in his means or obtrusive in his life style."[20] As for the Greeks, we may perhaps apply to them the words of the Gospel: "Mary hath chosen the better part."

References: Chapter Eight

1. *Greece Under Ottoman and Venetian Dominion*, G. Findlay (2nd Edition Vol.V) p223
2. *Ibid.* p223
3. *Memoire sur l'Etat de la civilization dans la Grece*, A Coray (1803)
4. *Pandias Stephen Rallis*, Timetheos Catsiyannis, Bp of Militorepolis (London, 1986) I am heavily indebted for information on the life of the founder of Ralli Brothers to this book
5. *Life and work of the Bishop of Chios, Platon Franghiardis*, N. S. Kroussouloudis (Thessaloniki, 1981) Extracts in Catsiyannis op. cit.
6. *The Age of Elegance*, A Bryant (Reprint Society, London, 1954) p296
7. *Ibid.* p341
8. *Victorian England as seen by Punch* (Book Club Associates, London, 1978) p51
9. Catsiyannis op. cit. p48
10. *Ibid.* p79
11. *India Britannica*, G Moorhouse (Book Club Associates, London, 1983) p156
12. Miscellaneous Bonds 1846-1865. Z/O/1/12 I.O.R.
13. Catsiyannis op. cit. p121
14. *Memoirs of William Hickey* (Century Publishing, London, 1984) pp40, 53
15. Catsiyannis op. cit. pp17-19
16. Moorhouse op. cit. p166
17. *Stones of Empire*, Jan Morris, Simon Winchester (O.U.P., 1983) p206
18. *A History of Calcutta Streets*, P. Thankapan Nair (Firma KLM Private Ltd., 1987) p643. Much of the information on Calcutta streets is taken from this source
19. *Hobson-Jobson*, Col H Yule & A C Burnell, Second edition (Routledge & Keegan Paul, re-issued 1968) entry on 'Jute'
20. *The City of the Sultan*, J Pardoe (London, 1837) quoted *The Greek Merchant Marine*, op. cit. pp36, 38

9

The Corfiots

Ye isles beyond the Adriatic wave,
Whose classic shores Ionian waters lave.

(Waller Rodwell Wright)

The Ionian Islands of Corfu, Paxos, Cephalonia, Zante, Ithaca, Levkas and Kythera between 1814 and 1864 were part of Britain's Empire. The administrative records of the islands are now housed in the Public Record Office at Kew where a perusal of the petitions which Corfiots submitted to the British Lord High Commissioners reveals that an extraordinary number of Corfiot names had the distinctive termination of 'chi' like Agrapidarchi, Augarichi, Mustachi, Neronichi, Slavichi, Triarchi and countless others. The records of Greek commercial firms in Calcutta also yield examples of names with the same ending whose holders were presumably Corfiots - Hulduvachi, Maniachi, Mizulachi, Micrulachi, Mallachi, Mayorachi, Pallachi, Tambachi, Zallichi and Sevelachi. Other families in mid and late Victorian Calcutta were certainly Corfiot like the Flamburiaris, who belonged to the Corfiot nobility, the Nicachis and, among the old Greeks of Bengal, the Revd Constantine Parthenios and the Ducas family.

Unlike the rest of Greece, Corfu never suffered the indignity of Turkish rule, as it formed part of the Venetian Empire. Until 1797 the Republic of St. Mark ruled and defended Corfu against the Turks. Twice their armies landed in the island in an attempt to expel the Venetians. In 1537 Sultan Suleiman the Magnificent sent 25,000 troops under the notorious Khaireddin Barbarossa who besieged the Old Fortress on the Island. His assaults were repulsed by a defending army of 2,000 Venetians and 2,000 Corfiots and the Turkish invaders withdrew.

In 1572 at the Battle of Lepanto, Don John of Austria, leading a combined fleet of Spanish, Venetian and Genoese ships decisively defeated the Turkish fleet. Ionians distinguished themselves in the conflict for Corfu by sending four galleys and 1,500 sailors. One Corfiot captain, Christofalo Kondakali, captured the Ottoman flagship and another was captured and flayed alive by the Turks. In 1716 the Turks made a second attempt to take Corfu with an army of 65,000 men under Kara Mustapha Pasha. This time Corfu was defended by a Saxon mercenary soldier, Count Johann Matthias von der Schulenburg, whose sister was the mistress of George I, the Hanoverian King of Britain. The Turks attacked the Old Fort but Schulenburg counter-attacked, routed them and forced them to retreat in disarray.

The Venetians set their seal on the cultural and social life of Corfu for, alone among the Greek lands, the inhabitants were influenced by Italian rather than by Turkish customs. The fabric of society was Venetian and in imitation of the Imperial city, Corfu produced its own Libro D'Oro, the Golden Book, in which the noble credentials of some 277 Corfiot families were solemnly recorded, amongst them the Ducas family, some of whose members emigrated to Bengal. The island was particularly valuable to Venice for its geographical position at the entrance to the Adriatic - a staging post to the far-flung outposts of her maritime empire and the last bastion of defence against her Ottoman rival. It has been described as "the Gibraltar of Venice".[1] In return the Corfiots gained from Venetian rule: "When you contrast the richly endowed Corfiot churches with their Cretan counterparts....where the eyes on icons and wall paintings have been cruelly scratched out by intolerant Turkish masters, the benefits of Venetian rule can be appreciated".[2]

By 1797 the Republic of St. Mark had reached a depth of political decadence that made it unable to resist the hungry advance of the legions of Napoleon Bonaparte. Corfu was seized by the French and until 1814, with one short intermission, remained under the Tricolour. When the Royal Navy liberated the island what the Ionians wanted was an independent state under British protection; what they got was a titular Septinsular Republic (Corfu and the other six Ionian Islands) under British rule. "A sort of middle state between a colony and a perfectly independent country without in some respects possessing the advantages of either".[3] Between 1815 and 1838, however, the island more resembled a colony with all significant powers in the hands of a British High Commissioner appointed by the Colonial Office. When the independent Kingdom of Greece was established in 1832, the Corfiots clamoured incessantly for union with Greece which the British Government, advised by Gladstone, conceded in 1864. Such a voluntary relinquishment of territory anywhere by a Great Power in the 19th century was almost unique.

The British contribution to the welfare of the Islands was considerable - security from external threat, a fair and independent judiciary, a good educational system and excellent public works. So much so that, despite some bitterness at the tardiness of the British Government in granting re-union, the British Occupation is on the whole remembered affectionately by Corfiots. Alone among the Mediterranean peoples they mastered the game of cricket and during British rule two Corfiot clubs flourished - the Megaloi, whose membership was restricted to the nobility, and the Microi who catered for the hoi polloi.

Descriptions of British life in Corfu have more than a passing resemblance, as far as the British were concerned, to the life of a secure cantonment in India. Complaints about the natives, certain discomforts and the elegance of some features of life were not dissimilar though the climate, the vegetation and the amenities in Corfu could hardly be equalled by any Indian station. Several distinguished British people experienced life both in colonial Corfu and under the British administration of India or Ceylon. The first Lord High Commissioner, Sir Thomas Maitland, born 1759, the second son of Lord Lauderdale, had rendered civil and military service in India and the Caribbean, been a Radical M.P. and was a notable Governor of Ceylon and Malta. His staff called him 'King Tom' and his critics thought that he was "insufferably rude and abrupt.... particularly dirty in his person.... constantly drunk and surrounded by sycophants".[4] He was, nevertheless, an efficient but autocratic High Commissioner who was concerned for the material welfare of his Corfiot subjects but distrusted their political ability. The Corfiot nobleman Joannis Capodistrias, who later became the first President of Greece, accused him of equating Greeks with Indians. On one occasion, clad only in a brief nightshirt, a red nightcap and a pair of slippers, he told the assembled Senate of the Ionian Islands to go to hell.[5] Viscount Kirkwall, who served with him in the Islands, described him as "a man of great abilities.... energy, resolution and soldier-like frankness.... counter balanced by an excessive coarseness and vagueness of language and manners". He was no mean tippler and Kirkwall delicately alludes to this fault as "the extraordinary lengths to which he carried his hospitable conviviality".[6]

Maitland's predecessor as Governor of Ceylon was Frederick North, the fifth Earl of Guildford, an accomplished Classical scholar who spoke modern Greek fluently and whose mission in life was to revive the spirit of Ancient Greece. To this laudable end he founded an Ionian Academy in Corfu Town, became its first Chancellor, bequeathed a valuable library of books and manuscripts to it, was received into the Greek Orthodox faith and was probably the most popular and revered Englishman in Corfu. Charles Napier has left us with a facetious description of him: "Lord Guildford is here again. He goes about dressed up like Plato with a gold band round his mad pate and flowing drapery of a purple hue. His students' dress is very pretty and said to be taken from ancient statues".[7]

Maitland's successor as Lord High Commissioner was General Sir Frederick Adam who took over in 1824 and left in 1832 to become Governor of Madras. A distinguished soldier who had lost an arm at Waterloo in command of the Light Brigade which routed Napoleon's Imperial Guard, he was a great favourite of Corfiots for whom he constructed the first efficient system of water supply in the island. Private William Wheeler, of the King's Own Yorkshire Light Infantry stationed in the Ionian Islands between 1823 and 1828, has the following intriguing story about him. "Sir Frederick is appointed Lord High Commissioner, nothing could have pleased the Greeks better. He is a very great favourite, his lady is a Corfiote, her husband and brother are living here. The story is that he was caught in such a situation with the lady that left no doubt on the mind of her Greek lord that Sir F. had just been measuring him for an outsize pair of horns, which everyone knows is a disagreeable appendage to one's brows, particularly in a warm climate. Whether there was any foundation for the husband's fears I cannot say. Be that as it may he soon applied for and obtained a divorce. The lady is now Queen of the Ionian Isles.... her complexion is dark, features regular, eyes black as sloes so is her hair, but the beard on her upper lip would ornament a hussar". Wheeler also chronicled a strange incident on the Esplanade parade ground in Corfu on November 10, 1825: "At times the General is very passionate when he will vie with any soldier under his command in swearing. A short time since while putting the Garrison through a Field Day on the Esplanade one of our sergeants made a mistake. It was noted by the General, he discharged a volley of oaths at the sergeant, then threw his gold snuff box at him". He must have made an interesting Governor of Madras and his Corfiot lady a fascinating consort.[8]

General Sir Charles Napier, conqueror of Sind, was yet another Ionian 'Colonial'. In 1819 he was appointed Inspecting Field Officer for the Islands and in 1822 Resident of Cephalonia, a mountainous island from whose harbour ships had sailed to America and South East Asia where one Cephalian sea captain at the end of the 17th century actually became Viceroy of Siam.[9] Napier combined the sentiments of a Whig radical with the restless, improving dash of a Victorian imperialist. Philip Mason describes him as "rough-tongued, hot-tempered, dogmatic, cynical, shrewd and honest, a man who put an edge on all he said".[10] He threw himself with enthusiasm into his Ionian work. "My Kingdom is of 60,000 souls and martial law exists. My predecessor is going home half-dead from the labour, but to me it is health, spirit, everything. I live for some use now".[11] His subjects were an unruly lot and included an Orthodox Bishop who was, according to Napier "an excellent, pious man, who used to live by sheep stealing, which he now calls his pastoral life, and who believes that Justinian wrote the Code Napoleon".[12] In eight years on the island he rescinded martial law, built excellent roads, drained marshes, cleared slums, widened streets, built prisons, market-places and a lighthouse, set up a model farm and new fisheries, expanded port facilities and arranged loans for the peasants. He made an enemy of Sir Frederick Adam for his criticisms of the Lord High Commissioner's wasteful expenditure on pomp in Corfu. His decision to courtmartial two subalterns who had seduced a Cephalonian girl did not endear him to senior army officers. His wife's health forced him to leave in 1830 but he never forgot Cephalonia where he left behind a native mistress. He named one of his daughters by her 'Emily Cephalonia' and left her and her two sisters two properties on the island and in his Will he remembered many islanders with bequests. In 1845 after his Indian campaigns had made him famous, he wrote to a Greek friend, Demetrius Kambitsi: "You give me great pleasure in telling me that the colony at Poros is to be revived. I am sure it will become again a great town and port. I would give all Sind for Poros. Here in Sind I am a King, it is true, but they say first love is truest and Cephalonia is mine".[13]

The memory of Bishop Reginald Heber, the famous Bishop of Calcutta (1820-1826) surprisingly surfaces in Corfu some years after his death. His second wife and widow, Mary, daughter of Cuthbert Allanson,[14] took as her second husband, Count Valsamachi, a Corfiot nobleman who led the Ionian delegation to the Congress of Vienna in 1815 and presented a memorandum to the Powers proposing the setting-up of an independent Septinsular Republic. The marriage was cattily noted by Emily Eden, the sister of a future Governor General of India George Eden, second Lord Auckland, who accompanied him to India between 1835 and 1842. Writing from her home in Greenwich Park in August 1830 Emily says "Mrs Heber, the Bishop's widow, has just published two more volumes of her first husband's life, and finding it lucrative has taken a second husband, a Greek who calls himself Sir Demetrius Valsamachi, and he has carried her off to the Ionian Islands where you will find her collecting materials for the biography of Sir Demitri".[15] For two years after her marriage she lived on Cephalonia. Many years afterwards, about 1860, Sir Henry Drummond Wolfe, on a visit to Corfu noted "there is a most interesting lady at Corfu, Countess Valsamachi. Her husband was an Ionian Count, an extremely handsome man, who had been very well received at Vienna at the time of the Congress. She was the widow of Bishop Heber, a lady very much sought after on account of kindness and dignified manner. She had one daughter by her marriage with the Count who, I think, married a Roumanian".[16] This daughter was probably Dionese Valsamachi who, in 1855, applied in Corfu for a British passport to travel to Constantinople.[17]

The most famous literary Englishman to live in Corfu was Edward Lear, whose reputation as an inspired writer of Nonsense Verse survives, but who was also a very talented painter who gave drawing lessons to Queen Victoria. Between 1848 and 1862 he lived off and on in Corfu, delighting in the magical beauty of the island, drawing and painting and observing, with amused detachment, the goings-on of its colonial elite. He even produced a Nonsense Rhyme about the island:

There was an old man of Corfu,
Who never knew what he should do;
So he rushed up and down,
Till the sun made him brown,
That bewildered old man of Corfu.

His letters are littered with passages that reveal his fascination with the island: "This place is wonderfully lovely.... if you come here I could put you up beautifully and feed you on ginger beer, claret and prawns". "I wish I could give you any idea of this island, it is really a Paradise. The extreme gardeny verdure, the fine olives, cypresses, almonds and oranges make the landscape so rich, and the Albanian mountains are wonderfully fine. All the villages appear clean and white, with here and there a palm tree overtopping them. The women wear duck;

the men - the lower orders that is - mostly red copes and full Turkish trousers. Here and there you see an Albanian, all red and white, with a full white petticoat like a doll's, and a sheepskin over his shoulder. Then you meet some of the priests with beards and flowing black robes. Mixed with them are the English soldiers and naval officers, and the upper class of Corfiots who dress as we do; so the result is most attractive". "The more I see of this place, so the more I feel that no other spot on earth can be fuller of beauty and variety of beauty." Just after he left Corfu he wrote to a friend: "I hope you got a letter from me just before I left Corfu - of which place I am now cut adrift, though I cannot write the name without a pang".

In 1873 Lear was invited by his friend, Thomas George Baring, the Earl of Northbrook, who had recently been appointed Viceroy, to visit India. All his expenses would be paid and in return he would paint for his friend one or two Indian landscapes. Lear accepted the offer and between November 22, 1873, and January 9, 1875, he carried out a massive tour of the sub-continent and left a fascinating account of his adventures in his 'Journal'.[18] The itinerary of his journey is breathtaking - Jubbulpore, Cawnpore, Allahabad, Benares, Dinapore, Calcutta, Darjeeling, Monghyr, Allahabad, Agra, Sikandra, Gwalior, Fatehpur Sikri, Bharatpur, Muttra, Brindaban, Delhi, Dehra Dun, Mussourie, Roorkee, Simla, Ambala, Bombay, Poona, Parbati Golconda, Hyderabad, Bangalore, Madras, Conjeeveram, Bangalore, Trichinopoly, Tanjore, Salem, Mysore, Conoor, Ooty, Malabar, Mahé, Calicut, Colombo, Kandy and Cochin. Amidst all his dusty travelling and constant sketching, he even managed to produce an Indian Nonsense Rhyme, the humour of which lies in the deliberate misunderstanding and misuse of Hindustani words. It was called 'The Cummerbund' and was first published in 'The Times of India', Bombay, in July 1874:

I

"She sate upon her Dobie,
To watch the Evening Star,
And all the Punkas as they passed,
Cried 'My! how fair you are'.
Around her bower, with quivering leaves,
The tall Khansammahs grew,
And Kitmutgars in wild festoons
Hung down from Tchokis blue.

II

Below her home the river rolled
With soft meloobious sound,
Where golden finned Chuprassies swam,
In myriads circling round.
Above, on tallest trees remote
Green Ayahs perched alone,
And all the night the Mussak moan'd
Its melancholy tone.

III

And where the purple Nullahs threw
Their branches far and wide -
And silver Goreewallahs flew
In silence, side by side, -
The little Bheesties twittering cry
Rose on the flagrant air,
And oft the angry Jampan howled
Deep in his hateful lair.

IV

She sate upon her Dobie, -
She heard the Nimmak hum, -
When all at once a cry arose, -
'The Cummerbund has come!'
In vain she fled - with open jaws
The angry monster followed,
And so (before assistance came),
The Lady Fair was swallowed.

V

They sought in vain for even a bone
Respectfully to bury, -
They said - 'Hers was a dreadful fate!'
(And Echo answered 'Very')
They nailed her Dobie to the wall,
Where last her form was seen,
And underneath they wrote these words,
In yellow, blue and green:-
Beware, ye Fair! Ye Fair beware!
Nor sit out late at night, -
Lest horrid Cummerbunds should come,
And swallow you outright."

Throughout his Indian travels Lear was accompanied by his Greek servant, Giorgios Kokali, whose name is mentioned on almost every page of the Journal, and without whose sterling help Lear could hardly have accomplished his fantastic journey. Several passages in the Journal bear witness to this: "I cannot be too thankful for the help I have had from such a man as Giorgio, in every respect so perfectly good a servant and so steady and faithful a friend". "Giorgio, my generally mute companion, is nevertheless really good company, being always in the way, and never in the way, a wonderful example of servant and friend or companion united". "Giorgio Kokali has been a good and faithful servant to me for many years, but how very many of his best qualities only come out now in this hard Indian journey! His quiet, content and unmurmuring patience, and his constant attention to me, his often wrong-doing master".

Kokali, born in Corfu, was a Souliote, Greeks who lived in the Thresprotian Mountains that tower from the Epirot coast between Igoumenitsa and Parga and whose menacing outlines can be seen clearly from Corfu. Many of the Greek villages here speak the Cham dialect of Albania and in the War of Independence these kilted mountaineers played an heroic part. Byron recruited a retinue of them as his followers and the great Souliote warrior, Markos Botsaris, 'the Leonidas of the Revolution' was fatally shot in the head in an attack on the Turks at Karpenisi a few hours after writing his last letter to the English poet. Near Souli, the stronghold of these Epirot warriors, stands the steep precipice of Zalango, where Souliote women, pursued by Turkish soldiery, flung themselves to their deaths.

Through the eyes of Lear we learn of the reactions of his Corfiot Souliote servant to the unfamiliar sights and sounds of India. He is bowled over by the sight of his first elephant at Jubbulpore and at Cawnpore one little boy with chicken pox took a great fancy to him and followed him about much to his annoyance. At Benares he is disturbed by shrieking jackals in the night and he tells Lear that their song is "Away! Away!" At Clark's Hotel they are given miserably furnished rooms but Giorgio is stoical while Lear is not. At Dinapore Sydney Coombe, Lear's old friend, tells him that travelling in India with a European servant is quite exceptional. Moving through Northern Bengal Giorgio spends a lot of time observing crocodiles basking on a stretch of sand. As they approach the Himalayas, Giorgio cries out in excitement "Presto, presto Padrone. Le Montagne"; and when Lear goes out one morning to attempt a sketch of Kanchinjanga, he is protected from the bitter cold by Giorgio constantly packing cloaks and blankets around him while he works. Giorgio keeps warm by shuffling about and smoking - perhaps he was reminded of the mountains of Epirus. Later, when Lear offers him some pineapple, he replies gruffly "No, I would rather have onions". (No vorrei mangiar cipolli).

At Monghyr, Lear's sketching drew around him a large crowd of Indians who drove him wild with exasperation so, with un-English venom, "I suddenly spat at them, whereat they ran away like mad, which made old Giorgio laugh as I had not seen him for many a long day". His calmness in the face of adversity is a constant wonder to Lear. On one occasion as they were tramping into the country for a picnic a bottle of beer broke in Giorgio's bag, playing havoc with the contents - "an event he bears with calmness". He is a remarkably useful servant who mends and sews linen "but he won't undertake to cover my, or his, solar topee". He loves his pint of beer but is not impressed with the ruined Mughal palaces of North India which, to him, do not equal the magnificent ruins of Samos and Norba. He prefers to watch the antics of thieving apes and the beautiful half-tame squirrels.

In Simla, he and Lear had to pass through a long, dark tunnel under a mountain. Lear could see nothing and began to panic but Giorgio made him hold one end of an umbrella and pulled him along to safety. Time and again, on his sketching expeditions, the Souliote came to Lear's aid. At Parbati Lear was drawing by a lake when a gust of wind carried his sketch into the lake and Giorgio plunged in to retrieve it. On another occasion, drawing in exceptional windy weather, he held the folio hard between his hands while Lear sketched. At Conjeeveram, the beautiful Indian children impressed him and he said to Lear "what fine colour they have! If white babies were here they would seem boiled or out of health". At Bangalore he was delighted when a Major Feneran gave him a box of a hundred cigars. He seems to have survived the unfamiliar food of India better than Lear though at Hyderabad he was sick from a surfeit of claret and cucumber, and he suffered a severe bout of dysentery in Ceylon. He was a stickler for table etiquette and in Mahé, where he was put up in a dark room containing only a table and chair and given a cold breakfast, he told the servants "before all things, you had better bring a table cloth".

He had left behind him in Corfu a young family about whose welfare he was always anxious and eagerly awaited letters from them. None came until the journey was over. At Bombay Lear says "Two letters were brought to me and the second was a dreadful one; I had to send on Giorgio to read it alone: Nikola (Giorgio's son) has gone all to the bad and Tatiane's illness is owing to her bad conduct, Lambi has also gone wrong, and ditto poor little Dimitri. It was bitter hard lines to tell my poor old Giorgio this, but he heard all except when I came to the last: the Greek Consul at Alexandria had written to say that Janni is dead". On that tragic note of the death of Giorgio's wife this Indian Odyssey came to an end. After many years of service to Lear Giorgio died on August 8, 1883, at Monte Generoso in Italy and was buried in the Protestant Cemetery at Mendrisio. In a letter to Tennyson's wife Emily, Lear wrote "I wish I could think I had merited such a friend".

To those who know both places it may seem far-fetched to compare Corfu Town to Calcutta. The advantages enjoyed by the former over the latter, the differences of climate, terrain and size make the comparison seem ridiculous. Yet, allowing for enormous geographical disparities, Victorian Calcutta and Victorian Corfu did have similarities which arose through their colonial situation. The Maidan in Calcutta, flanked by Fort William and Government House was not unlike the Esplanade in Corfu overlooked by the massive defences of the Old Fort. The residence of the Lord High Commissioners, the Palace of Saints Michael and George which, like Government House in Calcutta, was a classical building, was designed and built by an officer of the Royal Engineers. Just as Chowringhee runs by the side of the Maidan so the Liston, a beautiful arcaded thoroughfare designed by Matthew Lesseps, father of the man who cut the Suez Canal, with its cafes and fashionable shops, fronts the Esplanade. As on the Maidan, cricket matches took place on the Esplanade and in both places statues of famous dignitaries dotted the dusty terrain. Just as the Bengal Club was near the Maidan so, not many yards from the Esplanade, was the elegant Venetian building of the Reading Club. Behind Chowringhee stretched away the immense expanses of lanes and busties of the native town as behind the Liston lay the crowded, picturesque, winding streets of Old Corfu. The forest of masts and spars at Kidderpore Docks was not unlike the bustling quays of Corfu Harbour. In both places, religion was a powerful influence and, allowing for vast differences of creed, the worship of the Goddess Kali at Kalighat could be paralleled by the devotion paid to the mummified remains of St. Spiridon in the church dedicated to him. Perhaps it seemed so to the Corfiots of Calcutta and in particular to the members of the Nicachi family whose lives were closely connected with both places.

On May 17, 1854, while Britain was in the throes of the Crimean War, the Foreign Office issued passport No. 11545 which, in its customary dignity of language, declared "We George William Frederick, Earl of Clarendon, Baron Hyde of Hindon, a Peer of the United Kingdom of Great Britain and Ireland, a Member of Her Britannic Majesty's Most Honourable Privy Council, Knight of the Most Noble Order of the Garter, and Knight Cross of the Most Honourable Order of the Bath, Her Majesty's Principal Secretary of State for Foreign Affairs requests and requires in the name of Her Majesty all those who it may concern to allow Mr Constantine Nicachi (British Subject), a native of Corfu, going to Corfu, by way of Paris, to pass freely without let or hindrance and to afford him every assistance and protection of which he may stand in need". Creased and stained by use and age, bearing the lines of folding, this passport still exists today in the possession of Constantine's descendants.

The man for whom it was issued was one of twelve sons of a relatively prosperous businessman and landowner of Corfu, Panioti Nicachi. Like many Corfiots, he owned olive orchards and vineyards and his business prospered under British rule. The story of Constantine which follows was written down, the paper now yellow with age and the ink fading, by his son some seventy years later in Bangalore. Panioti Nicachi decided that his son Constantine should become a doctor. One of the complaints of Corfiots was that the British administration would not employ Corfiots in the higher echelons of service so that the only careers open to young Corfiots was in medicine or law. Corfu had no School of Medicine so Panioti decided to send his son to Paris to obtain a medical qualification. Constantine began his studies but some time later decided that a doctor's life was not for him and told his father that he wanted to emigrate to Australia.

Precisely why he wished to do this is unknown. We know, however, from an official correspondence of 1852 that a certain Charles Pridham in Corfu, researching for materials on colonial history, suggested to the Lord High Commissioner that the administration should endeavour to encourage the emigration of Ionians to New South Wales. The idea was rejected on the grounds that

145

the modern Greek race was totally averse to the idea of distant colonization because of their deep attachment to their native land. When we consider the presence in Bengal at this date of many Greek merchants and their families and the huge number of expatriate Greeks all over the world today, it is clear that the Lord High Commissioner had misread the situation. However, emigration to Australia was an idea that seemed to be circulating in Corfu in 1852 and so it is not surprising that an adventurous young Greek should have been influenced by it. Panioti Nicachi did not think much of the idea and vetoed it. Constantine persisted and a rift between father and son opened which was probably never healed in their lifetime.

It would seem as if Constantine's presence in London in 1854 was to enquire into the possibilities of emigration, but it was not until 1857 that he finally left Corfu and came to London to leave for the distant shores of Australia. Sometime early in 1857 he booked a passage on a sailing ship the 'Hylton Grove'. No details of the voyage have survived except for the fact that the vessel was wrecked off Penang. Crew and passengers took to the long boats in one of which Constantine found himself with eleven other members of the crew. After some days the scanty provisions had been consumed and the sailors, crazed with hunger, wanted to kill and eat a young cabin boy. Constantine wielded a six-chambered revolver to hold off the sailors, declaring that the only just course was to draw lots to decide who must be the unfortunate victim. Incredibly, not long after this incident, their boat was sighted by H.M. Steamer Simoom, bound for Calcutta. It picked up the survivors and landed them in Calcutta in October 1857. This extraordinary story was related by Constantine's son but two entries in the Bengal Directory of 1858 confirm it in part: "October 1857. H.M. Steamer Simoom from Penang berthed in Calcutta with survivors of the wreck of 'The Hylton Grove', wrecked off Penang" and the mention of Constantine's arrival in Calcutta though his name is misspelt.

He arrived there in the fateful year of the Mutiny. When he landed the worst dangers were over. Delhi had been retaken in September and Sir Colin Campbell's army was marching to the final relief of Lucknow. The 'Mutiny Panic' in Calcutta was a thing of the past, and while the outcome of the struggle was still awaited with anxiety, it seemed now that the Sepoy Rebellion would be crushed. But John Company's rule in India was moving to its close. In one other respect Constantine had arrived at an auspicious time, for by 1852 the Greek firms of Ralli Brothers, Ralli and Mavrojani and Schlizzi and Co. had established themselves in the city and he was, eventually, to find employment with the last named. He seems to have abandoned his original idea of going to Australia and took up employment in the Calcutta Customs Service as a Customs Preventative Officer and found lodgings at 11 Weston's Lane, an old street named after Charles Weston who was born in Calcutta in 1731, made a fortune in business and served as a juror at the trial of Nandkumar. There is a very old sepia photograph

146

of Constantine taken at this time which shows a short, burly, square-faced man with muttonchop whiskers, staring rather aggressively into the camera, dressed in a uniform that resembles that of an early London Peeler with a large top hat held firmly in his right hand. He was reputed to be a man of prodigious strength who could lift a sack of jute off the floor with his teeth.

In 1859 he moved to 26 Amratollah Street, the old haunt of Calcutta Greeks, and lodged with a descendant of Alexios Argyree, Demetrius Panioty who was Head Clerk in the Viceroy's Office and married to a girl of French extraction, Persine Eliza Fleury. With them lived her three brothers and her sister Maria Rose Fleury. It must have been a crowded menage but a happy one because in the next year Constantine married Maria Rose. The Fleury family, linked now with the Paniotys and Nicachis by marriage was swept into the Calcutta Greek social circle.

This family had connections with India which went back to the end of the 18th century when Jacques Fleury arrived in Calcutta in 1782. He was born at Saint Valery in Normandy in 1763 and, before his arrival in India, lived at the little town of Saint Pierre au Port, near to his birthplace in the Department of Fécamp in the District of Caux. 'Fleury' is a fairly common name in Normandy and among its holders was Cardinal Fleury, a minister of Louis XV. There were at least twenty-five Catholic priests of this name working in England at the very end of the 18th century, refugees from Revolutionary France. The name also appears in Indian Records - the death of Mons. Bertrand Fleury on September 3 1839 aged 31 years is recorded at Chandernagore and a mercenary soldier of that name served the Maratha Prince Scindia of Gwalior. It seems highly improbable, however, that any of these Fleurys were connected with Jacques. There is even a small town in Normandy which is called 'Fleury'.

In 1664 the English diarist, John Evelyn, visited Dieppe, close to Jacques' birthplace, and says that the port abounds in workmen that make and sell curiosities made of ivory and tortoiseshell and "indeed whatever the East Indies afford of Cabinets, Purcelan and natural and exotic rareties are here to be had with abundant choyce".[9] It seems probable that stories of East India trade and the fortunes to be made in India prompted the young Norman to leave his little town to emigrate to Calcutta. He was a tailor by trade and though the calling in Europe was a humble one, yet it offered opportunities of advancement in India as the Revd. James Long notes, "Tailors formerly made a rich harvest of trade at the beginning of this century (the 19th) but not so great as one Martin, who went out a tailor in the Lord Clive Indiaman in 1763. He found his trade so profitable that he refused to change it for an ensign's commission and in ten years he gave his friends a dinner served on silver plate and shortly afterwards retired to Europe with a fortune of two lacs".[20]

Jacques set up his tailoring business in China Bazaar and, like Mr Martin, seems to have prospered prodigiously for in 1805 he contributed one third of the

147

capital in and became a partner of the firm of Joseph Rondo & Co., Jewellers. Rondo was a native of Nantes who succeeded Hippolitus Poignand, watchmaker, jeweller and silversmith, as the director of a jewellery firm at 51 Theatre Street. But death, that familiar visitor to Calcutta Europeans, arrived at Jacques Fleury's door on November 15, 1806. His funeral service took place in the Portuguese Church and he was laid in Tiretta's Burial Ground in Park Street (Grave No. 11). In 1894 this cemetery was closed and finally cleared in 1977 to make way for a school. Many of the tablets were rescued by APHCI, the local Association for the Preservation of Historical Cemeteries in India (sister organization of BACSA), and removed to the South Park Cemetery where they have been re-sited in a small piazza of their own surrounded by a hedge, thanks to the generosity of the Compagnie Francaise Des Petroles.[21] Jacques Fleury's tombstone was one of those re-sited. Unfortunately, the French inscription recorded in BACSA's pamphlet on 'The French Cemetery' is incorrect and incomplete in the English translation provided. The full and correct inscription was as follows:

> Jacques Fleury. Né à Saint Vallery, Normandie, Agé de 43 ans et Mort le 15ème Novembre 1806. Il fut bon citoyen, bon Père, bon Ami, De tous les Malheureux le bienveillant Apui: sa generosité lui gagner tous les coeurs, et sa mort aujourd'hui nous fait verser des Pleurs. Calcutta. le 1er Janvier, 1807.[22]

His Will[23a] was sworn on 20 November 1806 and his friends and partners, Joseph Rondo and Nicholas Guillo, a Greek businessman of Calcutta[23b] were appointed executors. His wife is named as Joanna Rose and his son James Joseph, born on August 7, 1793, is the chief legatee of the estate which is to be managed by the executors until his son reaches the age of twenty-one. It is specifically stipulated that he is not to inherit if he contracts a marriage before this date. Other legatees are Jacques' sisters, Susanna Helen and Angelica, living at Saint Pierre au Port, and Mortais, his Bengali servant who has faithfully served him for seventeen years. Incidentally, he was owed fifty rupees by Alexander Panioty.

The inventory of his goods in 1807 makes fascinating reading and brings to life the professional and domestic establishment of a prosperous French tailor in Calcutta at the beginning of the 19th century. Among the numerous items listed are: 9 coats, 33 breeches, 39 Paris pantaloons, 37 waistcoats, 49 shirts, 30 jackets, 43 Paris stockings, 1 pair short drawers, 2 pairs slings, 4 Banyan gowns, 3 new sheets, 6 tablecloths, 2 black round hats, 15 neck handkerchiefs, 13 pieces remnants, 2 pieces white Nankeen, 20 pieces chintz, 11 pairs trousers, 1 roll cotton tapes, 1 bag button moulds, 19 Madras mats, 2 large copper stewpots with covers, 1 copper chunder, 2 copper frying pans, 1 gridiron, 6 iron spits of dogs, 2 copper mills, 4 flat irons, 7 brass and 4 tin candlesticks, 1 lot iron hooks, 6 pairs tailor's sheaves, 1 case with two razors, a pair of silverhandled scissors, 1 handsaw and 6 bits, 1 silver mounted sword, 1 swordstick with sword blade and much else including an office ink stand, a large pewter glister pipe in a box on a stand, a pipe of Madeira, 6 hogsheads of French claret, 70 dozen bottles of claret, 6 dozen bottles of brandy, 60 boxes of brandy and arrack containing 12 bottles each, 9 boxes of gin containing 15 bottles each.

His arrangements for the rearing and education of his son seem to have been faithfully carried out by his executors and there are careful accounts of the moneys spent in detailed inventories of 1809, 1811 and 1814.[24] They gave due attention to his intellectual and cultural development and paid out money for a Persian munshi, Richardson's English, Persian and Arabic Dictionary, a Music Master, Music books, a flute and a fiddle, fees to Mister Mauge, a Drawing Master and a case of red pencils. The young gentleman was clearly a keen horseman for money was paid out on a small horse with bridle and saddle, ropes and a horse blanket, iron horseshoes, a syce's wages, a jockey whip, a watering bridle, a currycomb and another pony from Messrs Gould and Campbell. He seems also to have had a penchant for a mild flutter, for money was also spent on a lottery ticket, and half lottery tickets bought from Mr De La Nougerede and from an Armenian, Arratoon Gaspar. There were miscellaneous items of expenditure for repair of a watch, a Savigny penknife, a box of fireworks, a Europe mahogany chest of drawers and fringes for a cot. The largest number of items of expenditure, however, were in the sartorial line - cloth for a jacket, waistcoat and pantaloons, velvet jacket and buttons, a pair of silk stockings and a hat, Nankeens, a pair of Europe shoes, a neck cloth, pieces of Madras handkerchiefs, Bengal stockings, a piece of fine Madras longcloth, a piece of Chandernagore longcloth, a looking glass from Messrs. Patterson and Company, a pair of yellow leather shoes and cotton gloves. Joseph Rondo and Nicholas Guillo seem to have carried out their duties in an efficient and not unimaginative manner. The former died in 1846 and was buried, like Jacques Fleury, in Tiretta's Burial Ground (Grave No. 23) with the following inscription:

Ce git Joseph Rondo, né a Couen près de Nantes le 30 Novembre 1767, Mort a Calcutta le 13 Novm, 1846. Il eut des vertus qu'il n'afflicha pas les défauts. Il chercha à seu corriger mais non à les cacher. Sa veuve eplarie a voulu laisser ici ce faible echos des sentiments vifs qui regnent dans son coeur des regrets et la reconnoissance.[25]

The young man for whom all this trouble was taken, James Joseph Fleury, married a Miss N. Paul on November 27, 1822, in Calcutta. It is possible that she belonged to a Greek family as there was a Greek merchant at Muttra called George Paul who died in 1822. James Joseph became a bookseller in Cositollah and is listed as such between 1824 and 1835 and then a printer of books in the Chitpore Road. Perhaps, after all, the money spent on a Persian munshi and an English-Persian-Arabic grammar had not been wasted. His mother, Joanna Rose, died in Calcutta on May 1, 1840, aged 60 years. He and his wife had at least six children, five sons, John Joseph, James, Lewis Charles, Peter, and two daughters, Persine Eliza and Maria Rose who married respectively Demetrius Panioty and Constantine Nicachi.

John Joseph, born in 1823, entered the Bengal Unconvenanted Service and spent his working life in the Mint which he entered in his eighteenth year, working as an Assistant Accountant, first on the Mint Committee and finally in the English Office of the Mint. He died on January 21, 1850, aged twenty-six. James Fleury worked as an auction dealer and commission agent in Calcutta from 1852 to 1862. In the latter year he became an assistant in the Greek firm of Argenti Sechiari and stayed with them till 1874 when he joined his sister in a commercial business, Nicachi & Co., founded by his brother-in-law Constantine Nicachi. His brother Lewis Charles, born in 1832, began as a teacher in Mr Montague's Academy in Armenian Street but in 1857 joined the Bengal Secretariat as an Uncovenanted Civil Servant in the Judicial Department where he spent the rest of his working life. The last brother, Peter W. Fleury, was a qualified engineer who worked for Jessop & Co., Founders, from 1855 to 1858, for the Goosery Rum Distillery from 1858 to 1864, was engineer, proprietor and architect of the Steam Soorkey Works and Iron Foundry from 1865 to 1866, and in 1868 founded the firm of P.W. Fleury & Co., 93 Lower Circular Road, housebuilders, electrical engineers, scientific instrument makers and contractors for electric light illuminations. In this last capacity he earned himself a modest niche in the history of Calcutta as the first person to demonstrate to the people of that city the marvel of electric lighting on July 24, 1879. 'The Statesman' of July 28 that year carried the following report: "Mr Fleury of P.W. Fleury & Co personally exhibited to a wondering crowd on Saturday evening one of the latest scientific wonders of the day - the electric light........ The new dynamo electric light apparatus is constructed on a totally different principle from the usual old-fashioned electric light apparatus in which the electric currents used to be generated, for a few hours only, by chemical decomposition and the use of expensive acids. The present machine consists of a steam engine, which imparts a rotary motion to a coil of wires in close proximity to magnets or metallic pieces, owing to which a current of electricity is generated..... at a distance of about 1,500 feet we could distinctly read a prayer-book in Brevier print. Lamps for interior illumination are also provided with reflectors for projecting the light to the ceiling - thus softening the rays of light. Mr Fleury deserves great credit for his enterprising disposition, and we would be glad to hear his efforts have met with the encouragement they deserve."

It did not take long for Constantine Nicachi to realise that he could do better for himself in the world of commerce. In 1861 he became an assistant at Schlizzi & Co. (London, Manchester and Continental Agents), the Greek firm with offices in New China Bazaar. He was, in fact, the only European assistant with M. F. Paspati and N. P. Caridia as managers until in 1864 the firm took on another assistant, J. P. Schlizzi, and in 1866 a third, F. Yakinthes. Constantine remained with the firm until it ceased trading in Calcutta in 1873. A few years previously he had moved from Weston's Lane to 19 Hill's Lane. It is probable that he had a notion, some time before the event took place, that Schlizzi & Co. were going to close their Calcutta branch and that he would like to set up in business on his own. It was a daring venture because the days of the lone Greek trader had long since passed away and Greek business in Calcutta was more and more dominated by the expanding London-based firms. It must have taken character, determination and nerve to establish the new firm of 'Nicachi & Co.', London and Shipping Agents at 101 New China Bazaar. To do this he went into partnership with two Bengali businessmen, Kistohurry Gupta and Koylas Chunder Bannerji, and received a loan of three thousand rupees from his friend and brother-in-law by marriage, Demetrius Panioty. The new firm had only just come into being when the cruel irony of sudden death overtook him in November 1873 - "made my square ship within a league of shore, Alas! To be entombed in seas and seen no more".

Probate of his Will - made on November 1, 1873, when death was fast approaching - was granted to his widow, Maria Rose, her brother Lewis Fleury and a Greek, Theodore Andrew Sypsomo, on January 7th, 1874. He bequeathed his household furniture, books, carriages and horses, plate, jewels and all his household goods to his "beloved wife". To his daughter Ellene Catherine his piano, to his son Menculaus Panioty his gold watch and gold pencil case. His loan from Demetrius Panioty is to be repaid and Rs 500 to Makim Sirdar. His business partners are asked to decide whether they will permit his wife to continue in partnership with them; if they refuse she is entitled to carry on the business of Nicachi & Co. on her own. The rest of his estate is to be sold and invested in Calcutta Municipal Debentures or in house property in Calcutta, the interest and proceeds of which are to be used for the upkeep of his family and the education of his daughter and son. On the death of his wife the estate is to be equally divided between his two children and the executors are empowered to pay the expenses of his daughter's wedding to the extent to which his wife deems reasonable. The cash value of the estate is estimated at Rs 12,000 and Administration of the Will after the death of his wife was granted on August 3, 1895, in favour of the children, the sureties being Philip Nicachi (nephew of Constantine) and Theophilus Lucas. The Inventory of the Will in 1878 records that the administrators had paid the profits of Nicachi & Co. to his widow, the expenses for a burial plot to the Warden of the Greek Church, four bills for pews in St. Thomas' Catholic Church, Middleton Row, presumably his wife and children attended this church and the children were brought up as Catholics. An interesting item was two bills to Stewart & Co., carriage builders, incurred in the lifetime of the deceased. An anonymous poet of Calcutta in 1811 commemorated the founder of this firm in the lines:

Bourne on the steed,
Or perched with whips and reins
In a dear specimen of Stewart's pains.

In a footnote the poet added that Stewart's workmanship was very superior so his charges were correspondingly high. The firm was situated behind the Old Court House and remained there from 1783 to 1907. A print of 1795 attributed to Francois Balthazard Solvyns shows the front view of his premises, a splendid classical building of handsome proportions.[26] Another bill was paid to Cook & Co. for the treatment of a horse. Constantine had a one-fourth share in the Ashcroft Press Company. All in all, the impoverished castaway from the 'Hylton Grove' had not done too badly for himself in Calcutta in less than sixteen years.

His widow, Maria Rose, was surely a determined woman for she carried on the work of Nicachi & Co. Constantine's Bengali partners must have pulled out for we hear no more mention of them. In 1875 the firm moved to 58 Strand Road and was joined by Maria's brother James M. Fleury, and Angelo Ducas, both of whom were formerly employed by Argenti Sechiari. In 1878 it shifted once again to 134 Canning Street and in 1882 the management was taken over by A. Panaghulides who set up his own firm, Panaghulides & Co., at the same address while continuing to run the affairs of Nicachi & Co. In 1902 the company moved once again to 6 Old China Bazaar, in 1905 to 2 Old Court House Street and in 1910 back to its old premises at 134 Canning Street. In 1912 it ceased trading. As a small firm it did fairly well in an age dominated by the great London-based Greek commercial giants and it might have done better if it had not been deprived of the direction of its founder at its very inception. Maria Rose died in 1895. Her obituary card simply states "In loving memory of Maria Rose Nicachi, widow of Constantine Nicachi; Died on 2nd July, 1895 aged 58 years, 1 month and 24 days. Requiescat in Pace". She was born on May 8th, 1837. This and an old photograph of her with her small son and young daughter are all that survives of her memory.

In 1882 Panioty Stephen Nicachi, nephew of Constantine and son of his brother Stephanos, came out to Calcutta from Corfu to join Ralli and Mavrojani at 68 Clive Street. He took lodgings with his uncle's widow at 45 Elliot Road. This thoroughfare was named after John Elliot of the Bengal Civil Service who, as Chief of Police, was a great suppressor of dacoits in Calcutta in the early part of the 19th century. His fame was recorded in a contemporary song:

> Here's a health to the jolly dacoits,
> Who are hung in the Law's fatal chair!
> Here's a health to John Elliot
> Whose daring exploits I shall not witness again.

Elliot died in 1818 and a handsome monument was erected to his memory in North Park Street Burial Ground. At 45 Elliot Road the newcomer from Corfu met his first cousin Ellene Nicachi (born circa 1861) and they married shortly afterwards.

Panioty Stephen Nicachi, commonly known to his family and friends as 'Pano', was born in Corfu in 1855 and was therefore twenty-seven years old when he arrived in Calcutta. He was reputed to be a sharp, crafty man with a nose for a good deal and somewhat ruthless in his personal and business relations. When Ralli and Mavrojani ceased trading in 1886 he transferred briefly to F. C. Pallachi & Co. at 13-14 New China Bazaar and the next year joined Ralli Brothers to work for them until 1907. During this period he and his wife lived from 1890 to 1893 at 32 McLeod Street which was named after Lt. Col. K McLeod of the I.M.S. who served in Calcutta from 1879 to 1884. From 1893-95 they were at 9 Clive Row and from 1895-96 at 31 Royd Street. This street-name commemorated Sir John Royd, Puisne Judge of the Supreme Court from 1787-1816, who died in 1817 and was interred in the South Park Street Burial Ground. It was famous for its boarding houses run by Anglo-Indian ladies and it was, presumably, at one of these that Pano and his wife lodged. In 1896 they were at 1 Mission Row and in 1898 at 5 Chowringhee Lane and in 1903 at 1 Theatre Road, which ran from Chowringhee to Lower Circular Road and was named after the old Chowringhee Theatre which burnt to the ground in 1839. The constant shifting of residences that seemed to be quite usual with most Greeks in Calcutta suggests that they lived in boarding houses rather than rented accommodation.

Pano and Ellene had three children: Marie born in 1888, Stephania Theresia born on 31st July, 1894 and Stephen Constantine born on October 3, 1896. They were all baptized in the Greek Church but in 1909 the two girls were received into the Catholic Church probably through the influence of their mother, and the ceremony was performed at St. Thomas' Church, Middleton Row. Of the three children Marie had the most interesting life. She grew up to be an exceptionally gifted professional violinist whose performances were remembered by many Europeans in Calcutta long after she had left the city. A copy of the programme for one of her concerts reads "Miss Marie Nicachi's Concert in aid of the sufferers in the Messina Disaster on Saturday, 13th February, 1909, at the Grand Opera House". In addition to her solo performances on that occasion, she conducted an orchestra in which four other Nicachis took part - her cousin Ione Nicachi with the violin, Mrs Philip Nicachi, a relation by marriage, at the piano, her sister Stephania on the cello and another cousin Zoe Nicachi in the chorus. Two other ladies in the orchestra, Miss D. Klemis and Miss D. Manuel, and one gentleman, Mr D. Mangos, were also from Greek families in Calcutta.

Shortly after this event Pano and his family left India for good. Like Mozart's father, he was determined to play impresario to his daughter's talent and had arranged a concert tour in the leading cities of Europe. Unfortunately, a detailed account of her itinerary has not survived but she played in Vienna before the Emperor Franz Joseph and became engaged to a young officer in the Austro-Hungarian Army. At St. Petersburg, after a performance before Czar Nicholas II and his Czarina, she curtsied as the sovereign approached her. Gently, he raised

153

her up and said "After such divine playing it is I who ought to honour you with obeisance". This moment of glory amidst the roccoco splendours of the Winter Palace was the highlight of the musical career of the Greek girl from Calcutta. In 1914 the lights went out all over Europe and Pano took his family to Corfu. His financial position must have been fairly sound for he retired from work and never returned to India. His wife Ellene died on January 1, 1918, in Corfu and is buried in the Catholic Cemetery just outside Corfu Town. Pano lived on till 1931, dying at the age of seventy-six. One can imagine him sitting at a cafe on the Liston with a glass of wine or ouzo regaling his friends with stories of Calcutta and the glittering experiences of Vienna and St. Petersburg. Marie spent the rest of her life in Corfu and continued with her violin recitals. Some of the older residents in Corfu Town vividly remember her concerts in the splendid neo-classical Opera House, tragically destroyed by German bombs in the second World War. When she had finished playing the shouts of acclamation from the audience nearly lifted the roof and pigeons were released in the auditorium in enthusiastic appreciation. A Greek lady who knew her well in those days said of her "She was so impractical that she couldn't boil an egg but she handled her violin like one of God's angels". Her Austrian fiancé was killed in the War and she never married. Her brother Stephen was educated at the Jesuit Public School, Beaumont, near Windsor, fought in the trenches in France where he was gassed and suffered from frail health ever afterwards. After the war he became a foreign correspondent on 'The New York Times' and eventually retired to England to live in Welwyn Garden City. Nothing more is known of her sister Stephania after the family left India.

Pano had a younger brother, Alexandros Stephanos Nicachi, who was born in 1867 and was always known in the family as 'Dandy'. He was thirty-three years old when he followed his brother to Calcutta and began work in Petrocochino Bros. at 23 Canning Street and stayed with the firm until 1922 when he returned to Corfu. Like Pano he shifted from one boarding house to another: 49 Chowringhee Road (1900), 23 Canning Street (1902), 1 Lower Circular Road (1903), 7 Hungerford Street (1906), 13 Theatre Road (1908), 4 Moira Street (1910), the Continental Hotel (1911), 15 Elysium Row (1912), 20 Alexandra Court (1921) and the Grand Hotel (1922). Hungerford Street was named after the Marquis of Hastings, Governor-General (1813-1823), one of whose titles was Baron Hungerford, and Moira Street after the same man who was Earl of Moira before he became Marquis of Hastings. Elysium Row may have been so named because it contained an old cemetery. The Continental Hotel in Chowringhee Place incorporated an old house which, at one time, was occupied by Colonel Searle, the father of two pretty girls who captivated the hearts of many bachelors in Victorian Calcutta. It was eclipsed in grandeur by its competitor, the Grand Hotel, built on the site of three boarding houses kept by a Mrs Monk. It had a long foyer lined with shops leading into its shady interior, cooled by fans and excluding the perpetual din of traffic along crowded and noisy Chowringhee.

Dandy died in Corfu in 1942 when the Second World War had begun to disturb the tranquillity of the Island. He was 75 years old.

Dandy's cousin Philip Nicachi, son of Demetrius, a brother of Constantine and Stephen, was two years older than him and preceded him in Calcutta by several years. He began work at Petrocochino Bros., 4 Clive Ghat Street, in 1886 and worked for the firm until 1925 with a short break in 1908 as manager of the Societa Anomina Coloniale di Trieste, an Austrian firm which was the agent of the Austro-Indian Jute Mill. He married Myra Phillips in Calcutta, twenty years younger than himself, and like his cousins Pano and Dandy made the round of boarding houses and hotels: with his relations Maria Rose and Pano at 91 Dhuramtollah Street, then 38 Maitland Street (1888), 35 McLeod Street (1890), 49 Park Street, Miss Bobonau's Boarding Establishment (1893), 1 Theatre Road, Mme. Couret's Boarding Establishment (1899), 6 Hungerford Street (1906), 231 Lower Circular Road (1907), 13 Theatre Road (1908) and the Grand Hotel from 1911 to 1925. In the dank, steamy hot-weather days Philip often promised Myra that they would soon retire to "the heaven of Corfu" and in 1925 the dream came true.

They rented a handsome house with tall, white-shuttered windows and a delicate wrought-iron balcony hanging over the imposing front door with steps leading up from the lovely tree-lined Mitripol Athanasiou near the Douglas Column, erected to the memory of a British High Commissioner, Sir Howard Douglas, overlooking the calm waters of Garitsa Bay. On the death of Pano in 1931, Philip and Myra were joined by Marie. In 1929, when he was sixty-four and she forty-four, they had a daughter whom they christened 'Marietta'. They had a pleasant holiday home in the village of Magoulades in the northwest of the Island, not far from the entrancingly beautiful beach of Paleocastritsa with its blue waters and an old monastery perched on a rock looking out to sea. In 1935 this idyllic life came to an end when Philip died suddenly of a heart attack, leaving his financial affairs in some disorder. Myra, her daughter and Marie had to give up the grand house in Mitripol Athanasiou for a humbler dwelling in Corfu Town, living in genteel poverty which war conditions and the occupation of Corfu, first by the Italians and then the Germans, made worse. Marietta, always a sickly child, died from pleurisy at the age of fourteen in 1943 and the two older women went on living, bearing their grief, according to their Corfiot friends, with old-fashioned dignity.

In the last years of her life Marie was rather a disconsolate figure living in a small flat above a jeweller's shop at 30 Filarmonikes Street in the shadow of St. Spiridon's Church, talking to her friends of the great, happy days of the past, re-living her former triumphs, worrying about the health of her brother Stephen in England and remembering Calcutta. She died on April 13, 1968, and was buried in the same grave as her mother in the Catholic Cemetery of Corfu on the right hand side of its tree-lined central avenue with a simple tombstone in Greek:

Elene Nicachi 1 January 1918,
Marie Nicachi, her daughter 13 April 1968.

A Latin cross is erected above the stone. She was eighty years old. Myra lived on till 1972 and was eighty-seven when she died. She never learnt to speak Greek properly but seems to have been the last survivor of Stephanos Nicachi's family in Corfu Town.

In the small Greek Orthodox Churchyard of St. Spiridon in Magaritti Street on the edge of Corfu Town is the family grave of Stephanos Nicachi. According to the burial records of the Church the following persons were buried in it:-

Maria Nicachi, wife of Stephanos Nicachi. b. 1831 d. 1880.
Stephanos Nicachi b. 1832 d. 1894.
Victoria Nicachi, daughter of Stephanos. b. 1879 d. 1894.
Elene Nicachi, daughter of Stephanos. b. 1858 d. 1905.
Panaoitis Stephanos Nicachi, son of Stephanos. b. 1855 d. 1931. Philipos Nicachi, son of Demetrius Nicachi. b. 1865 d. 1935 Alexandros Nicachi, son of Stephanos. b. 1867 d. 1942.
Myra Nicachi, wife of Philip Nicachi. b. 1885 d. 1972.

Above the grave is a tall stone cross, whose point of intersection bears a stone wreath, mounted on a plinth, which carries the simple inscription in Greek: "The family tomb of Stephanos Nicachi." Around it are short stone posts enclosing the grave which is to the left as one enters the cemetery from the road. One cannot help feeling a pang of sadness to reflect that all that hustling activity in Bengal, all those voyages overseas, journeys in the sun, and work endured under brazen Indian skies is now reduced to a handful of dust in a remote cemetery on the edge of Corfu Town.

"Home is the sailor, home from the sea,
And the hunter home from the hill".

Not far away is a small stone cross simply engraved 'Marietta Nicachi'. The little Anglo-Greek girl sleeps alone.

Constantine's son, Menelaus Panioty Nicachi, was born on June 3rd, 1863, at 17 Joratallao Street. In 1892 he began work with Ralli Brothers and stayed with them until 1910 when he transferred to the French firm of Louis Dreyfus (the same family from which Captain Dreyfus, falsely accused of espionage for Germany in the 1890s, came). A photograph of him reveals a good-looking short young man with luxuriant moustaches, looking thoughtful and leaning on a table. On November 15, 1886, he married Ione Panioty, the niece of his father's friend, Demetrius Panioty, thus linking the old Greek family of Bengal with the newcomer from Corfu. They were twenty-three and twenty-two years old respectively. The marriage took place in his parish church, St. Thomas',

Middleton Row, because he was, like his mother and sister, a Roman Catholic though the bride's family was still Greek Orthodox. One of the witnesses of the marriage who signed the register was Ione's cousin Constantine Panioty who later became a Judge in the High Court. Their married life seems to have been lived almost wholly in Elliot Road but not at the same house. They started in the Nicachi-Fleury family home at No. 45, moving from there to 45 Cockburn's Lane in 1899, back to 50 Elliot Road in 1903, to 32 in 1905 and to 42 in 1907. In 1910, Menelaus purchased 92 Elliot Road, a large house with an extensive garden, which he named 'Ionian Villa'. Next door to it he built 'Ellene Villa'. From the former his eldest daughter and his son were married and in it his grandchildren were born. In 1924 he sold both properties and retired to Bangalore with his wife, two daughters and one of his grandsons. The properties were eventually bought by the Loretto Order of Nuns (in which Mother Teresa began her Religious life in Calcutta) who turned it into a girls' school which continues to this day.

The Bangalore to which he went was a haven for retired Domiciled Europeans and Anglo-Indians. In the 1870s Lear wrote of it "This station is very extensive and populous and seems in some ways the pleasantest I have known in India. A sort of homely quiet pervades everything and the air is delightful, ditto the flowers."[27] He lived with his family at 1 Stewart Road in Langford Town and later at 2 Prime Street, Richmond Town. These were houses of a type almost peculiar to this station in India. Apparently inspired by the Gothic revival in Europe, they were "romantic buildings with steeply-pitched roofs of Bangalore tiles often culminating in a row of intricate ridged tiles; the gables carry plaster motifs and, against the skyline, a number of decorative urns; the balustrades have become battlements or have taken even more elaborate forms; the corners of the buildings have occasionally become towers with pitched roofs or castellations, and cast-iron appears, used for railings, pillars and brackets. Most distinctive of all - almost the trade mark of buildings constructed between the 1880s and the 1930s - is the monkey top, a pointed hood over the upper part of the window".[28] In 1929 Menelaus moved to 3 André Road, Langford Town, a pleasant rural place on the edge of the Cantonment. Here his wife Ione died on February 24, 1933, and was buried in the Catholic section of the Hosur Road Cemetery. He and his remaining family moved back to Richmond Town and in 1936 he bought 3 Rose Lane, a house with a very large garden, part of which he used to build 3a Rose Lane. He seems to have had an urge to build new houses on any land surplus to his immediate needs.

In his last years as a widower he became a well-known social character in the Cantonment; an active member of the Bowring Club, an inveterate lover of the cinema (he went regularly twice or three times a week), a connoisseur of good food and wine, an expert maker of Christmas cakes, a dedicated whist player and a genial host. In appearance he was bald-headed, bold-eyed, sporting a magnificent pair of curled white moustaches. He had an infectious laugh but an uncertain temper. He was touchily proud of his name and race and once, at an auction, after he had made a successful bid, the auctioneer asked him for his name. When he gave it a gentleman standing near him tittered. Menelaus swung fiercely on him "What's your name Sir?" he enquired. The poor man quailed and answered meekly "Rolfe", to which came the unanswerable but untruthful rejoinder, "In my language your name means 'monkey'." Every evening he drove out in his phaeton, after having carefully selected from his garden a rose for his buttonhole. He died on May 12th, 1941, and is buried near his wife. The only material possession of his which his descendants still possess is a handsome Sheffield Close Plate tankard. He was never a beer-drinker so it must have belonged to his father, Constantine.

Menelaus Panioty Nicachi, grandfather of the author, in Bangalore

Menelaus' eldest daughter Ione married Vincent Adair De la Nougerede who was descended from a French family which arrived in India, like the Fleurys, in the late 18th century. On 18th August, 1781, Louis De la Nougerede petitioned Warren Hastings to allow him to remain in Bengal. He had been dismissed from the Paymaster-General's Office and threatened with expulsion from Bengal because he was a subject of the French King. Louis pointed out that, though his father was French, he had been brought up under the British flag. Fortunately, Hastings granted his petition. Vincent was an old boy of St. Joseph's College, Bangalore, a fine cricketer, a Captain in the Bangalore Rifle Volunteers and became an executive officer in the Bengal Nagpur Railway. Most of his service was in the Central Provinces and a photograph taken there shows Ione posing before the body of a leopard she had shot on shikar. They had no children and Ione died in 1935.

Ione's brother, John Constantine Nicachi, was born in 1896 and educated at St. Xavier's College, Calcutta, and North Point School in Darjeeling. A photograph taken of him when he was five years old shows him dressed in the costume of a Greek Evzone, the kilted warriors who formed the bodyguard of the Greek Royal Family. It was brought to India by Constantine and John Constantine's children, Paul and Marina, were also photographed in it as young children and it is still in the possession of the family. When war broke out in 1914 he was commissioned in the Royal Engineers after training at Sabathu, near Simla, and saw service in Mesopotamia. After the war he became engaged to an English girl, Alice Elizabeth Davis, in London. She came out to India and they were married at St. Thomas' Church in Calcutta on January 22, 1922. He relinquished his active commission on May 1st, 1922, but retained the rank of Lieutenant in the Indian Army Reserve of Officers. He had two sons by his first marriage, Paul Byron and Peter Mario. The first served in the Hampshire Regiment and as an Emergency Commissioned Officer in the 7th Rajput Regiment during the second World War and the second in the New Zealand Army after the War. In 1930 John Constantine divorced his first wife and in 1937 married a Dublin girl, Dorothea Eleanor Yoakley, whom he met in England. They had one daughter, Marina, who became a Sister of St. Joseph in New Zealand. After the First World War he had joined the East India Railway, retired in 1948 and emigrated to New Zealand. Before he and his wife left India they were presented with an address from the Railway Colony in Howrah in which Dorothea (Paddy Nicachi) was described as 'the Florence Nightingale of Howrah'. As a trained nurse she was often called upon to deal with emergency cases in the Railway Colony and was unsparing of her time and devotion. She died, a comparatively young woman, at Point Chevalier, Auckland, on July 25th, 1952, victim of multiple sclerosis. Some years later John Constantine married a Yugoslav lady, Klelia Commerato, and outlived this third wife who died in 1970. Due to complicated family reasons he changed his name from Nicachi to 'Norris' and became a New Zealand citizen. His last years were spent in a nursing home run by the Little Sisters of the Poor. He died in Auckland and is buried in the Waikumete Cemetery. The inscription on his tombstone is:

In loving memory of John Constantine Norris. Loved father of Paul, Peter and Marina. Died 11th Jan. 1973. Aged 76. R.I.P.

His second and third wives are buried near him:

Norris.

In loving memory of

Dorothea	Klelia
Beloved wife	Beloved wife
of John.	of John.
Died 25th July	Died 1st July
1952. Aged 43 years.	1970 in her 67th year.

Menelaus' second daughter was Zoe born in 1890. In her eighteenth year she suffered a paralytic stroke and for the rest of her life she was a semi-invalid living with her family until she died in her sister's home in Calcutta in 1968 and was buried at Bhowanipore.

The youngest daughter, Ellene, born on August 4, 1904, became a qualified Music and Singing teacher and taught at Bishop Cotton Girls' School and Baldwin Girls' School in Bangalore for many years. She married Arnold Munro of the Netherlands Indies Bank and lived in Calcutta at Park Circus from 1939 until her death at St. Catherine's Nursing Home, Kidderpore, on August 16, 1989, and was buried in the Lower Circular Road Cemetery. She had no children. On that day the last link of the Nicachi family with India was severed.

John Constantine Nicachi, father of the author, as a Lieutenant in World War I

References: Chapter Nine

1. *The Venetian Empire*, Jan Morris (Penguin, 1980) p137
2. *Corfu*, Margaret Hopkins (Batsford, 1977) p36
3. Sir Howard Douglas, quoted in *Britain's Greek Empire*
4. *Ibid.* p104
5. *Ibid.* p108
6. Hopkins op. cit. p51
7. Pratt op. cit. p110
8. Hopkins op. cit. pp55-56
9. *Greek Mercantile Marine*, op. cit. p388
10. *The Men Who Ruled India*, P Mason (Guild Publishing, 1985) p145
11. Pratt op. cit. p112
12. *Ibid.* p113
13. *Ibid.* p115
14. Bengal Obituary p11
15. *Bengal Past and Present* XLV (1933) p76
16. *Rambling Recollections*, Sir H Drummond-Wolfe (MacMillan, 1906) p366
17. P. R. O. Kew
18. *Edward Lear's Indian Journal*, Ed. Ray Murphy (Jarrods, 1953)
19. *The Diary of John Evelyn*, Ed. John Bowle (O. U. P. 1985) p39
20. *Calcutta and its Neighbourhood - history of Calcutta and its peoples from 1690-1857*, Rev James Long (1860) republished Calcutta Indian Publications 1974
21. *French Cemetery, Park Street, Calcutta*, BACSA (1983)
22. *Complete Monumental Register of Churches and Burial Grounds in and about Calcutta*, M Derozario (Calcutta, 1815)
23a. Bengal Wills I. O. R.
23b. *The Makers of Indian Colonial Silver*, Wynyard R T Wilkinson (London, 1987) p174
24. Bengal Inventories 1809 (Vol I), 1811 (Vol II), 1814 (Vol I) I. O. R.
25. *French Cemetery, Park Street*, op. cit.
26. *Calcutta, City of Palaces*, J P Losty (The British Library, 1990) plate 10
27. *Lear's Indian Journal*, op. cit. pp176-177
28. *Monkey Tops*, Elizabeth Staley (Tara Books, 1981) p13

10

The Paniotys: The Last Act

Give me the word and I'll attempt it well.
(Hilaire Belloc)

Towards the middle of the 19th century the Greek community in Bengal began to experience a crisis of identity. Since their forefathers had made the decision not to return to their fatherland and to settle in India, their descendants began naturally enough to lose close touch with their cultural heritage. All around them was the infrastructure of British Imperial rule which exerted a powerful, anglicising influence and, more subtly in its operation, did the sights, sounds, speech and customs of the indigenous inhabitants of Bengal. The impact of India influenced all Europeans who lived there but it was bound to bear more heavily on those who had lost immediate contact with their original culture. The one institution that might have preserved their Hellenism intact was the Greek Orthodox Church but its presence in Bengal was too circumscribed to effect this purpose - there were never more than two churches in Bengal. Greek marriages with Europeans from other religious traditions led inexorably to the abandonment of Orthodoxy by the children of these marriages to the benefit of Roman Catholicism and, to a lesser extent, of the Church of England.

The original impetus of trade and the social grouping of Greek families in Dacca which was its result, was running down with the decline of the economic importance of the city. There was a movement away from Dacca to Calcutta and other places as individuals looked for employment outside trade. Broadly speaking, two fields of work lay open to them - in the new Greek commercial firms like Ralli Brothers and in, what Bishop Heber described as, "the subaltern positions in government". The relative poverty and social insignificance of most of these men ensured that they could only aspire to the Uncovenanted ranks of Government service. The descendants of the old Greeks were becoming part of the Domiciled European and Anglo-Indian community of Bengal, inheriting all the disadvantages, social and professional, from which it suffered.

These alternatives of employment were experienced by the sons of Emmanuel Panioty in Calcutta. Emmanuel was the son of a Greek merchant of Dacca, John Panioty, who was the grandson of Alexios Argyree Panaghiotis. Emmanuel left Dacca in the 1820s to qualify as a solicitor and then practised in Calcutta. His elder brother, Constantine, also left Dacca about the same time to obtain employment in Calcutta with the commercial firm, Eglinton McClure.

Emmanuel had two sons, Nicholas born in 1829 and Demetrius born in 1830. Both obtained employment in the Bengal Secretariat as Writers on October 8, 1849, at the lowly salary of Rs 40. In the dingy, high-ceilinged rooms worked a legion of sweating clerks at long, shabby tables, piled high with the sacred files in which transactions of the administration were meticulously recorded. The work was dull and formal and all day long the clerks were metaphorically chained like galley slaves to their desks. Papers were shifted around from one section of the building to another, always by a peon or native bearer, but never by the clerks who were not expected to carry a single sheet of paper to a colleague in another section. If papers needed to be transferred, the Filing Clerk entered a record of them in his book and the file, tied with faded pink ribbon, was taken by a peon to its destination in some other corridor of this clerical labyrinth.

In 1853 Demetrius made two important decisions - he married Persine Elisa Fleury and he obtained a transfer on January 25 from the Bengal Secretariat to the Durbar Department of the Private Secretary's Office at a salary of Rs 150. Henceforth his clerkly labours would be concerned not with the internal administration of Bengal but with the Governor-General's administration of all the Company's territories in India, its relations with the client Indian princes, his correspondence with the Directors in Leadenhall Street and with the conduct of foreign policy. Not only would the work have been more interesting but it provided a larger stage for the professional advancement of an ambitious and able young man. He must have been efficient and hardworking for in less than three years he was appointed Head Clerk.

During his early working years the master he served was the Marquis of Dalhousie, Governor-General from 1848 to 1856, one of the most able and energetic holders of this office. He vastly increased the territory under Company rule by annexing Pegu, the Punjab, Nagpur, Oudh, Satara, Jhansi and Berar, planned and commenced railways, laid telegraphs, built roads and canals, developed trade and agriculture, forestry and mining, improved the postal service and took energetic action against thugee, suttee and female infanticide. All this activity must have impinged on the work of the Bengal Secretariat and the Durbar Department of the Private Secretary's Office, so that by 1856 the young Head Clerk must have had a fairly extensive administrative experience of the range of problems confronting British rule in India. While he toiled away at his clerical duties in Calcutta, the Mutiny raged in the up-country lands between Delhi and Cawnpore, bringing to an end in 1858 the rule of the Company he served. It was something to be able to tell one's children that he had been Head Clerk in the Durbar Department when Queen Victoria was proclaimed Sovereign of India and the first Viceroy, Earl Canning, became his chief.

The strain of taking over the Governorship from Dalhousie at such a critical moment, of coping with the aftermath of that great man's reforming schemes and the anxieties of the Mutiny, drove Canning to work himself and his staff to the bone. He was a hard, though slow and unmethodical, worker who allowed the mahogany despatch boxes to pile up unopened. He rose at five and worked almost without intermission till dusk and therefore his meetings with his colleagues and subordinates like Demetrius had usually to take place at night. For his Private Secretary, Lewin Bentham Bowring, and the rest of the staff, it was a hard life. Canning's only recreation was to walk in the grounds of Government House where passers-by would see his solitary figure moving quickly to and fro. When he heard the news of the massacre of the women and children of Cawnpore he spent the whole night pacing up and down the Marble Hall in Government House, overwhelmed with remorse at having been unable to prevent the tragedy.

The officials who watched the arrival of the new Viceroy, the Eighth Earl of Elgin, were impressed by the contrast between him and Canning who "looked pale, wan, toil-worn and grief-stricken...... Elgin, on the other hand, came up gaily ruddy in face, massive and square in forehead, buoyant in manner and stalwart in frame".[1] Despite the vigour of his health, Elgin did not last long and died of a heart attack on a trek through the northern hills. The next Viceroy, John Lawrence, was already a hero with the British public. The diarist and man of letters, Arthur J. Munby, in 1860 records in his journal "Passing through Kensington on Tuesday, I saw a man of all others worth seeing - Sir John Lawrence. He was riding down the street alone - without even a groom: and no one knew or noticed him. A large loosely made man; sitting grave and quiet on his horse; with sallow wrinkled face and grizzly moustache; riding along, an unappreciated King of men, with such keen eyes and such a solemn face! All one's memories of 1857 were revived by the sight of him". Demetrius' new master had none of the aristocratic ambience which other holders of his exalted office exuded. "A rough, coarse man, in appearance more like a navvy than a gentleman" was how John Beames, a young civilian, described him. He was a martinet, hardworking himself and determined to get the most out of his subordinates. He worked in his shirt sleeves with his collar removed. People in Calcutta complained of the dullness of Government House under his regime - more like a parsonage than a palace with family prayers and croquet in the garden. Pedestrians long after dark could glimpse by lamplight, through the railings of Government House, the Viceroy wielding a croquet mallet.

In one respect Lawrence's tenure produced a significant change in the working lives of his subordinates for he initiated the removal of the whole administration, including the Secretariat and External Affairs Department, from Calcutta to Simla during the hot weather. Demetrius was caught up in that vast annual migration of 1,170 miles with its horde of attendants, attached memsahibs, children and tradespeople with their belongings and goods conveyed in an army of bullock carts, creaking under the weight of their contents along the Grand Trunk Road and then up the laborious ascent to Simla. This middle sized village rapidly bloomed into a fair-sized town in which Lady Wilson, wife of an Indian civilian, observed "the rickshaws whirling past, their bells tinkling and their runners shouting 'take care' to the rickshaw men in front of them, all of them, carrying overwrought humanity to their twenty-third or possibly fortieth consecutive 'tamasha', a ball, a play, a concert, or more probably the inevitable 'burra khana'."[2] Demetrius in his lowly position was hardly likely to be caught up in this social whirl but at least he could have enjoyed the magnificent views that so impressed Lady Wilson: "We see the near ranges of hills covered with crimson rhododendrons and topped by gigantic pines, and beyond these, faraway peaks crowned by everlasting snows or wreathed in mist. At dawn or sunset, by moonlight or in thunderstorms, they are indescribably beautiful".[3]

When the time came in 1869 for Lawrence to leave India he greeted his successor, the Earl of Mayo, on the steps of Government House. Mayo leapt out of the carriage, bursting with health and confidence and strode confidently up the steps to where the retiring proconsul, looking old and shrunken, awaited to greet him. Old hands amongst the staff must have felt that they were watching a re-run of the meeting between Canning and Elgin in 1861, so punishing was the pace of Viceregal life in those days and the heavy duties which reduced men of vigorous health to tired, sickly ghosts. Mayo restored the sparkle of Government House after the austerities of Lawrence. He was an ebullient chief, popular with his staff. His Private Secretary, Major Owen Burne (later Major General Sir Owen Burne) maintained that working for Mayo was like recreation. The Viceroy, however, was no dilettante, for he laboured twelve hours daily and inspired the staff with his own tireless enthusiasm and energy. He started at daybreak to avoid working into the late hours of the evening. His consideration for his staff and his talent for saving time meant that the work never seemed to get out of control. The Viceroyalty of this popular figure, a former Master of the Kildare Hunt, ended in brutal tragedy. He was stabbed to death by a Pathan convict on a visit to the Andaman Islands in 1872. One of the sights that must surely have impressed the Head Clerk of the Durbar Department was the magnificent funeral of the Viceroy. The entire European population of Calcutta followed the coffin from Prinsep's Ghat to Government House where it lay in state in the Council Chamber for two days while crowds of British and Indians came to pay their last respects. He was buried near his home in County Kildare.

The new Viceroy was a very different character from the extrovert Mayo. Lord Northbrook, a member of the famous banking family of the Barings and a widower, was a dry, reserved, shy man. Sir Percival Spear describes him as having the exterior of a Dombey with the will of an autocrat. The lack of colour in the new Viceroy was somewhat offset by the choice of his cousin, Evelyn Baring, as his Private Secretary. Intellectually brilliant and totally assured, in later life, as Lord Cromer, he was the maker of modern Egypt and one of the greatest administrators the British Empire ever produced. He must have been quite the most interesting character that Demetrius had to work under. It was during this Viceroyalty that he climbed another rung in his Uncovenanted career. In 1872 he became Registrar of the Private Secretary's Office and was occupying this position when Northbrook's friend, Edward Lear, visited Government House at the invitation of the Viceroy. Lear took a rather jaundiced view of the place and dubbed it 'Hustlefussabad'. The Viceroy and the writer of Nonsense Verse were both lonely men and both attracted by children. The former often visited schools in Calcutta where he observed "the little urchins being very nice looking, like English boys with a touch of bronze; some lighter and some darker, and as sharp as possible".

To replace Gladstone's sober Viceroy, Disraeli made a startling choice who turned out to be the enfant terrible of all the Viceroys. Lord Lytton was a poet and career diplomat, a romantic, a fanatic for pageantry, a bohemian who startled Simla society by smoking between courses at dinner and betraying an indulgence for liqueurs. His portrait by G. F. Watts reveals a handsome, thoughtful face but Viceregal photographs show him in a totally inappropriate pose for so exalted a personage, lounging on his throne, an off-hand arrogant look on his face. It has been suggested that this undignified position was really due to the fact that he suffered from the unromantic ailment of piles. He was a great admirer of beautiful women and one of his favourites, Mrs Plowden, presented herself at a Viceregal function "with a lovely water lily stuck where she ought to sit". Another lady was so enamoured of him that she wrote telling him that she could not sleep for thinking of his eyes. He was also a gourmet who brought out with him an Italian confectioner, Peliti, who became the proprietor of Peliti's Grand Hotel in Simla and of the famous pastry cook's establishment in Calcutta. He was well served by Northbrook's Private Secretary, Owen Burne, one of whose successors in the post was the ill-starred Colonel George Pomeroy Colley, an Anglo-Irishman who spoke Russian, was interested in chemistry, served in the Cape, China and West Africa but, as General Sir George Colley, was killed by a Boer bullet on the peak of Majuba Hill in the Transvaal. Lytton's involvement in the second Afghan War brought on him the displeasure of Gladstone, and his reign terminated in 1880.

To replace him, Gladstone sent out the wealthy Yorkshire grandee, Lord Ripon - earnest, radically-minded and totally sincere. He was decidedly home-spun in appearance - bulbous-nosed with a mild expression and a distinct lack of sartorial elegance. The handing-over ceremony took place on the lawn of the Viceregal residence in Simla, in a huge tent into which was crammed the entire Government of India, the military high command, the Punjab Government, the neighbouring hill chiefs and many other dignitaries. As Registrar in the Private Secretary's office Demetrius would almost certainly have been present on this occasion. After the formal presentations were over and a select party retired into Viceregal Lodge for the swearing-in, the rest of the assembled crop began to make their way back to the town when the sudden firing of the first gun of the Viceregal Salute plunged the whole cavalcade into a scene of chaotic confusion.

"A struggling mass of men and horses, all presenting the appearance of circus riders doing tricks. A portly General endeavoured to stop his pony from jumping over the railings and down the precipice; another gentleman was badly hurt while trying to discourage his horse in its attempts to climb a tree. People were seen disappearing into the distance on madly galloping steeds; horses pranced amongst topees and plumed cocked hats strewn about the ground".[4]

With the advent of Lord Ripon in 1880, Demetrius Panioty was appointed Assistant Private Secretary to the Viceroy, probably the highest post of responsibility that an Uncovenanted official could achieve in India. To obtain some idea of the nature and scope of his duties it is necessary to evaluate the extraordinarily unique political post of the Viceroyalty of India. The Viceroy did not belong to the Indian Civil Service (the only exception to this rule was John Lawrence), but was usually chosen from the narrow circle of aspiring politicians of the Conservative and Liberal Parties, many of whom, after leaving India, went on to serve in important Cabinet positions. He had, therefore, no first-hand knowledge of India's problems before taking up his appointment. One Indian civilian, Aberigh Mackay, 1880, said "I never tire of looking at a Viceroy. He is a being so heterogeneous from us.... He who is the axis of India.... lisps no Indian tongue; no race or caste of Indian life is known to him".[5] On all matters of policy he was advised by a Council of five or six members and he had a Private Secretary who could be a soldier or a civilian but the bulk of the routine work of his office was conducted by a staff headed by the Assistant Private Secretary. With a Viceroy who was a complete stranger to the minutiae of Indian official procedure and a Private Secretary who was usually a young man and did not usually hold the appointment for long, a great deal of responsibility lay on the shoulders of the Assistant Private Secretary, especially an official like Demetrius whose experience of the Private Secretary's Office stretched back to Dalhousies's administration and the last years of Company rule. The chiefs whom he served were autocrats who had, in theory, only one superior: the monarch. "Even the Prime Minister in London deferred to him on any occasion when they were together, for the Viceroy was uniquely the monarch's deputy, a deliberate creation to signify the Crown's special attachment to Indians".[6] The de facto situation, however, began to change in the 1870s for by then the electric telegraph enabled the Secretary of State in London to govern India by remote control and the Viceroy's despotic power became, in practice, modified. It must have been an additional responsibility to his clerical staff to know that documents emanating from the Private Secretary's Office could come under the eagle eye of a distant Secretary of State.

Ripon's first choice of Private Secretary was Colonel Charles George Gordon. At a farewell dinner in England, Gordon insisted on eating all his courses off the same plate explaining "We shall have to rough it out in India, you know, so I may as well begin now". But the opulence of Government House in Bombay showed him how mistaken he had been and he immediately resigned saying that he could not live in such luxury in a country in which so many millions were deprived of their daily bread. So Demetrius Panioty narrowly missed serving under the future hero of Khartoum. In his place Ripon appointed a man who was to become famous in the annals of India, Mortimer Durand, who in 1904 settled the international boundary (the Durand Line) between British India and Afghanistan. Ripon's other Private Secretary was Henry Wilson Primrose.

Ripon had been sent out by Gladstone to liberalise Indian institutions and to give Indians some share in power. He was attracted to the Christian Socialism of his friend, Thomas Hughes, the author of 'Tom Brown's Schooldays'. With his earnest moral attitude to India's problems, he was something of 'a Tom Brown in Calcutta'. No Viceroy was so deeply loved by Indians and his friend, Wilfrid Scawen Blunt, records how, wherever he went in India "I heard the same story; from the poor peasants in the south.... from the high caste Brahmins of Madras and Bombay; from the Calcutta students; from the Mohammedan divines of Lucknow; from the noblemen of Delhi and Hyderabad - everywhere his praise was in all men's mouths. 'He is an honest man,' men said, 'and one who fears God'."[7] The fact that Ripon's political career had suffered because of his conversion to Catholicism endeared him to his Indian subjects and perhaps also to Demetrius Panioty who was himself a convert to that faith from Greek Orthodoxy. During these years Demetrius lived with his family at 2 Russell Street (Mrs Betts' Boarding Establishment) in 1880, in the third flat of 16 Loudon's Buildings in 1881, 4 Government Place West in 1882 and 1 Larkin's Lane from 1883-85.

Ripon's successor, Lord Dufferin, was a totally different character. He was a man of the world, a cultured and charming career diplomat with a talent for literature and the arts, a romantic and a dandy. His chief failing was his indolence and he worked less than almost any other Viceroy. He paid little attention to detail and left many decisions to his able Private Secretary, Donald MacKenzie Wallace (later Sir Donald), who had been a Foreign Correspondent of 'The Times'. The Viceroy, however, commanded respect as a very shrewd judge of character and was said by Mortimer Durand to have an almost uncanny flair for detecting anything like insincerity or weakness. Therefore, it is pleasant to record that it was such a chief who recommended Demetrius for the award of Companion of the Indian Empire which he received on January 1, 1885.

Dufferin was responsible for the building of new Viceregal Lodge on the summit of Observatory Hill, Simla, a tall Elizabethan-style mansion of grey stone with cupolas and towers rising above the trees, furnished and decorated by Maples of London. To people like Demetrius who could remember the Old Lodge, 'Peterhof', with its corrugated-iron roof, continually drummed on by the paws of legions of monkeys, it must have seemed a singular and attractive addition to the Simla skyline. In Calcutta in 1885 Demetrius moved to 6 Council House Street, the house he occupied for the rest of his life.

The two Viceroyalties of Lansdowne and the Ninth Earl of Elgin have been described as an "Imperial Siesta". As the 19th century moved to its close, to the superficial observer it might have seemed as if an Olympian calm reigned in the Raj and that British rule would go on for ever. This placid lake was to be disturbed by the surging tempest of Curzon's restless tenure from 1899 to 1905. But from 1888 to 1899 Calcutta, seen through European eyes, basked in a late summer of relatively tranquil prosperity. The period also covered the last years of Demetrius Panioty's life. In her letters, Lady Wilson captures some of the charm and variety of late Imperial Calcutta. "What a strange medley Calcutta contains! Such crowds of Bengalis as seem more than the sands of the sea in number; our Eurasian cousins, the business community; the various ecclesiastical establishments; the officials and lawyers and, crowding the large hotels, the strangers who come from the four quarters of the globe for the winter season. Dominating this cosmopolitan city stands Government House at the end of the long Maidan, where the statues stand of the greatest governors of India. And who dare say that the spirit of the past has failed to survive in that gigantic building, which they rendered illustrious by their lives, and where their high ideals are still exemplified. Calcutta, in which the business element largely preponderates over the official, is a mental holiday.... the streets filled with the tall, grey offices of the businessmen, the multitude of well set-up shops, the sight of the river lined with ships of many countries, remind me so much of Glasgow, that if I heard the thud of the mighty hammers of the Clyde it would not seem incongruous. The business community speaks of Calcutta as if it had a living personality. 'Calcutta has a heart' is an oft-used phrase, the truth of which one can already endorse. Calcutta is genial and hospitable and has some little social traditions which are all its own".[8] It also had a more sinister, ugly side to it but Lady Wilson captures its ambience from a European point of view. It must have been not unlike the view of Demetrius in his last years.

Lord Lansdowne, Viceroy from 1888 to 1894 was a great Whig nobleman with a large estate at Bowood in Wiltshire and a splendid mansion, Lansdowne House, in London. Therefore, it is surprising to learn that, for him, the main attraction of the post of Viceroy was its salary, for he was the inheritor of large debts. He boasted that he had saved £20,000 in six years out of his annual salary of £16,700. To some, he seemed Gallic in appearance: slight, dapper, a small-boned figure with moustached side-whiskers, always elegantly dressed. He had also the manners of a cultivated Frenchman, a polished grace, an unfailing, slightly ceremonious courtesy. His natural dignity impressed Europeans and Indian princes but he showed little enthusiasm for his task. Like Dufferin he left officials to get on with their work and interfered as little as possible. "Used as he was to the splendours of Bowood and Lansdowne House he was not particularly impressed by Wellesley's Palace in Calcutta and complained of the entire lack of homely comfort."[9] India bored him and he was deeply homesick. He was oppressed by "the crowd of black servants" and dreaded being entertained by the Indian Princes "garlanded and smeared by their horrible attar of roses some half a dozen times". Government House cannot have been a comfortable place on social occasions. A certain French lady who "apparently under the impression that a liberal covering of paint made amends for a corresponding deficiency in the matter of clothes" was made to squirm under the Vicereine's glacial stare which so overwhelmed her that she could eat no dinner. As the Viceroy left Prinsep's Ghat in 1894 he felt like a schoolboy going home for the holidays.

Demetrius' last Viceroy was a sound and sober Scot, the Ninth Earl of Elgin. Son of a former Viceroy, shy, reserved, kind, he was not cast in the mould of a great proconsul. He was short, bearded, careless about dress and not greatly interested in the ceremonial side of his duties. He left important decisions to the Home Government and the day-to-day administration of India to his officials. Soon after his assumption of power Demetrius died in Simla. He was buried there and the inscription on his tombstone reads:

> Demetrius Panioty, Assistant Private Secretary to His Excellency the Viceroy, son of Emmanuel Panioty, a Greek gentleman of Calcutta. Born at Calcutta 1830. Died at Simla 17th July 1895. A devoted husband, a good father, a true friend and faithful servant of the government. He tried to do his duty.[10]

Some years later in 1904 Lady Wilson described the funeral in Simla of Lady Elles and, though Demetrius' funeral may not have been so impressive, her description may give us some idea of the occasion. "The rickshaws moved so slowly along it [The Mall], carrying such varied occupants. They were people of all classes, of every profession, sunburnt soldiers, pale-faced clerks, some poor woman with a child on her knee and a bunch of flowers in her hand, young people, old people, all silent, all sad, because they were moving to a churchyard. It was large and full of the dead.... the sun was shining down on the Simla hills covered with deodars and rhododendrons, but the churchyard was black with mourners".[11]

Demetrius Panioty's services to the Government did not go unnoticed or unrecorded. On the Maidan, east of Government House, the Government of India put up a monumental fountain to his memory. The fountain itself was of Jaipur marble with a large canopy of white granite, resting on four richly carved pillars. It was designed by Colonel Jacob, Superintending Engineer of Jaipur State, and its erection was entrusted to Mr Finnimore, Executive Engineer of the First Circle, who brought two men from Jaipur State to help in its construction. The inscription on the fountain's pedestal facing west read "In memory of Demetrius Panioty, C.I.E, Assistant Private Secretary to the Viceroy, who died at Simla, July 17, 1895". On the east panel was another inscription: "This fountain was erected as a tribute to faithful and assiduous service extending over a period of forty years, by the Viceroys and Private Secretaries who gratefully remember it".

On top of the west side of the canopy there is inscribed: "A good name is rather to be chosen than great riches" and this may justly stand as the epitaph to the man. His name may not rank amongst "The Men who ruled India" but, given the restrictions of his birth and education, his achievement was remarkable. To have served the Raj from the days of Dalhousie, through the critical time of the Mutiny, the end of Company rule and the inauguration of Queen Victoria's suzerainty to the succession of Viceroys from Canning to the Ninth Earl of Elgin is a story not without its quiet brand of Imperial glamour. The young Bengal-born Greek was, in his own way, an outstanding imperialist.

Monument to Demetrius Panioty on the Maidan, Calcutta

172

His Will, dated 26th August 1895 declared the chief legatees to be his wife, Persine Eliza, and his sons, John Emmanuel and Constantine Demetrius. It stated that in the event of the prior decease of all these legatees the estate was to be divided between the Catholic Male Orphanage, the Entally Orphanage for Girls, and the Catholic Free School.[12] The first of these institutions was run by the Irish Christian Brothers and was situated at 15 Portuguese Church Street, named from its proximity to the Roman Catholic Cathedral, dedicated to the Virgin Mary of the Rosary, designed by Thomas Syars Driver and consecrated in 1797. An earlier chapel, built by the Augustinian Friars (to which Order, Martin Luther once belonged) about 1700, had existed on the site of the Cathedral.

The second institution was run by the famous Loretto Nuns who had a convent in Entally. From the railway bridge in Entally the view was bounded on two sides by jute mills and their massive chimney stacks. At one's feet were packed the mean streets and low-lying bustees of the factory workers. But in front was spread out a vista of green fields and shady trees. A pleasant tank bordered by cannas reflected in its clear waters the nearest of the four white buildings that surrounded the Convent compound. On one big lawn one could see toddlers at play or watch a line of girls in white frocks walking across from the great central block to the chapel in the foreground. It was a scene of great beauty, an oasis in the desert of industrial squalor that stretched away on all sides. The Roman Catholic Church bought the Convent property from John Asphar, an Armenian merchant from Aleppo in 1847 for Rs 24,000. The original bungalow on the land was greatly extended in 1858 to house a boarding school and a community of nuns and in the next year, a two-storied building was erected to accommodate the orphans mentioned in Demetrius' Will. The nuns of Entally were dubbed 'Bishop Oliffe's Female Brigade' by 'The Englishman' in 1857, perhaps because of the following patriotic but somewhat unrealistic verses by the Loretto Sister, Mother Mary Colmcille:

Calcutta needs no volunteers, the Papist Bishop cries;
From rebels he'll defend the town, by aid of womens' eyes.
Our Citadels are Convent Walls! each rosary a gun;
The leading Chief - an abbess fair; each sentinel - a nun!
Loretto's Dames will quite suffice, to batter Delhi down,
And save the gem that glitters most, in Queen Victoria's crown.

The Catholic Free School was situated at 58 Free School Street which opened into Park Street nearly opposite to Middleton Row. In 1780 the area was a bamboo jungle which people were afraid to pass at night but the earliest Free School was established there in 1790.[13]

Demetrius' two sons made a mark for themselves in Calcutta and reached a greater social eminence than he did, without achieving the same degree of posthumous fame. The eldest, John Emmanuel Panioty, qualified as a doctor and practising surgeon; L.R.C.P. (London) and L.R.C.P., L.M. and L.R.C.S. (Edin-

173

burgh). In 1884 he practised in Larkin's Lane which connected Old Court House Street with Wellesley Place and was named after William Larkins, an intimate friend of Warren Hastings and William Hickey, who was Accountant-General of Bengal. In 1886 John lived with his parents at 6 Council House Street and was practising at the Mayo Native Hospital in Ripon Street. In 1898 he was Resident Surgeon at the Park Street Dispensary and from 1890 to 1899 in the Chandney Dispensary at 7 Hospital Lane. In 1900-01 he was in practice with Dr E.W. Chambers at 10 Kyd Street, named after Colonel Robert Kyd, the founder of the Botanical Gardens at Sibpore. He lived at 35 Free School Street in 1902, 40 Chowringhee Street in 1903, 9 Middleton Street in 1904 (next door to Lt. Col. Havelock, I.M.S.), and from 1905 to 1919 at 19 Royd Street. He was made an Honorary Magistrate in 1915 and died unmarried in 1919.

Demetrius' second son, Constantine Demetrius, followed his grandfather's profession of the Law, qualified as a barrister and was practising in the High Court of Calcutta in 1886. From 1890 to 1892 he was Reporter of the Indian Law Reports, and from 1893 to 1895, the year of his father's death, he became Fifth Judge of the High Court, in 1906 Fourth Judge, in 1909 Third Judge and in 1918 Second Judge. He lived with his parents at 6 Council House Street from 1886-1891, at 3 Old Post Office Street in 1892, 6 Fancy Lane from 1893-95 and after his father's death, with his widowed mother in the Top Flat, 2 Vansittart Row. After her death he moved to 6 Government Place from 1900 to 1914 and to the Grand Hotel from 1915 to 1916. He moved out to 3 Bankshall Street in 1917 and back to the Grand Hotel in 1918. In 1887 he married Miriam Jane Blackett and they had one daughter, Mary Rosalie, born on April 10th, 1902, and baptized in the Catholic Church of the Sacred Heart, Dhuramtollah. His wife died sometime before 1918 and in that year he retired to England with his daughter where he died.

Demetrius' elder brother Nicholas was dogged by ill-health all his life. With his brother he entered the Bengal Secretariat as a Writer in 1849 but resigned for reasons of health in 1853 and went to live in Dacca until 1866. His occupation during this period is not known and the reason for his presence there remains something of a mystery. Sometime before he left Calcutta he married Angelina Speroos. This Greek family can be traced back to a Joseph Speroos who was resident in Khulna in Bengal from 1804 to 1807 and had arrived in India in 1789. His place of origin is not known but the name 'Seroos' is mentioned in the records of the British Administration of the Ionian Islands and the likelihood therefore is that 'Speroos' is a Corfiot name. Joseph had a son, Athanas Speroos, born in 1815. He entered the Bengal Uncovenanted Service in 1833 as a section writer in the Secret Political Department. In 1834 he transferred to the General Treasury as an Indexer in the Accountant General's Office and in that year married a girl whose Christian name was Catherine and who died on August 7th 1861. They had two children: Angelina, reputed to be a very beautiful girl, born

174

High Court, erected 1872.

Constantine Demetrius Panioty, Judge of the High Court, Calcutta

May 8, 1844, who married Nicholas Panioty, and a son, Theophilus, who worked for some time in Ralli Brothers in Calcutta and died on November 16, 1908. In 1855 Athanas became Accountant of Deposits in the General Treasury and lived at 3 Bow Bazaar with John Foscolo, a Greek assistant in George Grant & Co., watch and clockmakers, and in 1857 at 1 Weston's Lane. From 1865 to 1866 he was Head Assistant in the Government Stationery Office. He retired on pension in 1866 and died in 1867 at his home, 34 Emambough Road. From the brief details of his career he sounds as if he was "a Galilean without guile" who had served his masters well.

Nicholas and Angelina Panioty had four children, the eldest of whom was probably born in Calcutta and the rest in Dacca - Nicholas, John Constantine, Angelo and Ione. The dates of birth for the three boys are not known but Ione was born in Dacca on February 21st 1864. In 1866 Nicholas moved back to Calcutta to live with his father-in-law and to work for the well-known firm of Jardine Skinner & Co. He died suddenly in 1868 at his home, 18 Joratallao Street, which he shared with the families of Demetrius Panioty and Constantine Nicachi. In his Will he left Rs 14,000 to his wife and one of the sureties was Angelo Ducas, a Greek friend of his. Angelo married Nicholas' widow in Calcutta on 5th October 1869. He was the son of Alexander Ducas, originally from a noble family of Corfu, who was a Greek merchant in Dacca. They were married in St. James' Anglican Church in Calcutta. Angelo worked for Argenti Sechiari from 1864 to 1874 and as manager of Nicachi & Co. from 1875 to 1881 and then joined Nicholas & Co. another Greek-managed firm, ships chandlers and mastriggers, at 7 Strand Road. He remained with them until 1887 and it is probable that he died in that year. During this period he lived with his family at 7 Joratallao Street (renamed Marquis Street after the Marquis of Ripon in 1879) till 1871 when he moved to 8 Bepareetollah Lane, opposite the West Gate of Wellington Square, where he remained till his death. Family tradition relates that he was a careful and kind guardian of his Panioty stepchildren and brought them up in the Orthodox tradition of their mother though he himself was a devout Anglican.

The Panioty boys grew up to be tall, strapping young men who had a reputation for being hard fighters and wild pranksters. On one occasion when an aggressive young man offered to fight Nicholas Panioty the latter replied contemptuously "try my youngest brother Willy first, if you can beat him try Jack and if you can beat Jack then apply to me". He was not a diligent pupil and often stole away from school to haunt Kidderpore Docks. He was a particular favourite of Italian sailors who admired his plucky, resourceful manner and nicknamed him 'Garibaldi'. The name stuck and for the rest of his life he was known to his family and friends as 'Gari Panioty'. In 1881 he began work as an assistant in the firm of Sigg Suglar in Dacca and in 1890 joined Ralli Brothers at Seragunj, transferring to Dacca in 1893. At some time during these years he married Effie George. She was most probably from the Greek family, one of whom in 1788 signed the Hastings petition, Simeon George from Georgia. Two other Georges, Demetrius and Emmanuel, were resident in Dacca in 1795 and the mercenary soldier Adam George also belonged to this family. Three of their children were born in Dacca: Eirene on 6th January 1888 and baptized August 3; Nicholas on 8th December 1889; Angelo on 30th July 1893. All of them were baptized in the Greek Church in Dacca.

In 1894 Gari and his family moved to Calcutta where he worked in the Head Office of Ralli Brothers, joining his brother-in-law, Menelaus Nicachi, and Panos Nicachi and lived at 76 Wellesley Street. In 1899 or 1900 he and his family went to England either on a long holiday or because he was sent there by his firm. They lived in Ealing and it was there that their fourth child Dorothy was born on 26th June 1901. Either at the end of 1901 or beginning of 1902 the family returned to Calcutta to live at 12 Canal Street (Durham House) and then in 1903 moved to 50 Elliot Road to share the house with Menelaus Nicachi and his family. He continued to work for Ralli Brothers with a brief spell with Philip Nicachi at the Societa Anomina Coloniale di Trieste in 1908. He worked for Ralli Brothers at their office in Kidderpore Docks, the old haunt of his youth. On 10th October 1902 his fifth child was born, Ella Ione, who was baptized at St. Stephen's Anglican Church, Kidderpore, on 19th January 1903. It seems as if he had abandoned the practice of Greek Orthodoxy and regarded himself as an Anglican. A sixth child, Jessie, was born on 17th October 1904. His eldest son Nicholas emigrated to Australia in 1908. On arrival he lived in a boarding house in Melbourne run by a Mr and Mrs Hanson whose daughter Lyla he married in October 1911. His letters home from Australia must have encouraged his father to leave Ralli Brothers and retire there with his family. All of them left India for Melbourne in 1911. Their last home in Calcutta was at Waverley Mansions, 72 Corporation Street.

When he arrived in Melbourne he lived at first in the suburb of Northcote, five miles north of Melbourne and in 1917 moved to East Malvern, Carnegie, where he died in 1918. His wife was not happy in Australia. She had left her heart in India and always yearned to go back. After her husband's death she lived with her married daughter in Melbourne at Riversdale Road, Camberwell. At Christmas and on her birthday all her sons and daughters gathered there for a family celebration. Her grandson remembers these occasions with affection and says that "we were a very close family who cared a great deal for each other". Effie died in 1948 and was buried near her husband in Springvale Cemetery, Melbourne.

Gari's eldest son, Nicholas, joined the Melbourne and Metropolitan Tramway Board as a conductor, was promoted to foreman and then transferred to the Head Office in Melbourne and put in charge of its Stationery Department. He built his own house about two hundred yards from the maritime waters of Mordialloc Creek. He, like Ratty in 'The Wind in the Willows', was a dedicated

Nicholas (Gari) Panioty and family in Australia, c.1910

waterman and spent every weekend on his boat fishing and every morning of his life went down to the beach for a swim. On dark winter's mornings he took old newspapers to the beach and set them alight to act as a beacon for his return journey. On one occasion some unknown person lifted his clothes and towel from the beach and when he returned home, dripping wet, found them neatly stacked on his porch. He was short, wiry and extremely fit - very Greek in appearance. When he died on 8 August 1971 he was cremated and his ashes, according to his wish, were scattered over the waters of the Creek he loved so much. He had three children: Eirene, born September 1st 1912; Nicholas, born July 27th 1919, and Margery who was born August 14th, 1923. His son Nicholas joined the Australian Army in World War II and marched through Athens with his unit in the unsuccessful defence of Greece against the Wehrmacht. After service in the Middle East he was taken prisoner by the Japanese in Sumatra and died at Monbaulk in Victoria on January 26th 1991. His son John is the only person to bear the Panioty name in Australia today. One of Gari's daughters, Eirene, returned to India in 1933 and died there. Her sons joined the British Army in India during the war and returned to Australia after the hostilities.

Chance has preserved for us some more intimate details of the schooling of Gari's second son, Angelo. When his parents returned to Calcutta from England he stayed on in a private school, West Ealing College at 288 Uxbridge Road, West Ealing, and a reference from the Principal dated October 22nd 1906 has survived:

Sir,

I have much pleasure in stating that Master Angelo Panioty has been in my school about seven years. He is a lad of excellent abilities and has always shown himself a diligent and willing student, and most anxious to excel in all his school work: hence he has taken a high position in his class. His moral character is such that I have no hesitation in recommending him to any teacher or school. I much regret that he must leave my care and teaching and have for him the heartiest wishes for his future success in life.

I am, Sir,
Yours very sincerely,
E. Arthur Williams. B.A. (Lon)

Angelo left this school to return to India and was sent by his parents to the Jesuit Boarding School, St. Joseph's College, North Point, Darjeeling, which was founded in 1888. Three of his letters home survive and they give so many details of boarding-school life in a Hill School in Edwardian India that they are worth reproducing in full. They are written on stationery which has the school crest and its motto 'Sursum Corda' embossed at the top left-hand corner. The first letter is dated November 30, 1907:

179

Dear Mother and Father,

I have not received any letters from you, except Nick's, but I am glad to see from his that you are all quite well. On Tuesday evening the quadrangle was decorated with chinese lanterns and flags and the band played till very late. Before supper there was an acting held in the hall which was very good. Wednesday was another full holiday, and there was another acting. On Wednesday races were held out in front, four annas being the prize for almost everything and a little place was made for the bar, the whole thing reminded one of a holiday we had at the beginning of the year. I won two annas. There was one race where we got hold of cats, dogs, cocks, hens, goats and made them race. At 6 p.m. Thursday, the whole school was called into the hall, and there the Rector told us that he was called away to Ceylon and the Minister was now Rector. In the afternoon nearly all the boys went and saw him off at the Station. It does not matter much if I am not allowed to come home on the sixth, the eighth will be not long afterwards. Today, Saturday, we had a full holiday granted us by the new Rector. Altogether we have only two class days left before we come home, all the rest being holidays. There is going to be no woodcutting this year so the coolies have cut the wood for us. We are allowed to make fires in the compound as there is lots of dry moss and grass about the place, and you may be sure a good many are burnt. This is a very funny winter which we are having - it is rather cold in the mornings but in the day it gets very hot. If you have not already sent my four rupees, please will you do so as fast as you can. This is the last time I can write to you while I am up here because if I write next Saturday I will be home before the letter. With much love and kisses,
Your loving son,
Angelo Panioty.

The next letter carries the date 24th November but the year is not given. It should probably be dated either 1906 or, more probably, 1908.

Dear Mother and Father,

I was glad to see from Nick's and Eirene's letter that you are all quite well. I have not received any cake but it does not matter. Thank you very much for writing to the Rector, write and tell me if he says 'Yes'. Just imagine this time next fortnight, a good many boys will be starting for the station and I hope to have arrived home. Yesterday we had a Volunteer picnic. I am sorry I did not ride going but I had some fine rides at Senohill. I bet I could beat Nick at riding. Going, five of us rode in a bullock cart, and coming back we got inside three rickshaws so altogether we had a fine time of it, besides having good weather on the hill which, in itself, is a rare thing. I got a letter from Eirene this week, she is bragging about her flat such a lot. Please will you send me my pocket money and two extra rupees because in the night train we are going to have a good feast. On Tuesday we will have a half-holiday and will continue on till Thursday because of the Rector's day. On Monday there will be a test in Elocution, and after that one in a month which will be the end and then we can look forward to the holidays. The boys of the high class leave on the fifteenth of next month because they have some exams on. Yesterday and this morning we had extra sleep before and after the Volunteer picnic, a thing which is looked forward to very much by everyone of us, especially now it is so

180

cold. I have received one hundred and two letters counting those from England and from home and I have filled three cigar boxes packed full of them. I must now close my letter. With much love and kisses,

I remain,

Your loving son,

A. Panioty.

P.S. I wonder if Dolly, Ella and baby will remember me when I come back. Remember how Ella would not say goodbye to me.

The mind boggles at the one hundred and two letters. He must have have belonged to a very loving family and been a very popular boy. The third and last letter is dated 12th December, 1908.

Darling Mother and Father,

Thank you very much for your postcard, and for the parcel, which I received quite safely. Dolly got a prize at their distribution. I saw her name on the prize list, we were not allowed to go. [This suggests that his younger sister, Dorothy, was also at boarding school in Darjeeling, probably at the Loretto School.] I got two prizes, one for Mathematics and one for Excessit so I will bring home three this year [in the original 'two' had been written and crossed out]. The examination begins on Monday, it is going to be held in our Hall this year. We have just got the rules and our index numbers today, mine is 682. This time next week we will be in the night train past Siliguri. On Saturday, after the Distribution, the bonfire was held. It was a better one this year and lasted longer. The Senior Cambridge boys are having their last supper tonight in the Hall. I wish we could have got one up only some of the boys would not subscribe. The store room is being pulled down and a bigger one is being put up in its place. All the exam boys have gone to the "Small Dorm" refectory, while the Fathers have taken ours. We have had class as usual up to today but I am glad to say that this will be the last day.

I must now close my letter. With much love and kisses

I remain

Your loving son,

Angelo.

P.S. Mother please do not tell Dolly, Ella and baby when I am coming down, I want to surprise them. Please may I get three rupees from the Procurator out of my own money for travelling down.

Angelo Panioty left North Point at the end of 1909, probably as a result of his family's plans to emigrate to Australia. The Rector of North Point, Father F. X. Crohan, S.J., gave him the following parting reference:

Angelo Panioty was a pupil of North Point College for 3 years. His general conduct during this period was uniformly very satisfactory and he had applied himself to study with commendable diligence. He was successful in the Junior Cambridge Local Examination last winter and was preparing for the Senior Locals when he left us. He is an honest lad; of good parts and thoroughly reliable. His morals, while he was with us, were ever above censure.

181

The letters show that he was happy at school and there is an amazing lack of complaint about school food, discipline and teachers but perhaps letters home were censored and Angelo knew they were. It seems as if the regime was liberal enough with a generous amount of holidays and plenty of extra-curricular diversions. Many years later Angelo's nephew Nicholas recorded how his uncle taught him the tune and the words of his old school song and it is interesting to picture the two Greeks in Down Under lustily singing the song of a Darjeeling school.

Angelo worked on a farm when he first went out to Australia and in August 1917 joined the A.I.F. and left Australia in 1918 to serve overseas but the Armistice was declared before he saw any action. After the war he found difficulty in obtaining suitable employment for many years but eventually joined the Postal Department from which he retired on June 30, 1958. He received the following letter from his superior:

P M.G.   30 June 1958.
Dear Mr Panioty,
As you are retiring from the PMG Department I wish to take the opportunity of conveying to you the thanks of the Department for a long period of enthusiastic, efficient and devoted service. May you be blessed with good health, happiness and contentment in the years that lie ahead.

M. Skerrett. Director.

He married but had no children. He was very close to his nephew Nicholas and after his wife's death he went to dinner at his nephew's house most Sundays and on Christmas Day. He was a keen golfer who laid out a miniature golf course in his back garden to practise his putting. He became a skilled gardener who exhibited in local shows and won many prizes for his dahlias and carnations and sold his flowers to an exclusive florist in Melbourne. Like his brother, he was very Greek in appearance but of a heavier build and thickly moustachioed. He died in 1975 at his family home at 3 Graceburn Avenue, Carnegie, Melbourne, and was cremated.

The lives of Gari's brothers John Constantine and Angelo are shrouded in relative obscurity. The first, known to his family as 'Jack', worked for Ralli Brothers in Dacca from 1892 to 1901 and then for another Greek firm, J. Nicholas & Co., in the same place. The youngest brother Angelo was known to his family as 'Willy' and about his life hangs a cloud of tragedy. Somehow, things did not work out well for him. He married Agnes Susan Emma Jones and they had three children: Argus, born November 3, 1894; Carlisle, born January 9, 1897 and Inez Mildred, born December 23, 1898. All the children were baptized at St. James' Anglican Church, Calcutta. He had a shifting, restless career: a Junior Licensed Measurer in 1891, Ralli Brothers from 1892 to 1894, a guard on the East Indian Railway in 1897, a Job Master in 1898. There is a family tradition that he ended his days in poverty and gloom.

Ione, Gari's only daughter, married Menelaus Panioti Nicachi at St. Thomas' Catholic Church in Calcutta on November 15, 1886. She was received into the Catholic Church from the Greek Orthodox Church "in periculo mortis" - as the records of St. Thomas' Church put it - on August 11, 1902. With her husband, two daughters Zoe and Ellene and her grandson Paul she went to live in Bangalore in 1924 and never returned to Bengal. She was a stern matriarch, generally respected by all who knew her, strict with her children but indulgent to her grandson. In appearance she was a tall, stout, pale lady who ruled her household with a rod of iron. In her last years it was her custom to be driven out every evening in the family car, a black T Model Ford by Krishnaswamy, her Tamil chauffeur (ex RIASC), who lived in mortal fear of her. She was immensely proud of her family history, had a deep regard for the memory of her step-father, Angelo Ducas, and a sharp dislike of her husband's cousin Pano. She corresponded regularly with her brother's family in Australia. She died on February 23, 1933, at 3 André Road, Langford Town, Bangalore, and was buried, like her husband, in the Catholic section of the Hosur Road Cemetery.

That these Calcutta Greek families tried hard to keep some sort of Hellenic identity is shown clearly by the patterns of their domicile. They hung together, living with their families in the same rented houses or in closely adjacent ones forming, as it were, one extended family of Paniotys, Nicachis, Sperooses, Ducases and Fleurys. The following list of residences clearly shows the pattern:

1855	18 Scott's Lane:	Demetrius Panioty and his wife Persine Fleury; Nicholas Panioty and his wife Angelina Speroos.
1856	26 Amratollah Street:	Demetrius Panioty and family; J.M. Fleury, P.W. Fleury, L.C. Fleury, Maria Rose Fleury.
1859	ditto	As above, joined by Constantine Nicachi who married Maria Rose Fleury.
1860	17 Joratallao Street:	As above.
1865	ditto	J.M. Fleury, P.W. Fleury, L.C. Fleury, Alexander Ducas.
	18 Joratallao Street:	Demetrius Panioty and family, Constantine Nicachi and family.
1867	17 Joratallao Street:	As above.
	18 Joratallao Street:	As above, joined by Nicholas Panioty and family.
1869	17 Joratallao Street:	The three Fleury brothers.
	18 Joratallao Street:	Alexander Ducas marries the widow of Nicholas Panioty. They and their three children move in with Demetrius Panioty, Constantine Nicachi and their families.
1871	19 Mehndee Bagan Rd : (Park Lane in 1875)	D. Panioty, C. Nicachi and families.
	24 Mehndee Bagan Rd:	L.C. and P.W. Fleury.

1872	5 Lower Circular Rd:	D. Panioty, C. Nicachi and families.
	92 Lower Circular Rd:	A. Ducas and family.
1873	5 ditto	C. Nicachi died
1874	5 Lower Circular Rd:	D. Panioty and family, Mrs M.R. Nicachi and family, J.M. and L.C. Fleury.
	92 Lower Circular Rd:	A. Ducas and family.
1877		By this time Demetrius Panioty and family had moved away to 2 Russell Street and Alexander Ducas with his family went to live with his brother Constantine Ducas at 9 Wellington Square.
1878	45 Elliot Road:	Mrs M.R. Nicachi and family J.M., L.C. and P.W. Fleury.
1882	ditto	As above, joined by Panos Nicachi from Corfu who married Ellene Nicachi, daughter of Mrs M.R. Nicachi.
1885	91 Dhuramtollah St:	Mrs M.R. Nicachi and son, P.S. Nicachi and family, joined by Philip Nicachi from Corfu.
1886	ditto	As above but M.P. Nicachi marries Ione Panioty and they join the rest.
1895	ditto	Mrs M.R. Nicachi dies.
1903	50 Elliot Road:	M.P. Nicachi and family, N.(Gari) Panioty and family.

After 1904 with the deaths of many of the original characters this pattern of domestic proximity broke up.

The Panioty hold on Dacca was tenacious despite the deterioration of the family's commercial prosperity. Throughout the second half of the 19th century the descendants of Ignatius Constantine Panioty and his wife Dispinoo (née Lucas) could be found, marrying and begetting children. Their son Alexander Ignatius Panioty, born 1853, inherited his father's zamindari at Burrakar, Dacca, and married Sultana Lucas of Dacca. One of his sons, Panioty Alexander (it is interesting to note that the old Greek habit of inverting names still continued at this late date), died as a young man and was buried in the English Cemetery at Barisal (Grave No. 45) with the following inscription:

In loving memory of Panioty Alexander, son of Alexander I. Panioty. b 27 Aug, 1877. Died 21 Jan 1897.

The verse that follows is a pathetic reminder of the constant presence of early death amongst Europeans in India and the strain this sometimes put on a belief in Divine Providence:

This must be wise which Thou hast done;
It must be kind, for Thou art God[14]

He died of spleen and pneumonia.

The records of Panioty births, marriages and deaths in Dacca in the late 19th century make it difficult to trace the exact relationships of the persons concerned. It seems probable that the Paniotys listed below were all descendants of Ignatius Constantine Panioty:

1. Christos Panioty b December 1878 and Georgios Panioty b 20 August 1880, baptized 9 March, 1882. Parents: Alexander Panioty, merchant, and Ellen Panioty. Greek Church, Dacca.

2. Angel John Panioty b December 1889, baptized November 1890 Parents: John Ignatius Panioty, landlord, Dacca, and Alice Mary Ripsina Panioty. R.C. Church, Dacca.

3. Florence Panioty b July 8, 1891, baptized December 25, 1891. Parents: John Panioty, landlord, Dacca, and Anna Maria Panioty.

4. Helen Marie Panioty b November 18, 1892, baptized May 22, 1893. Parents: John Panioty, Zamindar, Dacca, and Alice Panioty. R.C. Church, Dacca.

5. Ellen Panioty d January 28, 1894; 1 year 2 months, daughter of John Ignatius Panioty. R.C. Church, Dacca.

6. Ignatius Constantine Panioty m Celine Athanas 1895.

7. Ignatius Panioty m Aline Panioty 1896.

8. Alma and Eveline b August 25, 1897, baptized November 21, 1898 Parents: Ignatius Constantine Panioty and Selina Athanas. Profession of Father: Assistant Jute Merchant. R.C. Church, Dacca.

There is even a mysterious entry in the register of the Greek Church in Calcutta: 'Aleco Panioty, d Sept 22, 1889, 21 yrs. Sailor'. One other death which is difficult to place in a Panioty family tree is that of Virginia Panioty who died on October 10, 1876, aged 51 years and was interred in the Bhowanipore Military Burial Ground.

As late as 1923 a survey of European graves conducted by the Education Department of India in Bengal says that the Greek Cemetery in Dacca (Golbadan in Moulvi Bazaar) was under the supervision of the Paniotys. It adds, with a touch of melancholy, that the graves near the edge of the cemetery are covered with jungle.[15]

The Greek families at Dacca and Naraingunj added an exotic touch to the European community as the writer Rumer Godden noted in her book 'Two under the Indian Sun' which described her days as a young girl in Naraingunj: "The Greek children were always a little remote from us; they were so showily handsome with alabaster skins made paler by the climate.... they had dark, lustrous eyes and dark lustrous hair.... and when we went to spend the day with them, the meals were strange: a queer lunch breakfast at eleven o'clock which began with a rich soup in which meat balls floated and went on to curries.... for afternoon tea-time they had coffee instead of tea and little tartlets of very rich pastry filled with chocolate. Jon was often bilious after a day spent with our Greek friends. When we went to (their) house their father's carriage came for us; it was a glorified sort of Tikka-gharri in dark green panelling with a large chestnut horse and two liveried servants".

The Calcutta Directories also mention a G. Panioty who was resident in Dacca from 1850 to 1873 and was probably a son of Alexander Panioty and Catherine (née Barros). This man had a son, George A. Panioty, born in 1867, who was an Excise Inspector at Kyauk Phyoo in the Arakan from 1898 to about 1906. In 1906-7 he was steward to the late Raja Rajendra Narayan Roy Bahadur's Establishment at Joydebpur, Dacca. He and his wife had at least two children, Arthur born January 6, 1898, and Evelyne born December 28, 1899, both baptized in the Anglican Church at Akyab. George Panioty went back into the Excise Department and died at Mandalay on September 23, 1935, and was buried in the Methodist Cemetery there. He fathered an illegitimate son, Richard, who was born in 1923 in Mandalay. It is more than likely that he had two other sons (?illegitimate), Henry and Spiros, who are mentioned in the following records of births:

Agatha Panioty. b. August 27th, 1934, bap Dec 24, 1935 at Christchurch, Mandalay. Parent: Henry Panioty, Excise Sub-Inspector. Ma Nyun.

Alexander George Panioty b Feb 4, 1927, bap Sept 24, 1930 at St. Andrew's Mongwa, Mandalay. Parent: Sperew (Spiros) Panioty, Sub-Inspector of Police.

This study has concentrated on the presence of a large number of expatriate Greeks who came to Bengal and worked, and sometimes settled and died there, but historically this was only part of a much larger and wider Greek dispersion all over the world. Like the British, the Greeks managed to combine a deep, nostalgic love of their native land with a restless pursuit of livelihood in far-flung foreign lands.

In his fascinating book 'Roumeli' Patrick Leigh Fermor describes how he visited a bar in Panama City: "The three barmen were taking their orders in Spanish but shouting them back in Greek; and when my turn came, I asked for something in the same language. Hence the question: are you a Greek? The place was run by a family from the little port of Karlovassi in Samos. They were the fourth Greeks I had met during nearly a year in the Caribbean and the Central American Republics; one, a businessman in Haiti; another, on the plain between Havana and British Honduras, a grocer; the last, a lonely innkeeper in Cordova, on the shores of Lake Nicaragua opposite the volcano of Momotombo".

Travelling in the wilds of Abysinnia in 1930, Evelyn Waugh encountered "a most delightfully amiable young Greek", the manager of a primitive hotel who talked incessantly in very obscure English and made lethal cocktails of whisky, creme de menthe and Fernet Branca topped up with soda water which he downed cheerfully, saying "Cheerioh, damned sorry no ice". He came from Alexandria and was involved in a love affair with an elderly Abysinnian lady of high birth. Another enterprising Greek in 1898 followed in the wake of Kitchener's Army in the Sudan and was selling soda water to the troops on the very eve of the Battle of Omdurman. When the battle was over, several of his compatriots were found to be prisoners of the Dervishes and were released by the British.[16]

To set beside these little cameos, here is another from rural Warwickshire. A visitor driving through Long Itchington, on his way from Coventry to Banbury will notice, near the village pond, a signboard with the direction 'Galanos House'. If his curiosity leads him to follow the sign he will find that it is the name of a purpose-built British Legion Residential Home called after a Greek business-man, Christos Galanos. There is no evidence to connect him with the family of the Greek Indologist. He was born in Macedonia but at the age of 16 emigrated to Egypt and from there he went to German East Africa and worked on the railways, building culverts and bridges and laying tracks. After the War, he became a sisal farmer in the now British colony of Tanganyika and by the mid-1950s he had made a fortune estimated at 6 to 7 million pounds. He had a tremendous admiration for the British character and was a generous philanthrophist whose activities won him the award of an O.B.E. When he died he left a considerable sum of money to build homes for disabled and elderly British ex-servicemen in England. One of these is Galanos House in Long Itchington.

Christos Galanos in Tanganyika, Patrick Leigh Fermor's Greeks in Central America and the Caribbean, Waugh's Alexandrian in the wilds of Abysinnia, the Greek traders in the Sudan are historic symbols of the wander-lust that has characterised the Greek race. Alexios Argyree Panaghiotis and his fellow merchants were part of this great Hellenic adventure. It was a long way from Philippopolis to Dacca and an even longer way to Mandalay and to Melbourne where the bodies of some of Argyree's descendants lie buried. Perhaps they were worth commemorating,

Before this fire of sense decay,
This smoke of thought blown clean away,
And leave with ancient night alone
The steadfast and enduring bone.

References: Chapter Ten

1. *The Viceroys of India,* M Bence-Jones (Constable 1982) p42
2. *Letters From India,* Lady Wilson (First published 1911, ed. P. Barr) p303
3. *Ibid.* p320
4. Bence-Jones op. cit. p115
5. P Mason op. cit. p208
6. *India Britannica,* Moorhouse p128
7. Bence-Jones op. cit. p128
8. Lady Wilson op. cit. pp290-291
9. Bence-Jones op. cit. p157
10. *Two Monsoons,* T Wilkinson (Duckworth, Second Edition1987) p145
11. Lady Wilson op. cit. pp305-306
12. Bengal Wills I.O.R.
13. P. T. Nair op. cit. pp270-271, 585
14. Indian Papers, unclassified (Society of Genealogists, London)
15. *Ibid.*
16. *Omdurman,* Philip Zeigler (Collins 1973) p57

Appendices

Appendix A

Signatures to the Petition and Address from the principal members of the Greek Church in Bengal to the Honourable Court of Directors of the East India Company concerning the late Governor, Warren Hastings.
13th December, 1788.

C. Parthenio: Rector, Greek Church, Calcutta, Corfu.

Nathaniel Cyphano: priest and monk of the convent of Mount Sinai, and Rector of the Church in Calcutta.

Panageotes Alexios: Philippopolis.

Marodes Thireacos: warden of the Church, Philippopolis.

George Leondeu: Smyrna.

Demetrius Georgius: Bythynia.

Shereen Hadjy Ibraheem: Caesaria.

Athenasius Theodore: Prusa.

Theodore Charis: Arta.

Joannes Demetrius: Metyline.

Jacobus Haujy Thosma: Caesaria.

Angelos Dadelco: Philippopolis.

Christodolo, son of Papa Nicolai: Isle of Neos.

Panageotis Demetrius: Thely.

Angelos Doucos: Corfu.

Christodolus Maurody: Philippopolis.

Emmanuel Demetrius: Albania.

Demetrius Galanos: Athens.

Georgius Panageotis: Philippopolis

Alexandros Panageotis: Philippopolis

Anastersius Panageotis: Philippopolis.

Joannes Panageotis: Philippopolis.

Potos Hauji Abraham: Caesaria.

Jacob Heuji Isaah: Caesaria.

Alexeus Hauji Abraham: Caesaria.

Simeon Hauji Abraham: Caesaria.

Joseph Hauji Abraham: Caesaria.

Johannes Hauji Abraham: Caesaria.

Lucas Theodoro: Magnesia.

George Careeda: Philippopolis.

Solinees Anthony: Philippopolis.

George Athanasius: Philippopolis.

Constantine Theodosius: Philippopolis.

Constantine Shahiny: Philippopolis.

Michael Andrew: Peloponesus.

Demetrius George Calograthy: Isle of Neos.

George Demetrius: Isle of Neos.

Nicholas Marinus Calonas: Isle of Neos.

Marinus Nicholas Calonas: Isle of Neos.

Demetrius Christodolo: Philippopolis.

Michael: Constantinople.

George Alexander: Philippopolis.

Leontheus Christodolo: Philippopolis.

Alexander Thuriacos: Philippopolis.

Basileus Hadjy Constantine: Philippopolis.

Simeon Georgia: Georgia.

Michael Anthony: Isle of Naseia(?)

George Anthony: native of Calcutta.

Theodorus Lameos: Isle of Lamos.

Nicholas: Crete.

Sabas: a Sclavonian.

Pannagiotes, Thely.

George Angelo: Philippopolis.

Constantine: Trapazandios.

Jordan: Caesaria.

Joannes Garganos: Georgia.
Anastersino Constantine: Philippopolis.
Soteres Slogen: Philippopolis.
Nicholas Spiridion: Crete.
George: Cephalonia.
Stamatis Demetrius: Rhodes.
Zacharias: Rhodes.
John: Thely.
Athanasius Demetrius: Philippopolis.

Demetrius Elijah: Philippopolis.
George Angerles: Philippopolis.
Antony Phoskolos: Isle of Irineus.
Matthew Antony: Isle of Irineus.
Joannes: Thely.
Thalisinos Haujy Peter: Trapizon.
Moikos Neno: Philippopolis.
Paulee Stratee: Metyline.

Appendix B

Greek Merchants in Dacca, 1795, recorded in 'Bengal European Inhabitants 1783-1807'.
Number of years resident in India follows each name.

Panioty Alexander.	24	Simeon Jessay.	8
Constantine Achilles.	16	Manuel John.	8
George Angely.	15	Stamaty John.	8
Demetrius Athanasius.	8	John Jessay.	5
John Bandalacos.	4	Joseph Jordonny.	7
Antony Bulga.	3	Alexander Kyriakos.	24
Nicholas Calonas.	17	Constantine Linies.	8
Constantine Christodolus.	7	Constantine Mavrody.	1
George Columbas.	3	George Menessely.	4
Constantine Angerry.	3	George Mector.	3
Anastasius Constantine.	8	Nicholas Malakos.	3
Anastasius Demetrius.	8	Constantine Nicholas.	2
Constantine Ducas.	11	George Primas.	8
Angelo Ducas.	12	Michael Polity.	24
Demetrius Elijah.	8	Constantine Shahen.	36
Antonio Foscolo.	9	Nicholas Spyriden.	14
Demetrius George.	6	Paul Straty.	8
Emmanuel George.	4	Constantine Theodosius.	15
Demetrius Galanos.	5	Angelo Vetelk.	7
Nathaniel Jerols.	15		
(Clergyman)			

Appendix C

Greek Merchants of Dacca and Calcutta who signed a Petition to the Archbishop of Sinai. December 13, 1811.

Panagiotees Alexandrou.
Theocharees Georgiou.
Georgakees Theocharous.
Theocharees Menzelees.
Tzortsees Menselees.
Loukas Theodorou.
Joseph Jordanou.
Konstantinos Theodosiou.
Theodorus Louka.
Andreas Louka.
Antonio Phasolees
Joakeem Phasolees
Andreas Konstantinou.
Nikalaos Kalona.
Michael Andreou.

Jacob X Esaias.
Demetrius Elias.
Nikolaos Demetriou.
Georgius Demetriou.
Demetrius Georgiou.
Nikolas Palaiologou.
Georgius Pemmou.
Alexandros Georgiou.
Joannes Bardalachos.
Joannes and Konstantinos Panagiotou.
Georgios Konstantinou.
Athanasius Konstantinou.
Athanasios Mitzou.
Georgios Emmanuel.

Appendix D

On the following pages, in tabulated form, is a list of Greek merchants known to be trading in Bengal sometime between 1750 and 1853. The list is arranged in an artificial alphabetical order. Greek patronymics are treated, in the majority of cases, as if they were surnames which they often later became. A question mark after a date or place indicates some uncertainty as to its correctness. Columns A, B and C refer to the signatories and those recorded in the corresponding Appendix with the figures indicating their place on the list.

Name	Date of arrival in India	Place of Origin	A	B	C	Other Details
ABRAHAM, Alexeus Hadjee	—	Caesaria	23	—	—	Calcutta. circa 1788
ABRAHAM, Joseph Hadjee	—	Caesaria	25	—	—	Calcutta. circa 1788
ABRAHAM, Potos Hadjee	—	Caesaria	21	—	—	Calcutta. circa 1788
ABRAHAM, Shereen Hadjee (Ibrahim)	—	Caesaria	5	—	—	Calcutta: Bengal Directory, 1790-1792
ABRAHAM, Simeon Hadjee	—	Caesaria	24	—	—	Probably Simeon Coja who purchased Greek Burial Ground, Dacca 1792
ACHILLES, Constantine	1779	—	—	*	—	Dacca. circa 1779-95
ALEXANDER, George (Alexandros, Giorgiou)	—	Philippopolis	40	—	23	Calcutta, circa 1788-1811
ANASTASIOS, the Thessallonian	—	Thessaly	—	—	—	Played a leading role in Greek affairs in Calcutta circa 1806
ANDREW, Michael (Andreou, Michalees)	—	Lacedemonia	33	—	15	Calcutta before 1774, Warden of Greek Church 1802, Bengal Directory 1790-92, traded in salt to Chittagong
ANGELEE, Argyres Hadjee	—	Philippopolis ?	—	—	—	Calcutta before 1774
ANGERLES, George (Angely)	1780	Philippopolis	64	*	—	Dacca circa 1788-95
ANGELO, George	—	Philippopolis	51	—	—	Calcutta circa 1788
ANGERRY, Constantine	1792	Philippopolis ?	—	*	—	Dacca circa 1792-95
ANTONIOU, Soterios	—	—	—	—	—	Partner of Pantazes, Constantine Calcutta, trading with Constantinople. circa 1780-90
ANTONY, George	—	Calcutta	46	—	—	Calcutta circa 1788

Name	Date	Origin	A	B	C	Details
ANTHONY, Matthew	—	Isle of Irineus	66	—	—	Calcutta circa 1788
ANTHONY, Michael	—	Isle of Naseia	45	—	—	Calcutta circa 1788
ANTHONY, Solinees	—	Philippopolis	29	—	—	Calcutta circa 1788
ARDEUR, Mixanly	—	—	—	—	—	Calcutta circa 1792
ARGYREE, Alexios Panaghiotis (Katzee Alexiou, Alexander the Greek)	1750	Philippopolis				Master, Guild of Cloth Merchants Philippopolis 1766 - obtained permission for British to trade with Suez 1770-71; founded Greek parish in Calcutta 1772; began Greek settlement in Dacca, died August 5 1777, Dacca; buried Calcutta Greek Church.
ARIKOGLOU, George Manolakee	—	Constantinople?				Calcutta before 1774
ATHANASS, Emmanuel (Manuel)	—	Philippopolis				Meerut 1816-35. b. 1778 d. May 25 1840. Friend of Keryack, Michael. Wife's name Elizabeth.
ATHANAS, Demetrius (Athanasius)	1787	Philippopolis	62	*	—	Conductor of boats between Naraingunj and other stations, 1792. Dacca circa 1795-1827.
ATHANAS, George (Primo)	1787	Philippopolis	30	*	—	Dacca: circa 1795; Naraingunj 1820-23; Dacca 1831-35
ATHANASS, John	—	Calcutta				Calcutta 1821-35 (Kenderdine's Lane); b.1753 d.1835 Buried South Park Cemetery, Calcutta. Protestant upbringing, Baptist by faith; wife's name Hannah.
ATHANASS, Joshua 1809	1809	Philippopolis				Shopkeeper, Nuseerabad, 1825. Probably brother of Athanass, Emmanuel
ATHANASIOU, Manolakees	—					Calcutta circa 1800; leading part in Greek affairs; friend of Demetrius Galanos
BANAS, A	—					Delhi 1835
BARAKTARAGLOU, Georgius	—	Constantinople?				Calcutta before 1774 - one of the leading merchants

Name	Date	Origin	A	B	C	Details
BARDALOKOS, John	1791	—	—	*	24	Dacca circa 1791-95
BULGA, Anthony	1792	—	—	*	—	Dacca circa 1792-95
CALOGREEDY, George Demetrius (Calograthy)	—	Isle of Neos (Nio)	34	—	—	Calcutta circa 1788; b.1730 d.1790; buried Greek Churchyard.
CALONAS, George N. (Kalonas)	—	Isle of Neos	—	—	—	Dacca 1831-35
CALONAS, Marinos Nicholas (Kalonas)	—	Isle of Neos	37	—	—	Naraingunj 1821; Dacca 1831-35. m.Catherine Spiridon 1812
CALONAS, Nicholas Marinos (Kalonas)	1788	Isle of Neos	36	*	14	Calcutta 1792; Naraingunj 1795-1823
CAREEDA, George	—	Philippopolis	28	—	—	Calcutta circa 1788
CHRISTODOLO, son of Pappa Nicolai (Nicolay)	—	Isle of Neos	11	—	—	Calcutta circa 1788-1802; Warden, Greek Church
CHRISTODOLOS, Constantine	1788	Isle of Neos? Philippopolis?	—	*	—	Conductor Boats between Naraingunj and other stations 1792, Dacca 1795
CHRISTODOLO, Demetrius	—	Philippopolis	38	—	—	Calcutta circa 1788
CHRISTODOLO, Leontheus	—	Philippopolis	41	—	—	Calcutta circa 1788
COLUMBAS, George	1792	—	yes	—	—	Dacca circa 1792-95
CONSTANTINE	—	—	—	—	—	Refugee to Fulta 1756. Put in a bill for provisions
CONSTANTINE	—	Trebizond	52	—	—	Calcutta. Possibly same as 'Constantine' above
CONSTANTINE, Anastas (Konstantinou Athanasius)	1787	Philippopolis	55	*	27	Conductor Boats between Naraingunj and other stations 1792. Dacca circa 1795-1811
CONSTANTINE, Basileus Hadjee	—	Philippopolis	43	—	—	Calcutta circa 1788

Name	Date	Origin	A	B	C	Details
CONSTANTINE, Mafseel	—	—	—	—	—	Conductor Boats between Narainguni and other stations 1792
CONSTANTINE, Nicolah	1792	—	—	*	—	Condcutor Boats between Narainguni and other stations 1792. Dacca circa 1795
CONSTANTINOU, Andreas (Constantine, Andrew)	—	Corinth?	—	—	13	Calcutta and Agra? b.1788 d.1855 buried Agra?
CONSTANTINOU, Georgios	—	—	—	—	26	Calcutta circa 1811
DADELCO, Angelos	—	Philippopolis	10	—	—	Calcutta circa 1788
DANIEL, Constantine	—	—	—	—	—	Conductor Boats between Narainguni and other stations 1792
DEMETRIOU, Nikolas	—	—	—	—	18	Calcutta circa 1811
DEMETRIUS, Athanasius	1779	—	—	*	—	Conductor Boats between Narainguni and other stations 1792
DEMETRIUS, Emmanuel	—	Albania	15	—	—	Merchant Calcutta circa 1788
DEMETRIUS, Joannes	—	Metyline	8	—	—	Calcutta circa 1788-92. Bengal Directory 1790-92
DRACOULIS, (name uncertain)	—	Ithaca?	—	—	—	Refugee to Fulta, 1756
DUCAS, Angelo (Doucos)	1783	Corfu	13	*	—	Dacca 1795-1852
DUCAS, Constantine	1784	Corfu	—	*	—	Conductor Boats between Narainguni and other stations. Dacca circa 1795
ELEAZAR, Stephen Gabriel	—	—	—	—	—	Gabriel and Co. Calcutta 1852-4
ELIAS, Demetrius (Elijah)	1787	Philippopolis	63	*	17	Conductor Boats between Narainguni and other stations 1792. Narainguni 1795-1823 d.1823
ELIAS, Constantine Demetrius	—	Philippopolis, born Bengal	—	—	—	Son of Elias, Demetrius. Dacca 1831-38. b.1803 d.1838. Buried Old Baptist Cemetery, Wari, Dacca.

Name	Date	Origin	A	B	C	Details
ELIAS, John Demetrius	—	Philippopolis, born Bengal	—	—	—	Son of Elias, Demetrius. Dacca 1831-36 b.1800 d.1836. Killed by tiger at Mirzapore. Buried Old Baptist Cemetery, Wari, Dacca.
ELIAS, Nicholas Demetrius	—	Philippopolis, born Bengal	—	—	—	Eldest son of Elias, Demetrius. Dacca 1831-45 b.1799 d.1845. Buried Old Baptist Cemetery, Wari, Dacca. m.Theodosia Mavrody.
EASU, Jacob Hadjee (Isaah, Isaias)	—	Caesaria	22	—	16	Dacca circa 1818-19 b.circa 1771 d.1819 Dacca
ESAU, Joannes Hadjee	—	Caesaria	26	—	—	Calcutta circa 1788
FOSCHOLO, Anthony (Phoskolos, Phasolees)	1786	Isle of Irineus (Irino)	65	*	11	Naraingunj 1818-23 b.1751 d.1833 Dacca
FOSCHOLO, A.	—	Isle of Irineus b.Bengal	—	—	—	Dacca 1834-39
FOSCHOLO, John	—	Isle of Irineus b.Bengal	—	—	—	Dacca 1836-39
FOSCHOLO, Joachim (Phoskolos, Phasolees)	—	Isle of Irineus b.Bengal	—	—	12	Dacca circa 1811. m.L'Aunette Benville 1820
GARAGANOS, Joannes	—	Georgia	54	—	—	Calcutta circa 1788
GEORGE	—	Cephalonia	58	—	—	Calcutta circa 1788
GEORGE, A.	—	—	—	—	—	Agra 1846-51
GEORGE, Demetrius	1788	Isle of Neos	35	*	19	Dacca circa 1788-95
GEORGE, Emmanuel	1791	—	—	*	29	Dacca circa 1791-95
GEORGE, Simeon (Georgia)	1787	Georgia	44	—	—	Calcutta, Crooked Lane, circa 1787-1811
GEORGIOU, Constantinos	—	Constantinople	—	—	—	Calcutta before 1774; Dacca circa 1806, also known as 'Manrologlou' d.24 July 1806 Dacca

Name	Date	Origin	A	B	C	Details
GEORGIOU, Theocharees (Godela, Theochan, Charis, Theodore)	—	Arta	7	—	2	Calcutta circa 1774-1811. One of the leading Greek merchants
GEORGIUS, Demetrius	—	Bythnia	4	—	20	Calcutta circa 1788
GIANACOPULOS	—	—	—	—	—	Meerut d.1810, buried Race Course Cemetery
JESSAY, John	1790	—	—	*	—	Dacca circa 1790-95
JESSAY, Simeon	1787	—	—	*	—	Dacca circa 1787-95
JOHANNES	—	Thesally	67	—	—	Calcutta circa 1788
JOHN	—	Thesally	61	—	—	Calcutta circa 1788
JOHN, A	1798	—	—	—	—	Up Country 1806-1812, Muttra 1834-39, Agra 1840-51
JOHN, C	—	—	—	—	—	Agra 1846-51
JOHN, George	1795	—	—	—	—	Agra 1804-12
JOHN, Manuel	1787	—	—	*	—	Conductor Boats between Naraingunj and other stations 1792. Dacca circa 1795
JOHN, Peter	—	—	—	—	—	Calcutta: Moorghihatta 1846-54. Warden Greek Church
JORDAN, Joseph (Jordanou, Jordonny)	1788	Caesaria	53	*	7	Naraingunj circa 1788-1819 b.1759 d.1819. Wives' names Magdalene and Sophia
KERYACK, Michael	—	Vienna	—	—	—	Delhi b.circa 1782 d.1828. Buried Lothian Bridge Cemetery, Delhi. Friend of Athanas, Manuel
LAMEOS, Theodorus	—	Isle of Lameos	47	—	—	Calcutta circa 1788
LEONTIOU, George (Leondeu, Leonidas)	—	Smyrna	3	—	—	Calcutta 1788-92. Bengal Directory 1790-92 d.1792 buried Greek Churchyard
LINIES, Constantine	1787	—	—	*	—	Dacca circa 1787-95

Name	Date	Origin	A	B	C	Details
LUCAS, Andreas (Louka)	—	Magnesia b.Bengal ?	—	—	10	Dacca 1811-51 (trading in salt)
LUCAS, Joannes (Loukas)	—	Magnesia?	—	—	—	Calcutta circa 1814-54, Armenian Street. Warden Greek Church.
LUCAS, Theodoro (Loukas)	—	Magnesia	27	—	6	Naraingunj 1788-1823. Called 'The Greek Servant'. Played a leading part in Greek affairs.
LUCAS, Theodorus (Loukas, Louka)	—	Magnesia	—	—	9	Dacca 1811-51 (trader in salt). Zamindar, Dacca, 1856-57
MALAKOS, Nicholas	1792	—	—	*	—	Dacca circa 1795
MANUEL, George	—	—	—	—	—	Cawnpore circa 1835
MANUEL, John	1787	—	—	*	—	Conductor Boats between Naraingunj and other stations 1792. Dacca circa 1795
MANUEL, John	—	—	—	—	—	Service of Sumer Raze Begum, near Cawnpore 1792. Calcutta, Hoozrymull's Lane, circa 1835
MANUEL, Joseph Antonio	—	—	—	—	—	Service of Sumer Raze Begum, near Cawnpore 1792
MAVRODOGLIO, Cellibi Constacki	—	—	—	—	—	Naraingunj. m.Panioty, Emiralda 1799
MAVRODY, Christodolus (Marodes, Maurody)	—	Philippopolis	14	—	—	Either Calcutta or Dacca or both circa 1788
MAVRODY, Constantine	1794	Philippopolis	—	*	—	Dacca 1794-1810 d.1810
MAVRODY, Kyriakos (Marodes, Thireakos)	—	Philippopolis	2	—	—	Calcutta circa 1790-95, Warden Greek Church, leading merchant in Calcutta. d.1795, buried in Greek Churchyard.
MECTOR, George	1792	—	—	*	—	Dacca circa 1792-95
MENESSELY, George (Menzelees)	1791	—	—	*	—	Dacca circa 1791-95

Name	Date	Origin	A	B	C	Details
MENZELEES, Theocares	—	—	—	—	4	Calcutta circa 1811
MENZELEES, Tzortzees	—	—	—	—	5	Calcutta circa 1811
MITCHOO, Athanas	—	Philippopolis	—	—	—	Assam buried Dibrooghur, Upper Assam d.55 years old
MITCHOO, Ducas Athanas	—	Philippopolis? Bengal?	—	—	—	Assam b.1817 d.1840 buried Dibrooghur, Upper Assam
MITZOU, Athanasios	—	—	—	—	28	Calcutta circa 1811
MUSCOVITE, Nicholas	1763	Moscow?	—	—	—	Administrator of estate of Seapoy, Demetrius sued Argyree, Alexios in Mayor's Court, Calcutta. Calcutta circa 1763
NAZORAS, Sonozaor	—	—	—	—	—	Calcutta circa 1792
NENO, Moikos	—	Philippopolis	69	—	—	Calcutta circa 1788
NICHOLAS	—	Crete	48	—	—	Calcutta circa 1788
NICHOLLS, George (Anglicized name)	1790	—	—	—	—	Rungpore 1790-1812, Indigo Planter Rungpore and Doomra 1812-17
OCORPE, A	—	—	—	—	—	Agra circa 1843
PALAIOLOGOU, Nicholas	—	Wallachia?	—	—	21	Calcutta circa 1811. Phanariot family claimed descent from dynasty of Byzantine Emperors
PANAGEOTIS, Demetrius	—	Thesally	12	—	—	Calcutta circa 1788
PANAGEOTES	—	Thesally? Thesalonica?	50	—	—	Calcutta circa 1788
PANIOTY, Alexander (Panageotes, Alexios; Panagiotakees, Alexiou)	1772	Philippopolis	1	*	1	Leading merchant Dacca and Narainqunj, trading in Chunam at Sylhet 1787-88, in salt to Chittagong, in Narainqunj 1784-1820, in Dacca 1820-21. Builder of Dacca Greek Church. d.1821 buried in Dacca Church.

199

Name	Date	Origin	A	B	C	Details
PANIOTY, Alexander (Panageotis, Alezandros)	1772	Philippopolis	18	—	—	Dacca? Seems to have given up trading, became Zamindar. m.Catherine Barros circa 1802. Son of Panioty Alexander above.
PANIOTY, Anastasius (Panageotis)	1772	Philippopolis	19	—	—	Dacca. Church Warden Dacca, Dacca Church. Son of Panioty, Alexander (Panageotes, Alexios)
PANIOTY, Constantine (Panageotis)	—	Philippopolis b.Bengal	—	—	25	Dacca 1811-44 b.1782 d.1844. Buried English Cemetery, Barisal. Son of Panioty, Alexander (Panageotes Alexios)
PANIOTY, Constantine P	—	Philippopolis? Bengal?	—	—	—	Fategarh 1811-17, Karnaul 1921, son of Argyree Alexios?
PANIOTY, Emmanuel	—	Philippopolis? Bengal?	—	—	—	Cawnpore 1801-15 b.1776 d.1815; buried Kacheri Cemetery, Cawnpore. Brother of Panioty, Constantine P? and son of Argyree, Alexios? Wife Irene
PANIOTY, Emmanuel	—	Bengal	—	—	—	Cawnpore 1817, Up Country 1818-31 Muttra 1834-9. Son of either Emmanuel above or Panioty, Constantine P
PANIOTY, George (Panageotis)	1772	Philippopolis	17	—	—	Dacca 1788-1839. Church Warden Dacca
PANIOTY, John (Panageotis Johannes)	1772	Philippopolis	20	—	25	Dacca 1788-1848
PANTAZES, Constantine (Pantazis, Pandaze, Pandajee)	—	Epirus. Came to India from Adrianople	—	—	—	Agra 1795-1817, Calcutta 1818-42, Amratollah Street, Warden Greek Church 1834-42 founded Greek School, friend of Galanos, Demetrius, executor of his will. b.1770 d.1842. Buried Greek Churchyard, Calcutta
PANTAZES, Panagiotes	—	Adrianople?	—	—	—	Calcutta with Pantazes, Constantine probably his son, furthered Greek education in Calcutta
PATTERSON, Charles (Anglicized name)	1791	—	—	—	—	Calcutta, Chitpore Road, 1804-17
PAUL, George	—	—	—	—	—	Muttra b.1752 d.1822

Name	Date	Origin	A	B	C	Details
PEMMOU, Georgius	—	—	—	—	22	Calcutta circa 1811
POLITY, Michael	1771	Constantinople	39	*	—	Calcutta circa 1771, Dacca circa 1795
PROTOPAPAS, Peter	1820 circa	Epirus, village of Coucoulias, district of Zagorios	—	—	—	Calcutta 1820s, active assisting Greek education, sent funds from India to Greek schools in Epirus
SEAPOY, Demetrius	—	—	—	—	—	Calcutta circa 1755, trading with Basra. Commissioned Argyre, Alexios to sell a consignment in Basra. d.Calcutta 1756
SHAHINY, Constantine (Shaw)	1759	Philippopolis	32	*	—	Calcutta circa 1759, Dacca circa 1792-95. Leading merchant in Dacca
SLOGEN, Sotores	—	Philippopolis	56	—	—	Calcutta circa 1788-93. d.1793 buried in Greek Church-yard
SPEROOS, Joseph	1789	Corfu?	—	—	—	Khulna 1804-6. Alive in 1815
SPIRIDON, Nicholas	1781	Crete	57	*	—	Dacca circa 1781-95
STAMATIS, Demetrius	—	Rhodes	59	—	—	Calcutta circa 1788
STAMATY, John	1787	Rhodes?	—	*	—	Conductor Boats between Naraingunj and other stations 1792, Dacca circa 1795
STRATEE, Paulee (Straty, Paul)	1787	Metyline (Kydonia)	70	*	—	Panioty, Alexander's agent in Sylhet 1787-88: Conductor Boats between Naraingunj and other stations 1792, Dacca 1795 b.1758 d.1826 Calcutta, buried Greek Churchyard
THESALINOS, Hadjee Peter	—	Trebizond	68	—	—	Calcutta circa 1788
TREANDAFFELOS, Anastas	1792	—	—	—	—	Fategarh Cantonment 1801-4
THEOCHAROUS, Georgakees (Theokan, George)	—	Arta?	—	—	3	Conductor Boats between Naraingunj and other stations 1792, Calcutta circa 1811, probably son of Georgiou, Theochares

Name	Date	Origin	A	B	C	Details
THEODORE, Athansius	—	Prusa (Brusa)	6	—	—	Calcutta circa 1788
THEODOSIUS, Constantine	1780	Philippopolis	31	*	8	Conductor Boats between Naraingunj and other stations 1792, Dacca circa 1795-1811, wife Theodosia d.Dacca 1807
THOSMA, Jacobus Hadjee	—	Caesaria	9	—	—	Calcutta circa 1788
THURIACOS, Alexander (Kyriakos)	1771	Philippopolis	42	*	—	Dacca circa 1795. Wife Sultana d.1800, Dacca
VERDDALOKO, John	—	—	—	—	—	Conductor Boats between Naraingunj and other stations 1792
VOSCONCELLOS, J	—	—	—	—	—	Chinsura d.1838
VETELK, Angelo	1788	—	—	*	—	Dacca circa 1788-95, Lieut. in Mahratta Service. Patna 1811
ZACHARIAS	—	Rhodes	60	—	—	Calcutta circa 1788